Alfred Caldecott

English Colonization and Empire

Alfred Caldecott

English Colonization and Empire

ISBN/EAN: 9783337320867

Printed in Europe, USA, Canada, Australia, Japan

Cover: Foto ©ninafisch / pixelio.de

More available books at **www.hansebooks.com**

English Colonization

and

Empire

BY

ALFRED CALDECOTT, M.A.

(CAMB. AND LOND.)

FELLOW AND DEAN OF ST. JOHN'S COLLEGE, CAMBRIDGE
SOMETIME UNIVERSITY EXTENSION LECTURER
UNDER THE CAMBRIDGE SYNDICATE

'Of all the results of English History none is comparable to the creation of this enormous, prosperous, in great part homogeneous Realm, and it can be paralleled by nothing in the history of any other State.'—PROFESSOR SEELEY.

NEW YORK
CHARLES SCRIBNER'S SONS
743 & 745 BROADWAY
1891

[All rights reserved]

PREFACE.

IN this *Manual* the broad principles laid down in the General Plan of the Series have been kept in view, expressing, as they do, the method of lecturing upon the subject adopted by the writer as a University Extension Lecturer in the years 1880–1890. The actual course of events is sketched in a general way, and afterwards the more important phases of the history are treated separately. The history is studied in the light of Political Science, Political Economy and Ethnology, and, at the same time, with close reference to the observations and opinions of travellers, statesmen, and colonists; while Poetry and Fiction have also been recognised.

The fact that so many problems of Imperial interest are still being worked out, and that this particular time is one of great activity and considerable change, has proved a difficulty. Some questions still open will be solved, or the conditions which give rise to them will be altered, before this century closes, and others will, no doubt, be opened. It is hoped that the treatment here given will enable the student to follow these developments with increased interest, and to place them in proper connexion with the history of the Empire and of Colonization generally.

MAPS AND DIAGRAMS.

		PAGE
France and Spain, before they were single kingdoms, circa 1400		7
Spain. Dominion of Charles V in Europe		19
,, Dominion of Charles V in America		19
The Early Partition of America		28
The Thirteen Colonies, 1664–1783		48
India. As left by Clive, 1767		62
,, As left by Wellesley, 1805		62
,, As left by Lord Hastings, 1823		63
,, As left by Dalhousie, 1856		63
,, As left by Lord Dufferin, 1888		64
British Empire, 1690		86
,, ,, 1790		88
,, ,, 1890		90
South Africa in 1890 (coloured)	*To face p.*	110
The Partition of Africa (coloured)	*To face p.*	112
West Indies. Leeward and Windward Islands		147
Fifty Years' Growth of the Trade of the British Empire		172
Trade of European Countries with their Dependencies		173
Distribution of the Trade of the United Kingdom		186
Distribution of the Trade of India		187
Map and Diagram comparing population of Australia and British Isles		209
The Growth of Aryan Predominance (coloured)	} *Between*	218, 219
The Races of Mankind before the European Expansion (coloured)		

CONTENTS.

CHAPTER I.

	PAGE
INTRODUCTION	1–13
European Civilization	1
The British Empire	8

CHAPTER II.

PIONEER PERIOD	14–26
Portugal	15
Spain	18
England	22

CHAPTER III.

INTERNATIONAL STRUGGLE	27–43
With Spain	27
With Holland	29
With France	32

CHAPTER IV.

DEVELOPMENT AND SEPARATION OF AMERICA	44–57

CHAPTER V.

THE ENGLISH IN INDIA	58–85

CHAPTER VI.

	PAGE
RECONSTRUCTION AND FRESH DEVELOPMENT	87–120
§ 1. West Indies	87
§ 2. Australia	97
§ 3. Canada	101
§ 4. Africa	105
§ 5. Scattered Acquisitions	116

CHAPTER VII.

GOVERNMENT OF THE EMPIRE	121–164
§ 1. Forms and Methods	123
§ 2. Confederation	145
§ 3. Imperial Federation	149

CHAPTER VIII.

TRADE AND TRADE POLICY	165–189

CHAPTER IX.

SUPPLY OF LABOUR	190–215
§ 1. Native Peoples	191
§ 2. Negro Slavery	192
§ 3. Coolie Labour	196
§ 4. Convict Labour	199
§ 5. Free Emigration	202

CHAPTER X.

NATIVE RACES	216–235

CHAPTER XI.

EDUCATION AND RELIGION	236–257

CHAPTER XII.

GENERAL REFLECTIONS	258–274

APPENDIX.

BOOKS OF REFERENCE	275–277

ENGLISH COLONIZATION AND EMPIRE

CHAPTER I.

INTRODUCTION.

The Movements of Civilization. European Civilization. The British Empire.

THE civilization of mankind has passed through many alternate phases of diffusion and concentration. There appear always to have been what we may regard as small areas of light gleaming out from wide fields where illumination was faint and dull. In the very early childhood of the race uniformity may have prevailed, but as soon as anything of the nature of what is usually known as history began, divergences appeared. Men moved away from the cradle and nursery in Central Asia, dispersing into different zones: and afterwards it is probable that Ocean and Land made some exchanges of territory, fresh islands and peninsulas appearing and aiding in the cleaving of the Human Family into Races. Some were to settle down, some to make progress, and some, it would seem, to degenerate. The chief centres of civilization appear to have been:—(1) the basins of the Chinese rivers, (2) the Ganges plain, (3) the Euphrates valley, (4) the Eastern coast of the Mediterranean, and (5) the valley of the Nile. In these, men had settled homes, agriculture and rudimentary manufactures were pursued, property was established; in short, there were here sufficient human relations, both industrial and legal, to form the basis of *States*, when in other regions men were still in tribes and hordes. Whilst in these favoured districts men were ploughing fields and building cities and temples, elsewhere there were such peoples as the Tartar occupants of the elevated lands of Asia, without any progressive civilization, making inroads into the settled countries, but vanishing again, having accomplished nothing; and such peoples as the Australian aboriginals, the Hottentots and Bushmen of Southern Africa, and the Negro tribes in incessant restlessness and unprogressive change. To Chinese civilization we can only allude, but we must not quite forget it: for it existed throughout historic times, and there is reason for believing that it was more perceptible in its influence upon other nations in early times than afterwards, until again quite lately. But its influence was scanty and indirect at most, and did not penetrate far westward during the centuries when the European nations were being formed. The Indian region will concern us more closely because the barrier between it and Europe was often passed, and, by means of intermediate nations, it had some important influence. With the peoples who inhabited the valleys of the Nile and the Euphrates, and the coast of Phœnicia, we had closer connexion, as they contributed some important elements to our own civilization. From the history of Nineveh and Babylon, of Tyre and her colonies, and of Persia, we pass to that of the cities, islands, and colonies of Greece, and then to that of the great State into which Rome welded the peoples of Western Asia, Southern Europe, and Northern Africa. When this welding had accomplished its purpose, the centre of progress moved slightly more to the North and West, and in the country between the Carpathians and the Atlantic was developed the first civilization that seems likely to be common to the whole human race.

The world to-day shows us our race still ranged in great masses, but all in some contact. The Chinese mass of 400 millions, the Indian mass of 300 millions, the European mass of 300 millions, having accomplished their separate developments in isolation, have been brought into touch with one another, and, with the looser fragments of the Malay races, the African tribes, and the Polynesians, are now being moulded into *a single community of mankind*. In all this change the history of Europe is of pre-eminent importance. If at first man found it easier to deal with Nature in the warmer zones of the earth's surface, he has since found that his own capacities were called into more intense activity in the temperate regions. 'The true theatre of History,' says Hegel, 'is the temperate zone.' It has always been found that long sojourning in the tropics enervates: at this moment the dwellers in the Ganges valley would be at the mercy of Afghan and Nepaulese mountain-nations were it not that we have undertaken to guard them. Again and again the cooler climes have sent their wholesomely nurtured hordes to reap the fruits of the labours of enfeebled nations dwelling in the milder regions, either to return with spoil, or to be mingled with the conquered; themselves after a time of brief prosperity to be subjected to a like treatment in their turn. It is in Europe that the greatest progress has been attained: in this temperate region permanence has been at last secured, and from it the unifying influences have sprung. And it is this that constitutes our subject: *the diffusion of European civilization over the face of the inhabited and habitable world.* All other movements were but preparatory, as it were, for this. The Celts and Pelasgians spread into Europe, other Aryans passed into India, the Saracens made a new Northern Africa, and the effects of these movements are permanent: but in the outward movement of Europeans we have what there is some ground for regarding as the last great movement of all, the final settlement of Man upon the earth. Here first we find—

(i) A knowledge of the whole surface of our planet. In its general aspects this knowledge is final: the shape of the earth, the proportion of land to water; its mountains, its great river-basins, its islands, all are marked down. Man surveys his home at last.

(ii) An increase of practical mastery over the surface of the globe, amounting to a transformation: the ocean is a high road; space-obstacles yield to steam, and time-obstacles to electricity.

(iii) A recognition, both scientific and popular, of the oneness of the Human Family. There may still linger in some quarters doubt as to unity of origin, and in others as to unity of destiny, but on the whole the science and the sentiment of Europe are now based on the idea of a single humanity.

(iv) For rendering this recognition widely effectual in action a material base is laid in the commercial and industrial organization which now regards, even if it does not yet actively embrace, the whole globe. A freedom and suppleness of organization are obtained, which allow men to move to and fro on the earth, and under the form of 'Capital' much wealth is available for world-wide use.

(v) A character of finality is won for physical science; not as to its limits or its actual content, but as to the reality of the truths in actual possession: regions have been secured absolutely. And thus knowledge has a world-wide significance; there is science which is the science for all. Literature must vary in its right to command allegiance; Art must vary; Moral Science has its 'schools'; but Physical Science is positive and for the world.

(vi) A religious basis is disclosed transcending peoples and nations and languages, 'lofty as the love of God and ample as the wants of man.' Religious ideas which embrace Humanity in their scope are making way, and thousands of men and women place Religion above Nationality and devote themselves to the union of all men in Faith and Hope.

Thus we are now in presence of a great consolidation. The world is becoming a single home, and the races of Mankind a single family.

Preparation.

It has been in Europe that the preparation for this final stage or epoch has taken place. By means of the nations cradled there the scattering of men is being counteracted: not indeed altered as a fact, but as a cause of differentiation and division. Upon the differences developed in separation, unity is now being superimposed. The races which cannot bear this are doomed; the Maori and the Red Indian seem unable to live in the whiter light, or, at least, are in peril of losing their hold on individuality. Those which can respond to the call out of isolation, and can fit into the world-wide scheme, live on and prosper; the Negro, for example, seems likely to be always the African branch of the family: although inferior to the leaders, they can accept a lead and find new life under guidance. Where the Chinese—the heaviest mass of all—will come, is a problem which cannot yet be solved.

It was not till the fifteenth century that Europe was ready to take the first steps towards assuming the guidance of the world. By this time she had won three *physical instruments* of first-rate importance for the work: (1) The Mariner's Compass, which gave guidance over the open sea, and made water less separating in effect than mountain: just as the Mediterranean had joined North Africa to Europe in one stage of navigating appliances, the Ocean was to join all the Continents together; (2) the Printing Press, which recorded and communicated the results of efforts as they took effect, and made the growing knowledge a common possession; (3) Gunpowder, which enabled small bands of Europeans easily to force their way against whole nations and tribes of the twilight and the darkness. And in the moral sphere, Europe had herself been 'schooled' for the work; disciplined by war, trained by commerce, moralized by religion.

The European nations who took part in the movement fall into two groups[1]: the LATIN—Portuguese, Spaniards,

---

[1] To define more exactly the area occupied by the expanding races, it must be remembered that the fifteenth century witnessed the withdrawal of South-Eastern Europe from Christendom, when the Ottomans took Constantinople (1453), and also the addition of

French, and Italians; and the GERMANIC — Germans, Dutch, Scandinavians, and British. The Celts were mostly absorbed in the other nations, and no distinct function, if any, can be assigned to them; while the Slavs had no part. Of the two groups, not all the nations were ready. The *Italians*, not yet disciplined effectively into nationality, continued to plod along old lines of connexion with the East; but they contributed very considerably in the way of science and art to the powers of the other nations. The *German* states were occupied with internal interests; and the *Scandinavian* nations, although for many years they had been contributory to a slight diffusion by the cold highways of Greenland and the North-West seas, had but little energy to spare for enterprises of a tentative kind. The work fell, therefore, to five nations—*Portugal, Spain, France, Holland*, and *Britain*. The centres of activity were in Lisbon, in Madrid and Seville, in Paris, in Amsterdam, in London and Bristol.

Some facts of European history illustrate the preparation of the races for an era of colonization. First, the *internal consolidating* of the five nations had attained a final stage. SPAIN had in 1474 become a single nation: the kingdoms of Leon and Castile had been united with Aragon, while the whole peninsula had been cleared of the Moor; so that Charles V wielded the resources of Spain, Naples, Sicily, Sardinia, Milan, and the Netherlands. Meanwhile the Spaniard was the outcome of the discipline of eight centuries of warfare with the Moors, warfare of a peculiar kind, not by armies but by the guerilla method. In FRANCE the year of the loss to Europe of Constantinople (1453) was the very date from which the modern French kingdom begins, when Aquitaine was joined to the central realm: the duchy of Burgundy was added in 1479, and that of Brittany in 1491; while a new height of moral and intellectual attainment was in view, to be reached not more than a century later, the 'age of Louis XIV.' As for the DUTCH it may be

South-Western Europe, when the Moors were driven from Spain (finally in 1492).

sufficient to say that in the sixteenth century they found themselves developed enough to desire and to deserve their independence, and strong enough to win it. In BRITAIN, Feudalism was broken; the middle class was

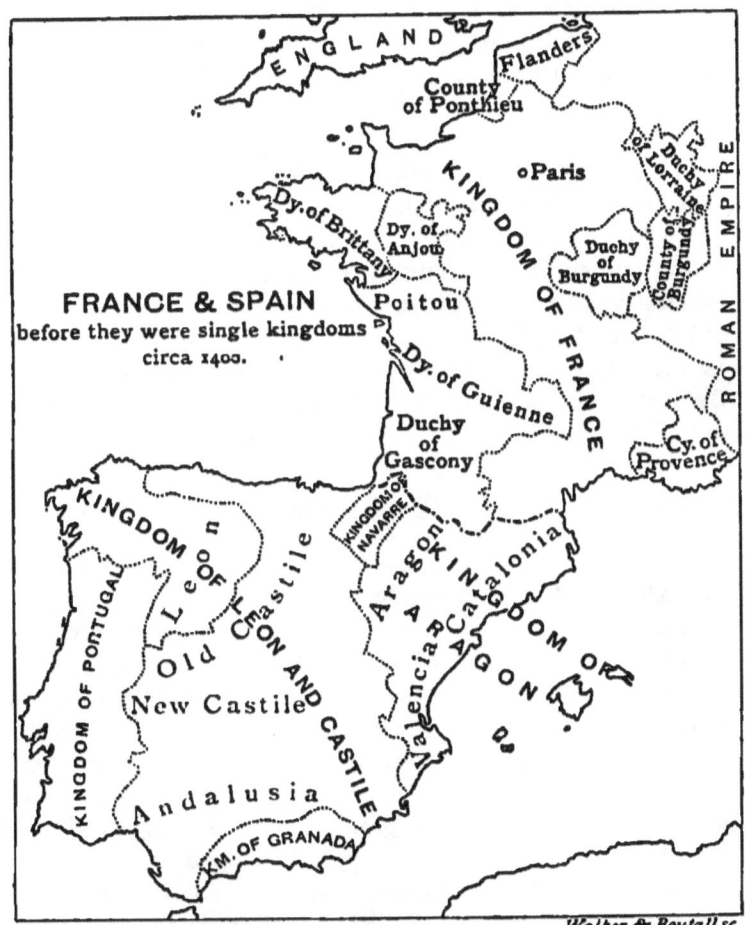

gaining power: England and Scotland were on the eve of union, and Ireland had been thoroughly subjected (Poynings' Law, 1479). Our maritime capacities were well established, and we were moving towards the new high-water mark of our Elizabethan period.

Secondly, in relation to one another these nations were drawing off from endeavours after mutual absorption, and taking up instead the position of competitors for a prize outside themselves: in their international policy the 'balance of power' idea was coming to the front.

A view of the whole situation, therefore, makes it clear that just as the voyage of Columbus was no sudden and isolated enterprise, but the greatest of a succession of efforts in navigation and discovery, so this new expansion was by no means casual and unprepared for. There was no discovery of a new world in the sense that a new world was given to an unenquiring race; and no outgoing of peoples in whom enterprise and energy and the discipline which gives success, were now first to appear. As Hegel says, the crossing of the Alps by Julius Caesar was an event of the same order as the crossing of the Atlantic by Christopher Columbus. By both events new spheres were opened out for peoples ready to unfold capacities which were pressing for development.

Colonization.

The spread of nations has sometimes proceeded by *migration*, i.e. by a whole tribe or nation changing its abode; sometimes by *overflow* into adjacent territories; sometimes by the *emigration* of companies of people quitting the national territory and taking up their abode elsewhere. This last is what is meant usually by 'COLONIZATION.' 'A colony,' says Dr. Johnson, is 'a number of people drawn from the mother-country to inhabit some distant place.' So expressed the general idea is caught; but the definition is too wide. It applies to people who live in foreign states, for we speak of the British 'colony' in Moscow, the American 'colony' in Paris. But we regard this as metaphor. The true definition must include the limitation 'remaining in political connexion with the mother-country or assuming political independence.' This last is the *Greek* sense of the term: the colony was not politically subordinate, but a strong sentiment of attachment was symbolized by the continuous keeping up of a sacred fire lighted in the first instance from the sacred hearth of the old home. The *Romans* had military colonies, of the character of garrisons, providing at once rewards for military service, occupation for disbanded armies, and order in newly conquered countries. The *Phoenicians*, with their seat first at Tyre then at Carthage, had trading colonies or factories, held for a time more or less in dependence. It is by colonization in the sense (1) of establishing new homes and (2) of assuming direction of native populations, chiefly with industrial or commercial ends in immediate view, that European expansion has been effected. America is the great example of the first kind, the subjugation of the natives not being of sufficient proportionate importance to make the element of conquest or rule prominent, except in Mexico and some parts of South America. India is the great example of the second kind.

We also, when speaking broadly, include under the term 'colonies,' places occupied for Imperial purposes. These are usually islands, harbours, or promontories; the *raison d'être* of their occupation is the attainment of some naval or military advantage for the empire.

Concentrating now our attention on England's share in what has been accomplished, let us glance rapidly at the condition of the English nation when its colonizing function began.

In the *England of Queen Elizabeth and James I* we see a state, with territories distinctly defined by water-boundaries, consolidated after centuries of strife out of the various petty dominions which had divided these islands of Great Britain and Ireland. The seven kingdoms of the Heptarchy, the princedom of Wales, and the various chieftaincies of Ireland, had for some time been united; the long-standing alliance with certain duchies on the continent had been more or less reluctantly renounced, and these had gone to their natural place in the French kingdom, while Scotland was just entering through union with England into the open field of history. The Reformation was in full tide of strength, and that not only in the sphere of ecclesiastical order and religious belief, and in renewal of continuity with the thought and art of Greece and Rome, but also in the freshness and vigour of independent endeavour to think, to admire, and to find aims and ends for conduct. The Church of England had received a certain degree of settlement, and the points of difference between those who could accept it and those who could not were being defined. The teaching of Erasmus, and Colet, and Ascham, and Cheke was operating in the Universities and in the new Grammar Schools; and Bacon was preparing the methods of knowledge for a wider and freer use.

Our population at this time was some five millions: Harrison, a contemporary, tells us that 1,172,674 men were enrolled as able to bear arms in 1574 and 1575, and he adds that this was probably about two-thirds of the actual number. In 1603 there were two million male communicants, including a few recusants; which fairly agrees with the above estimate. The people were engaged in a vigorous and, on the whole, a *progressive industrial* life. True, difficulty was arising from the increased practice of taking advantage of the excellence of our land as pasture, and the good quality of our cattle, to exchange cultivation for grazing, and so to employ less labour in agriculture. But our *manufactures* of broad-cloths, kerseys and friezes, of metal wares, of beer and of fells, were increasing, and our mercantile pursuits were rapidly requiring more money and more men. The looms of Norwich and of the West of England were prosperous, and Yorkshire towns were coming fast into importance; the ports of London, Bristol, Hull and Boston, and many others now insignificant, were occupied by busy mariners. Harrison gives it as his opinion that our shipping was incomparable for 'strength, assurance, nimbleness, and swiftness of sailing,' and he fortifies his position by foreign testimonies. The Queen had 24 ships, there were 135 merchant ships of over 100 tons, and 656 of between 100 and 40 tons. Abroad, our merchants were penetrating, on the heels of travellers of whom not a few were Englishmen, to the Levant, to the Baltic, and even to

Cathay and Tartary. We had colonies, or 'factories' as they were called, at Florence and Pisa, at Moscow, and in Norway, Sweden, and Denmark, which were so numerous and well-established as to have their own laws, administered by 'aldermen,' under treaties with the sovereigns of those states: all our trade was done in English ships. Looking outside, however, we saw that the New World was far from being an unoccupied field into which we might freely extend our activities. The Eastern routes were in the hands of Portugal or Holland, while the best portions of America were appropriated by the most powerful of the nations, Spain. The King of Spain held Mexico, Florida, Peru, and the largest of the West Indian islands; the mid-Atlantic and the Caribbean Gulf were regarded as his highway. The Brazils were in the hands of Portugal. If we were to grow it was clear that we must fight for room, and at the outset there was but faint prospect of much success. But the impulse was there, and the energy, and the intelligence, sufficient, as the event proved, to give us the supreme place in the outward movement.

What the result has been is briefly shown in a conspectus of the British Empire in the reign of *Queen Victoria*. The EMPIRE now consists of:—

(i) THE UNITED KINGDOMS OF GREAT BRITAIN AND IRELAND under a Crown and Parliament with a single Executive administration. This kingdom is the head and the heart of the whole organism, and the centre of a commerce in which the whole civilized world has concern.

(ii) Certain great DAUGHTER COLONIES in the full sense of the term 'colony'; predominantly blood of our blood and bone of our bone, with our language, our laws (in the main), and our manners; namely, the seven colonies in Australia and New Zealand, the Dominion of Canada, and Newfoundland.

(iii) MIXED COLONIES: where English people are predominant in influence as well as in government, but where there are native populations exceeding in numbers the English residents: the older colonies in South Africa (Cape

Colony and Natal), Sierra Leone, the Gold Coast and Lagos, Mauritius, the British West Indies, including Guiana and Honduras, the settlements at the Straits of Malacca.

(iv) DEPENDENCIES: where we are present as rulers, the well-being of the native populations being now recognised to be the purpose of our staying, whatever may have been the original motive of our going: namely, the Presidencies, Provinces, and Native States of India; Ceylon; Burmah; Fiji. Some of these are incompletely under our rule under the designation of *Protectorates*, as Zanzibar, Niger Territory, Bechuanaland, British New Guinea; and in some places we have agreed with other European nations that they will not interfere with our predominance if we wish to assert it: these are called '*Spheres of influence.*'

(v) OUTPOSTS for military, naval, and commercial purposes: Gibraltar, Malta, St. Helena, Ascension, Bermuda, the Falkland Isles, the Seychelles, Socotra, Chagos and Oil Islands, Aden, Singapore, Labuan, Hong Kong, Norfolk Island, the Kermadec Islands, the Louisiades, Rotumah, Tonga.

Three salient features in the colonizing and governing achievement of the British people are so remarkable and so important that they should always be brought into the field of view when we feel in danger of being confused through the variety and the multitudinousness of our colonial history:—

(*a*) They have colonized and started in full course the *largest pure colony* ever yet seen—our thirteen colonies in North America, now the United States. No development by growth of offshoot has been exhibited in ancient or modern times on a scale so extensive before; compared with this, the Spanish daughter-nations in South America are puny in strength, besides being hybrid in race.

(*b*) They stand before the world as rulers of the many nations summed up under the term '*India*'; a government by an outside people carried on *for the welfare of the governed* such as has never yet been attempted on anything approaching the same scale.

(*c*) They have an Empire so placed that they are brought

into *direct and effective contact* with all the great nationalities in the world. Their islands give them a place in the European home; they have a footing on all the ocean-coasts of Africa and are extending inland from several sides; they are neighbours to China and Japan; they have important interests in America; and are without serious rivals in Australasia and the Southern Oceans.

Upon this basis is erected a *Commerce* which causes nearly a thousand million pounds' worth of goods to pass in and out every year: the corresponding figures for France being 350 millions, Germany 350, the United States 300, Russia 150. This commerce gives employment to a mercantile Marine which the first complete Lloyd's Register (in 1886) showed to be 52 per cent. of the shipping of the world, 63 per cent. of the steam tonnage taken separately; and it gives rise to a Banking system which makes London the centre of the business of the world. Upon this imperial and commercial basis, and by means of a language becoming more and more necessary as an equipment of educated people, there flourishes a system of book and journal circulation by which English ideas are rapidly communicated to the educated classes of every nation.

CHAPTER II.

The Pioneer Period: Portugal, Spain, England.

The Motives.

IN the formation of our Empire we shall see in action *motive powers of various kinds* controlled towards one end. For the early stages it is not necessary to make much analysis. We may very well allow that with nations as with men, and with animal life generally, there is such a thing as *spontaneous* activity, especially when the nation is young and vigorous. The English nation had energy to spare, and was soon aware that new opportunities were offered, especially to those of her people who were already occupied with commerce and were familiar with the sea. In her ports and all along the sea-board of the southern counties the movement was soon intensely felt. Gentlemen and merchants banded themselves together for 'ventures' and found no lack of mariners to man their little ships. There can be no doubt that in many minds the aim was for *Gold:* but somehow the gold-yearning of an early period hardly carries with it the sordid associations of later times. When a man takes his life in his hand, and sallies forth with all his wits on the *qui vive*, and all his courage required, even the pursuit of gold has some nobility about it; and when his life is risked not only in stormy wind and tempest, but also in conflicts with savages in unknown lands, and in still greater jeopardies from jealous and angry rivals, we feel that we must allow him some claim upon our capacity for admiration. In England, too, we find that gold had far less share in the attraction than it had in Spain. We can best describe our aim as *Trade:* the acquisition of bounties of Nature not bestowed on our own land, in exchange for products of our own industrious people.

In looking at the great expansion of trade in the new era we must note that to some extent it was a *diversion* of enterprise, and not wholly a creation of new lines. The commerce of Venice and Genoa with the East had before this given birth to a wealth and luxury of life which for many years was not more than replaced, if it was ever replaced, by the prosperity of Lisbon and Seville and Antwerp. The sea-voyage to the East made traffic easier in certain points, but it is a fact that large regions of Asia,—the Bokharas, Thibet, and China,—were better known to Europe before the New World was discovered, than they have been until this century. But of course there was also a great expansion over a *new field*, and the glory of Italian commerce was to pale before the rising stars of the more Western States.

Portugal first in the field.

The honour of *priority* in the move seaward belongs to PORTUGAL. In Portugal we see a compact nation, owning a long coast-line well out to the West, and trained by her long wars with the Moors. She found herself free in 1385, about one hundred years earlier than her neighbours of the then separate kingdoms of Aragon and Castile, and she produced a man capable of stimulating and directing the new movement, though never himself an active participator in it. *Prince Henry the Navigator*, younger son of the Portuguese king, devoted himself to the fostering of discovery. He took up his abode on the sea-coast of Portugal and for forty-three years directed a School of Geography and Navigation; never marrying, but taking the Advance of Knowledge of the Earth as his bride, in the mystic spirit of mediaeval chivalry. Securing the property of an effete order of knighthood, Prince Henry obtained leave to reconstitute it as the 'Order of Christ,' with himself as Grand Master; and by this means expeditions were equipped throughout his life and for years after his death. The Navigator's efforts were directed to the determination of the coast of Africa. It is of interest to remember that this enterprise was only in a sense a new one. The Renaissance was a re-conquest of Knowledge in many ways, and one of the last fields re-discovered was that of the Carthaginian and Greek navigations. If we may trust Herodotus (Book iv. § 42), Africa was circumnavigated before his day, by close clinging to the coast. The voyage took two years, and the explorers went ashore to raise crops.

> Rude as their ships was Navigation then,
> No useful compass or meridian known;
> Coasting, they kept the land within their ken,
> And knew no North but when the pole-star shone.

Still, we must not depreciate Portugal's glory, for all this was as if it were forgotten. Prince Henry found that what lay beyond Cape Bojador was unknown: modern navigators had sailed only 700 miles out of the 6000 between the Strait of Gibraltar and the Cape of Good Hope. They had indeed ventured away to the west 500 miles, sufficiently far to secure the Madeira Isles—which still remain to Portugal—and Prince Henry at once showed the quality of his ideas by providing that the islands should not be used simply for their indigenous produce, but improved by the planting of sugar from Sicily and grape-vines from Crete. Gradually his sailors pursued their way along the coast. The Senegal and Gambia rivers were discovered, and then Prince Henry died—1460. But the mark of success was on his work, for his own death could not stay it. The Sierra Leone mountains were sighted and named; the great bend of the coast eastward was followed round the Gulf of Guinea until it turned southward again; and so on and on, until at last in 1492 one of the successful Diaz family, Bartholomew, found the coast again trending eastward—he had rounded the Cape. After placing a pillar on the shore of what is now Algoa Bay he returned. Immediately an expedition of three first-rate ships, three-masters of 400 tons burden, were fitted out in the dockyards of Portugal, and Vasco da Gama, their commander, had the honour of showing Europe the ocean-road to Asia. In July 1497 his expedition left the Tagus, in May 1498 it landed at Calicut on the Malabar coast of India. Here a 'factory' was formed, and after Da Gama's return a large fleet followed him up and planted factories all along the coast. Forty years had been required to push from Cape Bojador to the Gambia river, less than 1000 miles; the next forty saw Portuguese factories in India. Prince Henry's School of Navigation had worked out the mission of the new 'Order of Christ.'

Following up these efforts, Portugal's merchants were soon busy from the Tagus to the Canton River in China. She attained the height of her power under her Governor-General, *D'Albuquerque*, 1508-1515, while England and Scotland were engaged in conflict at Flodden, and Henry VIII was occupied with continental intrigues. But Portugal did not either colonize or rule, except in the Brazils. Her factories were *trading-stations* to which a few miles of adjacent territory were annexed, and the native potentates in the neighbourhood were entirely undisturbed. In Goa and Panjim she still holds relics of her Indian possessions, and it was from her that we acquired Bombay, as part of the dowry of Catharine of Braganza. Portugal was very nearly being the first in *Western* discovery also. Columbus first offered his services, and all his ideas about the western roadway, to the nation for which Prince Henry had won so noble a name. The fatal mistake was committed—this was some years after the Prince's death—of referring Columbus and his proposals to a Committee; his plans were misunderstood and despised, and his offer refused. But, even so, the Prince's work was still bearing fruit; his school largely contributed to the triumph of Columbus, and later on Magellan and Portuguese sailors were engaged in the Spanish expedition which went beyond the River Plate, and they were eventually the first Europeans who entered the Pacific Ocean from that side. But when the New World had been discovered, by a curious blunder Portugal obtained a share. She was to be left free by Spain to all the regions east of a certain line of longitude, while Spain was to be free on the western side. But by an error in their geography, South America was pushed too far east on the map, and the Brazils were marked as on Portugal's side of the line, as if, in fact, in line with Africa, the breadth of the South Atlantic not being known. Accordingly, Brazil became Portugal's chief colony, and, though now not in any way politically connected with her, she has left her mark upon it. Portugal figures so little in later colonial history that we may dismiss her here by saying that when she came under the dominion of Spain, 1580-1640, her factories and dependencies in the east fell one after another into the hands of the Dutch, leaving only the Azores and the Madeiras, Goa and Macao, and long lines of African coast in Mozambique and Angola, where the hold was so slight that there was nothing which the Dutch took the trouble to secure. In thinking over our recently evoked controversy with Portugal in East Africa, we do well not to forget that her past history entitles her to a degree of regard which her own present position would not justify. And we may still hope that the tradition of her ancient glory may enable her to be of some use to civilization in her African territories; if not, we shall have to leave her to be dealt with by our South African colonies. But at least the historian of colonization will always have a warm regard for the gallant little pioneer nation—the land of Prince Henry, of Diaz, of Da Gama, of Magellan, and of D'Albuquerque.

Spain.

An ampler and more varied page in the history of European colonization is filled by SPAIN. There is something attractive to the imagination in the record, and yet a very mixed impression is caused by its study. Gorgeous with show of wealth, and sometimes splendid with heroism, it is also stained indelibly with cruelties, and gloomy with almost inexplicable failures. How was it that so much of the best of the New World fell to Spain and gave her a magnificent appearance in the world, and yet whenever she

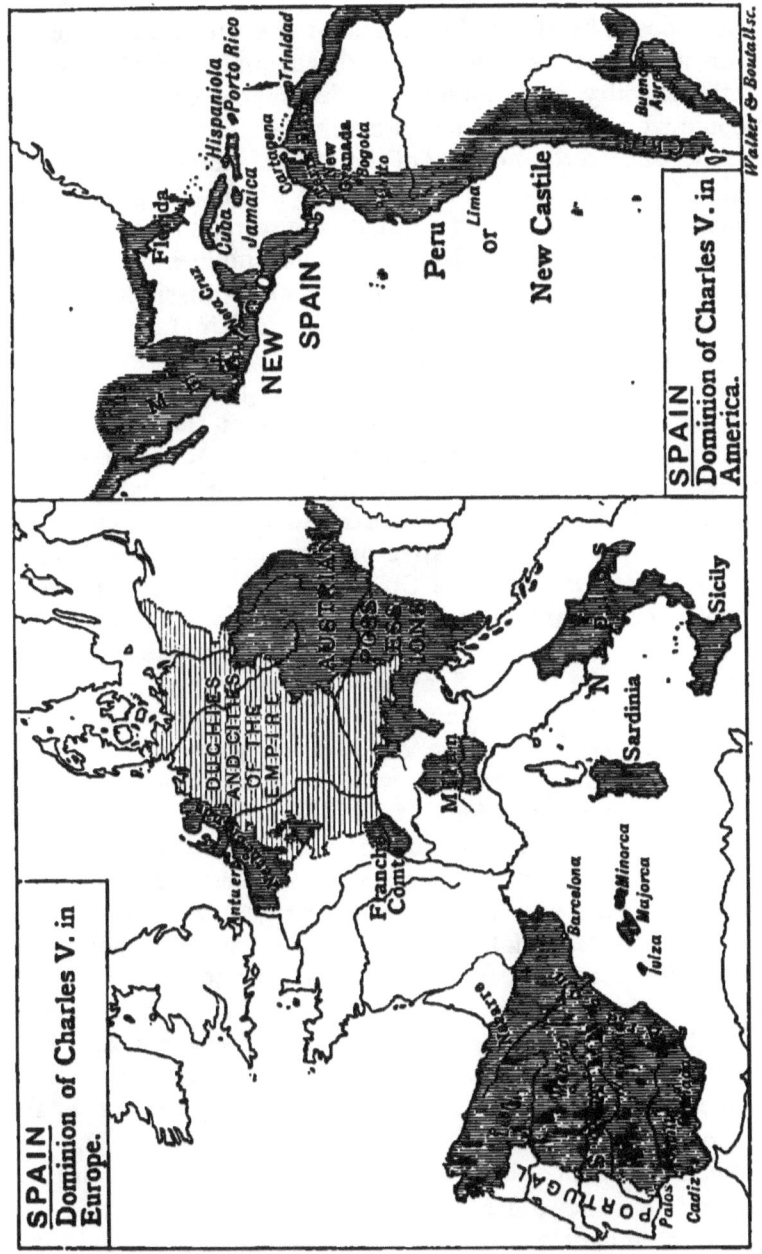

was opposed by Holland or England she had the worst of it? How is it that we associate with the name of 'Spaniard' both chivalry and blundering in their extremes? The people who carried Mexico with a *coup de main*, who in naval conflict shared the honours of the critical victory of Lepanto, were of the same nation as those who when setting about the chastisement of England seemed only to pass from one kind of blundering and ineffectiveness to another. The same country produced in Las Casas a flower of missionaries, and a queen of singularly high and tender soul in Isabella; and also a ruffian-leader like Pizarro, and the godless inhumanity which harried out of life in fifteen years fifteen-sixteenths of the natives of Hispaniola. The wrath of the Devonshire gentry was kindled by narratives of the ruthless dealings of the 'Spanish Papists' out on the main; and yet the heart of generations since has been touched to the quick by that incomparable imaginative picture of the true gentleman, Don Quixote, drawn by a Spaniard and Spanish in every detail of colour and character. To reconcile this opposition is not now our task: we need here only notice three advantages on the side of Spain in these early days:—

(1) Her *training* in the wars with the Moor, rendering the bearing of arms and the conduct of guerilla warfare a matter of common education with the Spanish gentleman.

(2) Her position under Charles V and Philip II as *chief of a quasi-confederacy*. The looms of Flanders and the industrial organizations of her Italian dominions and allies were ready to absorb and work up what the gentry of Castile and the mariners of Andalusia and Biscay might bring home.

(3) Her readiness to bring the valour and the enterprise of others into her own service. Columbus of Genoa and Magellan of Portugal learned their business apart from her, but it was under her flag and with her resources that they sailed, and in the prestige of their achievements Spain claimed the Western World.

Securing at once the greater islands in the Caribbean Gulf she set to work to get their gold and silver. But this was not an abundant source of wealth in those islands, and from them sallied forth in farther quest bands of disappointed adventurers. Cortez led one to Central America and secured Mexico; Pizarro led another and seized Peru; and Balboa first of Europeans crossed the isthmus and gazed upon the Pacific waters. These expeditions absorbed her strength, and furnished her with ample spoil of conquest and an adequate field for fresh development. The mines of Mexico and Peru fed her with the precious metals, and emigration from Spain proceeded with sufficient continuity to give a colonizing character to her new provinces. Intermingling with some freedom with the natives, a considerable mixture of population ensued, and a civilization which is semi-European has characterized the colonies of Spanish America. There are not wanting persons who think that true colonization should give rise to new nationalities by admixture of race, not merely to transplantations of existing races. In this aspect it is maintained that the United States is somewhat of an intrusion, a make-shift which was all that the English people had the genius to accomplish, but that a higher function has been discharged by the Spanish people in the formation of the hybrid populations of Central and South America. This question will be again before us in the chapter on Native Races. Of the Spanish *method of Empire* we need only say that it was an unmitigated exploitation of the new lands on behalf of the old; despotic in government, it was also monopolist in trade-policy. Trade was limited to a single Spanish port, first Seville, afterwards Cadiz; and, in reality, to a few rich houses of business both there and on the other side of the Atlantic; and to two annual fleets, one to and from Carthagena, the other to and from Vera Cruz.

The history of the decadence of Spain in Europe does not concern us except to note that it was naturally followed by a weakening of her hold upon her American colonies, until they one by one broke off; and they are all now independent Republics, partly in touch with Europe, partly pursuing a somewhat turbulent course of development of their own and not likely ever to be prominent in general history. The splendour of the entrance of Spain upon world-history has, therefore, in no way been maintained. The national character was not of the fibre out of which the world-dominating nationalities are made. The expulsion of Moors and Jews undoubtedly inflicted irreparable loss on the Peninsula, a loss which was disguised at the time by the abundant supplies of silver from Mexico and Peru. But if character of the right stamp had been there, the gap so caused would have been filled up by movement of the Spaniards themselves into the places occupied by the aliens expelled. That they did not fill up their place is a proof that they were unable to play a really great part on the world's stage. And yet this could not have been predicted. It might have been thought that the nation of Loyola and Saint Theresa could have inspired and organized, that Velasquez and Murillo and Cervantes might have had worthy successors in art and literature, sufficient to keep Spain and her daughter-colonies permanently in the front rank of the nations. But it was not so in fact, and Spain had to make way for other nations.

England's appearance on the scene.

For the roots of the history of our own colonizing activity we must dig in the portly volumes of RICHARD HAKLUYT, preacher and sometime Student of Christ Church, Oxford, who in 1582 began to publish, under the title of *The principal Voyages, Traffiques and Discoveries of the English Nation*, the results of years of labour upon the records of British enterprise beyond the seas. Hakluyt was a thorough student, but he was a student of human action, not of thought or learning. His taste was early formed; he tells us of a worthy uncle, a lawyer in the Temple, who showed him some charts which were to his boyish mind 'a high and rare delight.' With his ears always drinking in tales of adventure, and his thoughts turning upon the wonders of the new geography, we may easily conceive his disgust at having to hear reproof from foreigners that Englishmen were behindhand in this glorious contest for knowledge and fame, and that this was in spite of our having some manifest advantages for this very pursuit—

our insular position, our excellent shipping, and, as was handsomely alleged, our valour. Perplexed though the Oxford student may have been by the peremptory way in which this charge was brought and passed about, he dealt with it as Charles II did with the problem of the floating fish, by questioning the fact. He then set to work methodically to show what Englishmen had so far done; and rich was the harvest of his toil. He was able to fill one large volume with the narratives of English ventures *before the reign of Queen Elizabeth*, and proceeded to occupy other volumes with narratives and original documents bearing upon *the Elizabethan voyages and discoveries*. To summarize all these would be merely to give a catalogue: some noteworthy facts must suffice.

Hakluyt prints at length the patent issued by Henry VII to two Venetian mariners, John and Sebastian Cabot, for discovery in North America. Their achievement is modestly recorded by Sebastian upon a map in a note which, as translated by Hakluyt, runs: 'In the year of our Lord 1497 John Cabot a Venetian and his sonne Sebastian (with an English fleet set out from Bristol) discovered that land which no man before that time had attempted, on the twenty fourth of June about five of the clocke early in the morning.' This was the beginning of our many voyages under the Cabots; Gilbert, Frobisher, and many another continued along the coast and towards the North-West passage; while Jacques Cartier and others for France were surveying the river of Canada, and making voyages southward of our coast to Florida. In the patent to the Cabots we see leave given to raise ships and crews to navigate under 'the banners, standards, and ensigns' of England, and to have a monopoly of royal protection and of trade in such places as they might discover. The return for this was to be one-fifth of the net proceeds of each voyage; later, in Queen Elizabeth's patent to Sir Humphrey Gilbert, for example, it was one-fifth of gold and silver only. This is inserted, it would seem, less as means of gain on the part of the Crown than as an equitable return for the protection and countenance of the State. In the East India Company's

Charter (1600) the balance of trade was the object in view: as much gold and silver was to be brought back on each return voyage as had been taken out. As a clue to the causes of our success we note with pleasure Elizabeth's special commendation of the company who returned from one of Frobisher's expeditions for 'their so good order of government, so good agreement, every man ready in his calling,' and this in spite of the great opening for looseness of discipline, as there were several on board who sailed as neither officers nor seamen, but as gentlemen-adventurers. The religious cast of mind of the time is indicated in the watchwords given for Frobisher's third voyage to the North-West passage—Watchword, '*Before the world, was God;*' Reply, '*After God came Christ his Sonne.*' Sailing under such words we are not surprised to find that order was taken for Daily Service twice in the ships, that 'swearing, dice, card-playing, and filthy communications' were to be 'banished.' And when they landed, the bonds of Church and State were not to be dissolved. The first three laws of Newfoundland under Gilbert, 1583, were (1) public worship to be according to the Church of England, (2) attempts against English rights to be high treason, (3) speaking against the honour of the Queen to be punished with loss of ears, of ship, and of goods. And Mr. Hailes, the writer of the account of Gilbert's voyage and the sole 'gentleman' who survived it, commends as among its purposes religion as the chief, other motives being valuable as giving place for this. We find an early instance of the '*valour*' of our forefathers beyond the sea in the statement of our position at the Newfoundland fisheries in 1578 (before Gilbert went there). We had only 50 sail of fishing-ships to Spain's 100, Portugal's 50, France and Brittany's 150 (small), and 20 or 30 Biscay whalers. But it is said that 'the Englishmen are commonly lords of the harbours where they fish.' We kept off rovers from other fisher-vessels in return for help in our fishing, if we required it, and the payment of a boat or two of salt; and this had been in vogue for some time, being said to be 'according to an old custom of the country.'

In *relation to other countries*, we find that the letters patent to Sir Humphrey Gilbert read in the same international sense as do our late treaties of partition in Africa. They explicitly suppose that the expedition aims only at countries 'not actually possessed by any Christian prince or people'; and it is provided that if Sir Humphrey or his successors should give offence to any foreign princes, or their subjects, in league and amity with England, and should decline to make amends when ordered by proclamation of the Crown, he or they should be put out of allegiance and receive no further protection. The connexion of the new country with England was to be maintained therefore by its being under *protection* in return for *allegiance*. Our 'Empire' was beginning.

An *internal bond* was retained; the settlements were to be *colonies*—the *patria* was not abandoned but carried over the seas. All natives of England and Ireland—this patent is made out before the union of the Scottish Crown with the English—whose names were on the registers of Courts of Record at home, continued in allegiance and privilege. Civil and criminal authority was placed in the hands of Gilbert, his heirs and assigns, for ever; and it is worth noticing that the reason given for this is no other than the one which Hobbes was presently to make so much of as the reason for government, namely, the ensuring of peace by fixing of power *somewhere*. But it is enjoined that the statutes made were to be as near 'as conveniently may be' to the laws of England, and 'not against the Christian faith or religion now professed in the Church of England.' A wise elasticity: within bonds like this an enduring connexion could be maintained. The spirit of Bacon and the method of Burleigh and Walsingham are here in operation: sagacious, practical, trustful.

We note also that other purposes besides that of extending empire or gaining means of livelihood were already being taken into account by thoughtful men. Richard Hakluyt the uncle, in his instructions to some friends going out with Frobisher (H., vol. iii. p. 72), mentions—besides 'private enrichment and increase of Navie'—*independence* of Spain for our supply of 'oils, sacks, resignes, orenges, &c.,' and of France for woad, baysalt, Gascoyne wines, and of 'Eastland' for flax and pitch. But he also catches a glimpse of other needs when he speaks of the cities to be built in the New World as a *refuge* from civil or religious troubles at home.

This storehouse for the record of our early achievements was worthily extended by SAMUEL PURCHAS, B.D., of St. John's College, Cambridge, who in 1624 published four volumes entitled, *Hakluytus Posthumus, or Purchas His Pilgrimes*, wherein he exhibits 'the English Mariner making the Seas a Ferry, and the widest Ocean a Strait,' and presents to us the formation of 'Englands out of England.'

How vigorously and with what promise the work of colonization was begun may be seen by noting that by the death of Queen Elizabeth we had

- established ourselves as leaders in the Newfoundland fisheries;
- made several attempts to plant colonies on the coast between the St. Lawrence and Florida;
- made numerous attempts to work a North-West passage to China and India;
- sent two expeditions round the world;
- over and over again spoiled the great monopolist Spain of some of her Mexican and Peruvian cargoes.

And we note also some of the characteristics which fitted our forefathers for their parts, viz.

- their reputation for skill and valour at sea;
- their disposition for order and discipline;
- their preference for general commerce over mere acquisition of gold and silver;
- their solicitude for religion and humanity, at least on the part of the organizers and supporters at home.

No one can rise from a few hours' reading of Hakluyt and Purchas without an impression that the men of whom he is reading were laying down lines of national enterprise with a spirit and an intelligence which might lack something of the pomp and romance of the Spaniard, but were of a kind and degree that made permanence and progress a moral certainty.

CHAPTER III.

INTERNATIONAL STRUGGLE: SPAIN, HOLLAND, FRANCE.

Spain.

THE expansion of Europe was not to be a struggle with Nature alone, nor a conflict only between civilized nations and barbarians. It was to be worked out in fierce *rivalry* among the colonizing nations themselves. Aggrandisement and monopoly were supreme objects at that time, and a new cause of hostility between England and her competitors was to mark our history. With Portugal we had little strife; she herself was in decay before we entered the field in any force: but with Spain we had to grapple for our place. We entered vigorously upon the struggle, and pursued it unfalteringly until our end was gained. Our warfare with Spain was very much after her own manner in her own earlier days, irregular and almost private; not with fleets and navies, but with small squadrons and single ships, attacking, harassing, plundering. The State was only partially concerned: approval was not always sought, but acquiescence, hearty if informal, was relied upon and not wanting. Elizabeth ('Mother of English Sea-greatnesse,' as Purchas calls her) well knew how to play the monarch in this. The salient features of the conflict can be well traced in a perusal of the life of our greatest sea-captain of this period, *Sir Francis Drake*, a life of constant prowess but varied fortunes. The principal concentration of forces took place in 1588, when the great Armada was despatched to crush us. All Spain's enemies, political and ecclesiastical as well as colonial, witnessed with intense interest and unbounded triumph the preparations, the attempt,

MAP to illustrate the Early Partition of AMERICA

the colossal failure, the ruined prestige. As our Queen attended a thanksgiving service at St. Paul's, so also the Kings of Scotland and Denmark (including Norway) and Sweden and Navarre, and the citizens of Geneva and of several German Protestant cities, did the like; England's lead of the Protestant nations was secured at home, the colonial monopoly fatally weakened abroad. For a space France—with its industrious Protestants not yet oppressed— was with us, and joined us in attempts to settle the West India islands in the reign of Charles I, planting royal colonies of each nation by agreement as to certain islands. But though Spain's supremacy was mortally wounded, the hostility to her lingered on, and, whenever any mind was strongly affected with dread of Papacy, Spain still loomed as the most dreaded foe. This was the case with *Cromwell*. He did not discern that the power of France was growing while that of Spain was in decay, but still held Spain and the Pope to be the chief obstacles to freedom and progress. 'The Lord Himself hath a controversy with your enemies,' he wrote to the Vice-Admiral in Jamaica, 'even with that Roman Babylon of which the Spaniard is the great underpropper. In that respect we fight the Lord's battles.' Later in the same year, 'we think to strive with the Spaniard for the mastery of all these seas.' Although he sent Blake to the Mediterranean against the Duke of Florence and the Bey of Tunis and secured justice from them, he exclaimed in the House of Commons, 'Why, truly, your great enemy is the Spaniard. He is your natural enemy.' He found Spain refusing both liberty of religion and liberty of trade in the Indies; he found English Papists looking to Spain rather than France: and his bias prevented his seeing that the effective power of Spain was declining, that however bad her principles might be, Spanish chivalry was gone, 'laughed away' or otherwise. After Cromwell's days all Englishmen regarded her as dangerous only when swelling the resources of France.

Holland.

But before France became our chief rival, another conflict had to be waged. The little nation of HOLLAND made an effort for the vacant supremacy; and for her size and resources a gallant effort it must be considered. The provinces which had broken away from Spain and are usually known as *Holland* had become the successors of Portugal in the choicest parts of her Eastern possessions. Dutchmen were established at the Cape, along the coasts of India, in Ceylon, in the Straits, and in the archipelago between the Indian and Chinese seas. They had worked hard for a North-East passage, sending many expeditions round by Nova Zembla and Spitzbergen, and it was a Dutch captain and crew who first of Europeans had to know what it was to be icebound and to spend a winter in the Arctic regions in (1596, on the east coast of Nova Zembla), the first of Europeans to live through the three months' night, and to penetrate up to 80° N. The practical result was, not a useful North-East passage, but the whale-fishery of Spitzbergen, which presently employed a hundred Dutch ships and proved an admirable nursery for Dutch seamen. It was when they were foiled in this direction that they insisted on going round by the Cape, and at that very time Portugal collapsed, and they took her place. They also made good a temporary footing in America, where their *New Amsterdam* was the precursor of the present 'Empire City' of the West. Of the first six *voyages round the world* the Dutch had the honour of making the last three. It was on the latest of these that they were the first to round Cape Horn, and some twenty years after that a Dutchman (Tasman) discovered New Zealand and Tasmania. And to other nations they contributed no slight help by the excellence of their globes, sea-charts, and atlases.

The strength and the weakness of the Dutch extension lay in their method. They owed their very existence to their industry. Bacon in his Essay on *Seditions* epigrammatically says that the Dutch had the best *mines above ground* in the world, that is, their own work and trade. Their strength lay in their intelligence and readiness to labour and to thrive, not in any physical advantages. And so their enterprises were placed upon an essentially business footing. Some of their expeditions were fitted out at public expense, but most of them by private subscription. The Joint-stock principle was thoroughly worked—advantageously, in calling into active operation the capital, however slight, of all her thrifty citizens; perniciously, in making the principal object the payment of dividends, heavy, prompt, and continuous. Far-sightedness was wanting because the shareholders would not wait; generosity, greatmindedness in Aristotle's sense, was out of the question. In education we should hardly expect a proprietary school system to work out new and unpopular lines of progress; in colonization and empire immediate returns of profit can hardly be the best means for attaining permanent success.

But for a time Holland flourished exceedingly, and her wealth greatly moved the envy of English merchants. While Cromwell was denouncing Spain, the London Exchange was occupied by men whose attention was directed rather to Holland. It was her immense *carrying trade* which was her great instrument, for she of course could not 'consume' more than a fraction of the produce which she brought to Europe: she 'carried' merchandise on commission. Of the 25,000 ships which conveyed the trade of Europe (writes Colbert in 1669) between 15,000 and 16,000 belonged to Holland; only between 500 and 600 to France. When they had settled down to their carrying trade they very shrewdly contrived to get Great Britain's consent (including Cromwell's) to a change of Maritime Law in their favour. Hitherto the old *Consulat de Mer* had allowed neutral goods in enemies' ships to pass, but enemies' goods in neutral ships were forfeited. The Dutch had this reversed; the ships were to be the points of favour and to protect the goods they carried. But to be a common carrier and trafficker was a position widely open to attack, and from what is known of England's vigour at that time it is at once manifest that we were unlikely, and indeed unable, to accept the situation, in spite of the religious sympathies which kept Cromwell from perceiving the antagonism between Holland and ourselves. But commercial rivalry was bound to tell, when men thought of the situation in such words as Dryden's:

> Trade, which like blood should circularly flow,
>   Stopped in their channels, found its freedom lost:
>   Thither the wealth of all the world did go,
>   And seemed but shipwracked on so base a coast;

and at length Cromwell had to act, the hostility being at first confined to legislative enactments. The famous *Navigation Acts* of 1651–5 struck directly at the heart of Holland. No Dutch—to save appearances it was expressed as 'no foreign'—ships were to carry to England other goods than those proceeding from Holland itself. This was fatal, of course, if it could be enforced, and to enforce it we had to fight. Here again the 'valour' and seamanship of Englishmen were not lacking, and in 1652 the naval warfare of Blake against De Ruyter and Tromp commenced. It did not last very long. The sea-fights of Cromwell's time were succeeded by the sea-fights of the reign of Charles II, but the wavering success of the actual fighting issued in a definite success for England. We made good our position; the Navigation Act was enforced, and Holland was obliged to be contented with a substantial share instead of having almost a monopoly of the traffic of the East. As a sign that our desire was for room for ourselves, not for interference, we agreed after the war of 1667 to allow all the merchandise from the Rhine districts, far away beyond Holland, to count as 'Dutch,' because they passed through her hands at Rotterdam and Amsterdam and we were in no way concerned with them. When France entered into conflict with Holland we were already on terms that made Holland and ourselves natural allies, only that the disloyalty of Charles II to his trust forced us into an alliance with France for some time longer. Holland was very nearly ruined; but when the Stuarts had gone and William of Orange wielded the combined strength of England and Holland, these nations were united by both religious sympathy and trade-interests against the threatening power of Louis XIV.

France.

In our ANTAGONISM WITH FRANCE we entered upon the last great stage of struggle; fierce, bitter, and prolonged.

The seventeenth century had brought France to the summit of her strength and placed her supreme among European States. If we must make considerable deduction from Voltaire's panegyric of the *Age of Louis XIV*, still we must frankly allow a stage of general development which marks this as one of the great periods of the world's civilization. If we ourselves produced in Milton a mind of loftier powers than either Corneille or Racine, we had no Molière, no La Fontaine or Madame de Sevigné. Boileau in criticism led an ephemeral taste, but he constructed a definite and delicate instrument of culture. Bossuet and Fénélon were not superior to our theologians and preachers, but Hobbes can hardly rank with Descartes in philosophy; and whom shall we place in a line with Pascal? If our policy was more profound it was not administered with such ability as was shown by Richelieu and Mazarin, and we never had in our history an administrator of the comprehensiveness and inventiveness of the great Colbert. COLBERT'S name, indeed, would have to be painted in large letters on a roll of those who have stimulated European colonization. Perhaps no other man of first rank, except Prince Henry of Portugal, could be placed as high as he, for no other so definitely made colonization a fixed element in his public policy, and had plans and systems so sagacious and far-sighted. He discharged at the same time five of the great offices of State—the Household, Finance, Agriculture and Commerce, Public Works, and the Marine, yet he was not overwhelmed and therefore confined to a hand-to-mouth policy. In finance he changed in twenty-two years a revenue *gross* 84 million francs, *net* 32, to *gross* 112 (in spite of reductions), *net* 94. He established five great commercial companies and induced princes of the blood to take shares. He added to the French West Indian Islands, occupied Hayti, sent out colonists to Cayenne and Canada, occupied Louisiana, Goree, the east coast of Madagascar, and established factories at Surat, Chandernagore, and Pondicherry. He raised the register of sailors from 36,000 to 77,000, and the Navy from 30 to 176 ships. With all remembrance of what England owes to Raleigh and

Cromwell and Chatham, it must be allowed that no single statesmen occupies in our history a place like Colbert's. In all interests of the human mind France was then laying the foundations and rearing the structure of the moral domination which was to last so long over the continent. Her literature and art and science and learning were known among other nations while England's had no vogue beyond our shores.

In colonization France had, by 1690, taken up a strong position and one of considerable promise. In the outer world she had positions alongside our own. In *North America* she was developing Canada, Acadia, and Cape Breton Island, and had her place on the fishing banks of Newfoundland; further south she held the mouth of the Mississippi; in the *West Indies* she had Martinique and Guadeloupe; in *Africa*, Senegal; and in *India* she had Pondicherry and Chandernagore. Her navy and her mercantile marine were of great volume, and, for a time, competently directed and manned.

Our Second Hundred Years' War.

The contest went on from the time when *William of Orange* took his seat on our throne until *Wellington* finally sheathed his sword at Waterloo. In this period of 127 years England and France, as Professor Seeley points out, were at war for sixty-four years. Not that it was always and solely as rivals in the attainment of dominion beyond Europe. Besides the fact that minor and comparatively trivial difficulties, dynastic and other, had some influence, there were two other great causes of hostility—the endeavour of France to upset the balance-of-power solution of European relations, and the breaking out of the anarchical element in the French Revolution. But throughout this period there was always in the rivalry for colonies and empire a constant ground of thorough hostility and real national animosity.

But, before bringing forward some evidence of this, we note that, in 1661, when England's population was some seven-and-a-half millions, France was a solid nation of probably twenty millions. A French historian, *M. Victor Duruy*, thus sums up the situation at that time :—

'Louis XIV had able ministers and the most united and best situated kingdom in Europe. After the breaking up of the Fronde resistance his own authority encountered no obstacle whatever. His finances were being put in order by Colbert, his army organized by Louvois under skilful generals. His strength was great and was augmented relatively by the feebleness of his neighbours.' M. Duruy then speaks of 'the decadence of Spain, the chaos of Germany, the inability of Austria to do more than hold her own against the Turks, the effacement of Italy, the weariness of Sweden after her efforts under Gustavus, the slender territorial basis of Holland.' He points out that England was terribly hampered for a quarter of a century by the opposition of the Stuarts to the national sentiment in reference to foreign affairs; a condition which disappeared when William ascended the throne.

But, just as the contest began, signs of decay in the condition of France could have been discerned. *First*, the spirit of *intolerance* gained ascendancy in the national policy; the Protestants' privileges were withdrawn in 1685; and numbers of the most industrious and steady of her citizens left for England, where there were thirty-one congregations formed in London alone, and for Holland, Germany, and America. The aged Chancellor of the kingdom ejaculated his *Nunc dimittis* of supreme thankfulness for the purgation of the Church, but did not see that he was participating in the infliction of one of the greatest misfortunes of France. In spite of the police, at least 250,000 crossed the frontier, carrying with them the secrets of their manufactures and a sense of hostility to a land they now identified with despotism and bigotry. And it may be noted that, as the French control of colonies was closer than ours, this intolerance was extended to them also : Louisiana could not play the part of New England, for the interdicts were extended to the colonies. 'The King has not expelled Protestants from his kingdom in order to set up a republic of them in America,' said a French statesman.

Secondly. The *personal character of government* was not

adapted to the needs of the situation : great ministers and generals are not always found in continuous succession, much less are upright and devoted officials of all ranks to be always secured. A despotic government may be well adapted for the organization of an invasion, or for resistance to a sudden attack, but in a prolonged contest its weakness is proved. Corruption, embezzlement, private interests and ambitions, these and similar malignant influences ruined the government of France. And at the very outset a terrible disaster befel them just where, for the conflict with us, they had most need of strength—in their navy. The story of the battle of *La Hogue*, 1692, and its consequences, is well told by Macaulay, and Michelet entirely agrees, stating that for a generation afterwards the French admirals had orders to avoid meeting our fleets, and that in consequence the English seamen were possessed with the idea of their own prowess, while all Europe was obliged to recognise that the imbecility of England in recent years had ceased with the departure of the Stuarts. When the ruler who inaugurated our resistance to French ambition had passed away it is possible that we might again have acquiesced in the superiority of France, but that she went too far when Louis XIV accepted the crown of Spain for his grandson, and thus brought on the *War of the Spanish Succession*. It was indeed a dilemma for England : whichever alliance had been thus cemented— Spain with France, or Spain with Austria—we should have been its enemy sooner or later, because, as Michelet says, 'we were looking at the Spanish Indies, the trade and the contraband of America and Asia.' Only, he adds, as it was France that took up this disputed crown, the English general desire for increase of commerce was supplemented by the English hostility against the particular nation. The council at which Louis XIV sat before he made up his mind is a scene of intense interest, and we see the terrible responsibility of despotism in the fact that his personal decision led to one of the most terrible wars of modern times, 1704–1713. Still, it was no idle butchery, nor an unaccountable madness of anger or ambition. Everything cannot be made plain by old soldiers to little Peterkins. *The Sea is a British common*, says Sir Andrew, of the Spectator Club; and Englishmen felt that they could not allow Spain and her monopolies to pass into the hands of the mightiest kingdom of the time, to our exclusion for indefinite years to come. The Marlborough series of victories confirmed our faith in the future of our nation; the first stage of the last great struggle was decided in our favour.

A glance over the *Treaties of Utrecht* (1713) shows the place which colonial interests occupied with us. Whilst allowing the family union of the French and Spanish crowns (our own candidate having become Emperor) we provided that no advantages to French commerce and navigation should be given by the King of Spain; and by means of the 'vaisseau de permission,' a ship of five hundred tons which we might send once a year to the Spanish colonies, we were able to work a gigantic contraband and smuggling trade.

After *Robert Walpole's* long efforts for peace, England was gradually driven into a new war (1743) because Spain refused frankly to permit trade to be open. The war was with Spain first; but, apparently on account of a new question, the *Austrian Succession*, France soon joined her, and the campaigns signalized by Dettingen and Fontenoy were fought. As instances of the real importance of our colonial interests at this time, it is remarkable that while the experienced Walpole was for maintaining peace, the commercial classes felt that he was wrong and that hostilities must be prepared for, if not precipitated; and it was afterwards discovered that their instinct had led them right, for a secret family treaty between France and Spain had been arranged, entirely to our detriment. This brief war ended in a 'peace' (Aix-la-Chapelle, 1748), which was merely a truce, a suspension of hostilities in the field; 'made in a hurry and without wisdom, it was badly made,' says Michelet; it may be taken as a warning against attempts to have 'peace at any price.' The weakness of the situation was shown beyond the seas: in America and India our plans and those of France were irreconcilable, and campaigns were going on even before the peace was publicly broken. In *America* the French were making an attempt to connect their two colonies, Canada and Louisiana, by a line of forts, occupying the territory behind our backs, and thus shutting us up to the country between the Atlantic and the Alleghany mountains. The Ohio valley was the scene of conflict, and the colonists of Virginia were supported by British soldiers in resisting the French and their Indian allies. It was here that Washington, in command of colonial forces, first saw active service. At this time, too, we carried out,—under the plea that it was necessary to remove people of French nationality, and therefore of doubtful loyalty, from our own territory near the St. Lawrence,—the banishment of the *Acadians*, brought home to us in its sadness in Longfellow's *Evangeline*. At the same time the two nations were joining issue on the question whether France or England should represent Europe in India. Four considerable men appeared on the scene for France, La Bourdonnais, Dupleix, De Bussy and Lally; and it was one of these, DUPLEIX, who first put into active operation the idea of going beyond the factory system of the Portuguese and Dutch and establishing 'a *colonial empire in India*, built upon the power of the native peoples.' But he was inefficiently supported from home: an empire could not be established by means of such offscourings as his Government supplied him with; he had to give way; and Lally, in his turn, was so ill-supported with funds, that the genius of CLIVE and the energy of the *East India Company* soon settled the question on the Carnatic coast, and the French position was gone. It is sad to reflect that La Bourdonnais was shut up in the Bastille, that Dupleix died in misery, and that Lally was executed.

Chatham.

At length the *Seven Years' War*, which was practically to settle the controversy, broke out in full flame in Europe. Our alliance on the continent had changed. Gradually the Austrians had begun to feel that France was their true friend, and these countries formed an alliance in 1756, an enmity of two hundred years' standing being effaced by the appearance on the scene of a fresh centre of force in the person of Frederick of Prussia and by the beginning of the unification of Germany. To Frederick we turned; and early in 1757 we stood forth with him as joint champions of 'the liberties of Europe and of the Protestant religion in Germany.' We were to keep an army in Hanover of 50,000, and a fleet in the Baltic, and to supply him with substantial subsidies, whilst France did much the same for Maria Theresa; they in their turn declaring for 'the liberty and tranquillity of Europe' too. The position on the continent was not hopeful for our cause. In front of Frederick was a hostile line of nations from St. Petersburg to Lisbon, and a shower of disasters marked the beginning of the struggle. Braddock lost his life and his little army in the *Ohio Valley; Minorca* was taken by the French Mediterranean fleet; *Gibraltar* was in danger; the *Duke of Cumberland* was out-manœuvred and obliged to disband his troops in Hanover; and Frederick was driven back from *Bohemia.* 'We are no longer a nation,' said Lord Chesterfield.

But in England there came to the front one who drew from Frederick the declaration that England had at last brought forth a Man. WILLIAM PITT, or CHATHAM, as we oftener call him now, confident in himself and trusted by the great bulk of the middle classes as no one ever was before or since, took the helm of state, and in conjunction with the Frederick whom Carlyle 'defined to himself as the Last of the Kings,' soon changed the aspect of affairs. Expeditions were sent from England to aid Frederick, subsidies were poured into his coffers, and he made a fresh invasion of Germany, and won over the French the critical battle of *Rosbach*, besides driving the Austrians out of Silesia. Frederick had, indeed, to give way again afterwards, but our victory at Minden made all clear once more, and Frederick poured his troops along the old line of victory, and this time with permanent effect. About the same time *Clive* was establishing our power in BENGAL, Pitt's chosen general *Wolfe* was storming QUEBEC, and our *Admirals*, Hawke at Quiberon and Boscawen off Lagos, were shattering both the great divisions of the French navy. The year 1759 alone saw the following successes: in June, *Guadeloupe* taken; in September, the news of *Minden* and of the driving ashore of the *Toulon fleet*; in October, the capture of *Quebec*; in November, the *Brest fleet* attacked in its shelter among rocks and shoals, and ruined. A contemporary remarked that if this went on 'it would soon be as shameful to beat a Frenchman as a woman.' 'Our bells,' writes Horace Walpole, 'are worn thread-bare'—we must pardon the mixture of metaphors—'with ringing for victories. I don't know a word of news less than the conquest of America. Adieu. Yours ever.—P.S. You shall hear from me again if we take Mexico or China before Christmas.'

Again, he puts his finger on the seat of disease when he writes more seriously, 'Sure universal monarchy was never so put to shame as that of France. What a figure do they make! They seem to have no ministers, no generals, no soldiers. If anything could be more ridiculous than their behaviour in the field it would be their behaviour in the cabinet.' As France could not pay in time the interest on her National Debt, a line was inserted in an English newspaper among the list of Bankrupts—'Louis le Petit, of the City of Paris, peacebreaker, dealer, and chapman.'

Three great *results of the Seven Years' War* will always give it a distinguished place in modern history:—

   The firm establishment of the *Prussian Monarchy*, and the beginning of a new German State;
   The decision as to which European nation should make the attempt to *dominate India*;
   The securing of *North America for the British people*.

This signal advance on our part must always be associated by Englishmen with the great name of Chatham. An almost reluctant contemporary opinion is worth quoting. Horace Walpole (Letter, June 3rd, 1778) writes, 'I do not know yet what is settled about the spot of Lord Chatham's interment. I am not more an enthusiast to his memory than you. I know his faults and his defects—yet one fact cannot only not be controverted, but is more remarkable every day. I mean, that under him we attained not only our highest elevation, but the most solid authority in Europe. When the names of Marlborough and Chatham are still pronounced with awe in France, our little cavils make a puny sound. Nations that are beaten cannot be mistaken.'

The next stage of the century of war shows *France joining our American colonists*, thereby supplying them with a navy and making our permanent victory over them impossible. Again there was a terrible situation before us: an accumulation of dangers such as recalls the direst straits of the Roman Republic. In 1780 we had to face the following perils and obstacles: powerful French and Spanish fleets were besieging *Gibraltar*; large hostile fleets were in the *West Indies* (sixty of our merchant ships were carried into Cadiz in one sweep); the *Armed Neutrality of all the Northern nations* was like an ice-wall before us; *Holland* had just passed from neutrality to actual war; our *chief colonies were in revolt*, and we had lost one of our two armies there; the ablest of Indian native rulers, *Hyder Ali*, was threatening our new position in India; *Paul Jones and other privateers* were damaging our ships; *Ireland* was seething with discontent; and in Parliament the Ministry were faced by an *Opposition* composed of abler men and better speakers than themselves. But there was no despair. The spirit of Chatham worked on after his retirement and death. Elliot saved Gibraltar; Hastings preserved India; and Rodney, after ruining the Spanish fleet, sailed to the West Indies and gained a splendid victory over the French fleet there: the net result for France in 1782 being that, though somewhat restored in prestige, as compared with 1763, she regained not a single foot of territory from us, and was again proved to be our inferior on the seas.

Against Napoleon.

The other two wars were waged after the fall of the old monarchy in France, and, so far as our empire is concerned, we were mainly occupied in holding what we had already while keeping France within bounds in Europe also. These *Napoleonic wars* were not carried on by us so evidently for our Colonial Empire as the others had been, especially in the later period after Nelson had succeeded in reducing their navy to impotence. Opposition to the revolutionary spirit counted for a great deal in the first, and afterwards opposition to the designs of Napoleon took its place. But Napoleon had had his eye on the East, and when his prodigious successes in Italy gave him the peace of Campo Formio, 1797, he turned to deal with England. Buonaparte himself found out that we could not be attacked in our islands, and so he proposed to gain glory in Egypt, and strike us from there—'la frapper au cœur en y détruisant son commerce et son empire.' Madame de Stäel, for instance, acknowledges (*Le Directoire*) that Napoleon, after having, under the instructions of the Directory to prepare an attack on England, examined our coasts and discovered our impregnability, tried the conquest of Egypt and the Mediterranean, and eventually of our establishments in India. Nelson's victory at the Nile and Sidney Smith's stubbornness at Acre were timely and successful obstructions to great designs against us. Napoleon aimed a more direct blow at us by his *Berlin Decrees*, but we never paused in our opposition until we had cleared the French from Spain. When at Vienna in 1814 England and her allies settled the boundaries of France, we left her on her former lines of territory, but relatively a weaker nation, as Prussia, Russia, and Britain had all aggrandized themselves; meanwhile the English were confirmed in the possession of all the colonies acquired since 1783 that they thought it essential to keep.

Result.

In looking back upon this persistent and desperate conflict for empire an Englishman naturally feels a glow of patriotic pride at the evidence it gives of the strength and the spirit of his nation, not more manifest when Chatham and his son in turn guided and inspirited her government than when, in the interregnum between these great statesmen, men of mediocre ability had to hold the helm. When we turn to form our judgment upon the *failure of France* we must frankly acknowledge the justice of the claim of her historians, that she was placed in a more difficult position than we: she had her continental foes to deal with as well as ourselves. *C'est le double effort qui l'épuisa.* But France, it must be remembered, was a mightier nation than England at the outset; and, as has been pointed out, she was at the height of her moral power when the contest began. We have to conclude that she suffered from internal degeneration; that she became enervated, whilst we were strong and healthy, with a liberty sufficient for our needs, and an aim not at dominion over other nations, but at legitimate development of the material sources of national prosperity.

To learn that the acquisition of colonies and commerce was the cause of our fierce hostility to France eases the minds of those who have been taught to look upon these wars as ebullitions of passion or efforts of ambition. The warlike spirit which breathes through Bacon's essay on *The true Greatness of Kingdoms and Estates* (xxix) was neither ambition nor passion, but is quite consistent with the declaration of President Garfield in our own day—' Ideas are the great warriors of the world, and the war that has no ideas behind it is simply brutality.' The ultimate object of this long and severe strife was, as Professor Seeley points out, neither trivial nor brutal, but 'a prize of absolutely incalculable value,'—free room for national development.

CHAPTER IV.

DEVELOPMENT AND SEPARATION OF AMERICA.

THE birth of our American colonies fell so far within the era of printing that their history, though not yet of three centuries' stretch, is already voluminous and detailed almost beyond control. The hasty generalizer finds abundant material for epigrams, and the laborious investigator of human history finds masses of documents capable of absorbing his toil for years. Their importance has not been adequately recognised: but even Professor Gardiner, interested as he is above all men in upholding the importance of the home history of England in the first half of the sixteenth century, declares that 'Englishmen of future times will turn from questions of the Palatinate or Parliamentary privilege of James I's time to contemplate the fortunes of a little band of exiles.' An interest in the early days of the American colonies can perhaps best be acquired by calling in the aid of fiction and poetry. For New England we have *Miles Standish* and *The Scarlet Letter* and *The Seven Gables*; with Campbell's *Gertrude of Wyoming* for Pennsylvania; *Esmond* and *The Virginians* for Virginia, supplemented with the gruesome romances of our colonizing life on its roughest side in Defoe's *Colonel Jack* and *Moll Flanders*; and for the romantic side of our contact with the aboriginal Red Indians we have Fenimore Cooper's novels and Mayne Reid's. Then would come that remarkable book, Smith's *History of Virginia, New England, and the Summer Isles,* where fiction and fact are unrecognisably intermingled by a writer who was himself a chief actor in the scenes described; the story of the *Pilgrim Fathers*; and a life of *William Penn*. By means such as these the history of the formation of the American nationality can be introduced with the advantages of local and personal colour or the attractions of literary art.

The colonization of America dates back to the surveys of the Atlantic coast by the Cabots; then came the voyages of Gilbert, and Frobisher, and Hudson (only partly under our flag), followed by the attempts of Gilbert to plant a colony at the fishing-stations of Newfoundland and the repeated attempts of Raleigh to found one farther south in the vast and undefined region marked as Virginia. But it was not until Elizabeth had been dead three years that the *Companies* were formed which were to achieve permanent results in colonization. These were the *London* and the *Plymouth Companies*; and it was a venture of the former which despatched 143 emigrants, who, in 1607, founded the *first permanent centre of our colonization*, under the name of *James Town*, on Chesapeake Bay. This little settlement, too, was nearly abandoned, through lack of the means of livelihood; but on a change in the constitution of the Company at home,—which brought in among others Francis Bacon, who added in a later edition of Essays the one on *Plantations*, already referred to,—500 more settlers, with stores, were sent out. But these unfortunately represented a new policy; the emigrants were mostly rascals: and all went so badly that once again the precipice was neared: in fact the whole 'colony' had embarked to start for Newfoundland when a reinforcement arrived under Lord Delaware. He set the people to tilling the ground and fortifying themselves against the Indians, and from his landing the colony was really established: although the early struggles of the settlement will always be bound up with the name of that hero of Thackeray's boyhood, 'CAPTAIN JOHN SMITH.'

The first nail is often enough to hold a plank in its place for a time: by the James Town settlement English energy found a centre on the American continent, and development soon followed. Another motive for emigration—foreseen some time before by the elder Hakluyt—was soon in operation, *refuge from oppression.* The party of English refugees in Holland, revered by their posterity as the 'PILGRIM FATHERS,' compelled to seek some other refuge than monasteries or mendicant orders, obtained a royal but 'private' promise that the Companies should not molest them and sailed for America. They landed, 102 'strong,' in 1620, at a point already named Plymouth by Smith. The climate was their chief difficulty; they arrived in November, and their capacities for endurance were severely tried; at one time, when corn was gone, shellfish was their principal diet. However, things cannot have been so very bad, as by 1627 the little community was able to undertake to buy up the shares of the Company which had fitted them out, and in six years more had paid off all the instalments; but it was twenty-three years before they numbered 3000 people. A colony close by them was planted by a new Company in 1629, which became the colony of *Massachusetts*, and eventually absorbed the original Plymouth settlement. Massachusetts must not, however, be confounded with Plymouth and the Pilgrims. The former numbered in its ranks some squires and merchants, and even relatives of prominent public men, and was very nearly including Cromwell; the Pilgrims were poorer, and unlettered; and, while the latter were thorough-paced Independents, the men of Massachusetts were of the main body of the Puritan party and had the countenance of its leaders at home. From Massachusetts the colonies of *Connecticut* and *Rhode Island* were afterwards formed. Maine was separately founded.

The growth of the American colonies was due partly to a stream of immigrants, partly to natural multiplication when Nature had been grappled with and brought into service. The stream of migration was *a conflux of people from four sources :—*

(1) People whose main desire was to get *homes*, by the assistance of the Companies in England;

(2) People who found *political or ecclesiastical laws oppressive;*

(3) People whom the Government desired to rid the country of, for their *misdemeanours;*

(4) People from Africa carried over as *slaves* and regarded as chattels.

Of those in category (2) it is sufficient to notice that the tolerant application of the laws of Maryland, rather than the constitution itself, gave the Papists one place of refuge; that the Quakers went to New Jersey, but afterwards founded a colony of their own, Pennsylvania, on 'liberal' principles; while Cavaliers and Churchmen naturally turned to Virginia, where the Church of England was established by law; and the Presbyterians and Independents flocked to the New England settlements. Repression was not, however, a thing of the past. Nonconformists were at one time disallowed in Virginia, and Churchmen were evicted from New England colonies; in 1704, for example, there was no congregation of the Church of England east of New York, except a single privileged one at Boston. But after the seventeenth century greater toleration prevailed.

The Colonies in 1765.

The colonies had become thirteen in number by 1765, when the movement for independence was begun. The physical qualities of the territories and the characters and tempers of the people cause them to fall into three groups.

I. THE NEW ENGLAND GROUP, four: *Massachusetts, Connecticut, Rhode Island, New Hampshire.* These were Puritan in religion, and popular in government and in social organization: industrially occupied in corn-growing, timber-working, fishing, shipbuilding, and maritime enterprise; and in fur and skin-trading with the Indians. This group was the region where popular rights were asserted, and became the centre of literature and science: it was the home of Jonathan Edwards and Daniel Webster; of Irving, Hawthorne, and Longfellow; of Channing and Emerson; of Motley and Bancroft; of Dr. Holmes and Mr. Lowell.

II. THE SOUTHERN GROUP, five: *Virginia, Maryland,*

North Carolina, South Carolina, Georgia, all cut out of the original 'Virginia,' and occupying the territory between Chesapeake Bay and Florida. They adhered to the Church of England nominally; they were aristocratic in government and society, a class of planters with two large servile classes ('mean whites' and negroes); industrially occupied on the *Plantation* system, with tobacco for a long time as their staple product. This group furnished such leaders of the Independence struggle as Washington, Jefferson, and Patrick Henry.

III. THE MIDDLE GROUP, four: *New York, New Jersey, Pennsylvania,* and *Delaware.* Of these four, New York was taken over from the Dutch, and Delaware from the Swedes. They were not marked in religion, or in social organization; but were cosmopolitan in character. To this group, for example, came 3000 German Protestants from the Palatinate, French Huguenots, Dutch Calvinists, Swedes, and Welsh. Occupied in agriculture and mining, they were more like New Englanders than like Virginians. There was a strong taint of selfishness about the group: it supplied few leaders for the time of strife; on the contrary, they more than once nearly drove Washington to despair, and nearly wrecked the Rebellion. Their character is largely redeemed, however, by their greatest man, Benjamin Franklin, a native of Boston but a citizen of Philadelphia, and what he, with Alexander Hamilton, born in the West Indies but a citizen of New York, did for the formation of the new Union of States.

Their French Neighbours.

As time went on it became important to consider the position of *our colonies relatively to others.* Both north and south of us France had persistently continued to colonize. Quebec city was founded only two years after our James Town, and, under Colbert, definite attempts to develop French colonies were on foot. Later on, it was after the truce of Aix-la-Chapelle, 1748, that French colonies were at the height of their prosperity. Not only were the islands of Bourbon, Mauritius, and their West Indies the chief contributors of sugar and coffee to Europe, but Louisiana also was in a condition which might be called flourishing. Yet the French colonies in America were very far from being so flourishing as ours. In 1740, when our colonies could have hardly numbered less than a million people, the French in both Canada and Louisiana had not fifty thousand Europeans. Their advantage lay (1) in their magnificent position; (2) in their being united under one government and thus ready to act together, and (3) in the very friendly relations which the French succeeded in establishing between themselves and the Indians. On this last head we read their record with some jealousy. 'No other Europeans,' says Merivale, 'have ever displayed equal talents for conciliating savages; or, it must be added, for approximating to their usages and modes of life. The French traders and hunters intermarried and mixed with the Indians at the back of our settlements, and extended their scattered posts along the whole course of the two vast rivers of that continent. Even at this day (1841), far away on the upper waters of these mighty streams, and beyond the utmost limits reached by the backwoodsman, the traveller discovers villages in which the aspect and the social usages of the people, their festivities and their solemnities, in which the white and the red man mingle on equal terms, strangely contrast with the habits of the Anglo-Americans, and announce to him on his first approach their Gallic origin.' But in spite of these advantages, the secret of success was not in French keeping. They were not supported by that volume of emigration from home which was feeding the English settlements. And in Europe, as we have seen, England was improving her relative position. Acadia was given up by the Treaty of Utrecht, and when the boundary question both there and in the Ohio valley came to the front, the Seven Years' War was precipitated, and France lost all but Louisiana, which she transferred to Spain, as in isolation it had become practically useless to herself.

France retained in North America only the little islands of Miquelon and St. Pierre near the Newfoundland shore, in connexion with their right to share in the great cod-fisheries which was reserved in the treaties. Spain never made much of Florida. The Dutch settlement in New Amsterdam seemed at one time, under Governor Stuyvesant, likely to do better, but the population was not homogeneous: Walloons and Huguenots were so numerous that some public documents were issued in French as well as in Dutch; in fact it is said that eighteen different languages were spoken within the little colony. It was absorbed in 1674, and Irving's *Knickerbocker's History of New York* remains as a reminder of the early days of the great commercial centre of the West. Before the colony was absorbed, however, it had itself had time to swallow up the little Swedish settlements on the Delaware, so that after 1674 the future lay only between the French and the British.

Government.

The *government* of these colonies was in essential features a reproduction of English institutions. Representation was a ground principle, and it was distinctly associated with taxation; and as there was considerable personal authority attached to the governorships, our combination of King and Parliament was reflected there. The common law of England was supposed to be in operation unless specific alteration had been made. The main organs of government were a Governor, a Council, and a Representative Assembly. The Governor was nominated in some cases by the Crown, in others by the company or the personage at home who was proprietor of the patent or charter. In Virginia a *House of Assembly* was formed very early, 1619; it was composed of eleven representatives of the eleven 'parishes' then existing. The public history of the colonies until 1700 is full of struggles, sometimes degenerating into rancorous quarrels between the different members of government, and between these and the proprietors or the Crown at home. It is wearisome reading except for the purpose of acquiring actual insight into the working out of political problems on a small scale. The *Trade* was regulated so as to secure the export of American produce to the British market, and to keep up a character as markets for British produce. This will be further explained in Chapter vii: it must suffice here to remark that the broad effect of this did not give any serious ground for complaint, as the course of trade thus artificially regulated was very much what it would have been in a natural way. England could supply America at least as well as any other country could, and was the best market for American produce.

Separation.

But the time of *separation* was drawing near. There is undoubtedly a general *à priori* ground for thinking that 'Colony' is a temporary and unstable 'status.' A colony is in need of nursing and fostering, but when grown up the question of separation or reorganization has to be faced. Carthage separated from Tyre, Syracuse from Athens; and the question was to arise how these thirteen colonies would finally stand related to their mother-country.

The Immediate Cause of Quarrel.

Their separation from England is one of the best-known chapters of history. On both sides speakers and writers well able to express themselves were found, and every detail of the struggle with tongue and pen and rifle is before us. The immediate cause is of course quite clear; an attempt was made to raise REVENUE from these colonies without application for their *assent*. This was touching English communities in the point where English temper has always been sensitive. An Englishman believes that if you have the heart to rob him or extort money from him, there is really no crime to which you will not presently stoop. 'The feelings of the colonies,' Burke asserted in the British House of Commons, 'were formerly the feelings of Great Britain. Theirs were formerly the feelings of Mr. Hampden when called upon for the payment of twenty shillings. Would twenty shillings have ruined Mr. Hampden's fortune? No! but the payment of half twenty shillings, on the principle it was demanded, would have made him a slave.'

This is all quite true, but we must at this day insist strongly on what lay in the background. The cardinal event which had just taken place was *the deliverance of the colonies* from all fear of French aggression, or even rivalry. And this had been done chiefly as an imperial measure for the good of the empire. Should it not therefore have been paid for by imperial contributions? and, if so, who should levy these except the imperial authority? Or, if it be taken that the Parliament of England was not superior to, but only co-ordinate with, the colonial parliaments—a position repudiated by Burke—where was the gratitude of the daughter-communities for the essential assistance rendered against the power of France? Gratitude certainly seems to have little place among national motives. De Garden, the historian of Treaties, says that even after France had helped America it would have been unwise to reckon gratitude for this help as a force of any value in determining the future: such a confidence would have been *un calcul erroné en politique*. It was this feeling that the colonies were ungrateful that rankled in many English minds, and, combining with the widespread opinion that their assemblies were rather *municipal* than national in character, more like borough corporations than parliaments, gave ground for the determined endeavour to hold the colonists to the principle at least of contributing to the imperial revenue. To allow that their consent must be asked, that their contributions should be voluntary benevolences, was to make a breach in the constitution of the empire, and to diminish the authority of the Parliament in which we so much trusted, and which foreigners like Montesquieu so heartily called upon us to admire. Chatham had a view which led him to take up without reserve the colonists' side. He considered that their assemblies were full *parliaments*, that the Crown was the imperial authority; the colonies were originally planted by royal patents or charters and had never come within the jurisdiction of the English Parliament. 'I rejoice therefore,' said he, 'that America has resisted.' Burke supported the colonists because they were strong and desired this power for themselves; he took it as a matter of expediency, not of abstract right; they had always been consulted, he said, and even now were willing to contribute voluntarily; the old plan should continue. And so the most philosophically minded of all our parliamentary statesmen was found for once leaving philosophy and deciding by the expediencies of the situation. Lord Mansfield, the great lawyer, solidly and calmly vindicated the supremacy of Parliament, and Dr. Johnson wrote his pamphlet *Taxation no Tyranny* on the same side.

The Conflict.

The story of the crisis and its issue is very easy to follow. Its chief events were the *Stamp Act* of 1765, the protest from a congress of nine colonies, the repeal of the Act; the *Six Duties*; the retaining of the solitary *Tea Duty and its preamble* asserting the right to tax; the disturbances at *Boston, the closing of that port*; the decision of *Virginia*; the gradual acquiescence of the other colonies, and the *Declaration* that *a new Nation* was formed, *July 4th*, 1776. Physical force was the only means of settling a dispute in which strong reason and powerful sentiment were found on each side. The military campaigns were marked by varying fortunes. Washington earned a military fame like that of William of Orange, great after defeat and between defeats. And Franklin as the representative in France of the new nation proved himself a first-rate diplomatist, and an imposing advocate of the new Republican principles. The employment of Hessian troops by the British Government[1] was a great blunder; it introduced

---

[1] We hired 4000 men from the Duke of Brunswick, 12,000 from the Landgrave of Cassel, 608 from Hesse Cassel. On this the Americans declared themselves independent, partly in order that they in turn might be able to resort to foreign aid; France not only lent them money freely, but also guaranteed a loan from Holland.

an alien element, and led to the *intervention of France and Spain* with their navies, 66 line-of-battle ships, and so, by affecting our communications, weakened our greatest advantage. To some degree their interposition led to a softening of our animosity against the Americans, on the principle that a stranger is in peril who interferes in contentions among members of a family. Chatham had urged that we should leave America alone and deal with France, but he died soon after Franklin had negotiated the treaty of alliance between France and the new States. Then in all minds animosity took a new direction, and anxiety to keep the colonists in allegiance gave place to eagerness to cope again with our continental foe. And so it was that the shame of the capitulation at York Town was softened into sorrow for the ordinary fortunes of war as our troops filed past the French regulars (landed from their navy), paying them the salutation due to conquerors, but ignoring the American militia who stood by them.

Reflexions.

Some reflexions upon the history of the separation suggest themselves.

(i) *It is surprising that Great Britain so nearly held her own.* The distance was great, but it was not so serious a difficulty as that caused by other dangers then threatening us. That we held on for seven years before relaxing our efforts when our minds were full enough of perplexities at home and abroad is itself a fact to be borne in mind. As a matter of fact we were ready to give up the effort two years before we were compelled to do so: it was regard for our loyalists in the colonies and in Canada which compelled us to persevere so long as there was any reasonable hope.

(ii) *There is also ground for being surprised that we did not hold our own altogether.* The colonists were only nominally a 'nation' at first. The Congress—whose officer Washington was—had no powers except by the voluntary consent of the constituent states, and some of these were supine in the extreme. The middle group—Pennsylvania and New York—thought more of the disturbance of business than of political principles. There was always a strong body of Loyalists, some of whom resented the Independence measures so strongly that when the war was over they crossed to the British territory in Canada. The militia system was not adapted for a prolonged struggle; at the end of each year many returned to their farms and their merchandise. If the French had not appeared on the scene it is possible that a considerable party might have wearied of the struggle, and deferred the solution of the question at least for a time.

(iii) It is only by hasty or prejudiced judgment that we are impelled to throw ourselves with enthusiasm completely on the side of the resisting colonists. There were some ignoble motives on their side, and some honourable motives on the side of the British Government. For an unbiassed opinion we may turn to De Garden (*Treaties*, vol. iv. p. 208), where he finds no question of rights and liberties in any high sense on the side of the Americans, but sees simply a desire to quit a connexion grown useless. 'It was only,' he points out, 'after the disappearance of France from Canada, and the Spaniards from Florida, that British dominion was suddenly discovered to be intolerable.' And on our side that we fought for a preamble attached to a single unremunerative tax shows that it was not substantial revenue but a principle of government that was set in the very front of our policy, and we cannot allow the charge of narrowmindedness or petty tyranny to pass unchallenged into history. Until the introduction of the German mercenaries by us and the acceptance of French support by the Americans, the contest was of the nature of a Civil War for a principle, and it is hardly rash to say that our sympathies ought probably to follow our political views: if we have 'high' theories of government, we shall think that Mansfield and Johnson and Grenville and North were in the right; if we consider constant operation of the popular will to be fundamentally necessary, we shall side with the assemblies of America when they claim that by them alone was American will effectively expressed. And after all, it will be allowed by both that it was only a question of time. Sooner or later the spirit of the English constitution would have required either that the local assemblies should be recognised as parliaments, or that representatives should be sent to the British Parliament.

(iv) There were great compensations for our loss. The departure of the colonies from our political system, and from our monopoly system in trade, came just at the time when the axe was being laid by Adam Smith to the root of the monopoly system of trade. And De Garden points out as compensations,—

1. That our trade increased by virtue of the increase of prosperity of the new nation.
2. That the agricultural development of the United States continued to extend demand for our manufactures.
3. In the East, England was at this time obtaining several new markets hitherto monopolized by Holland. Special articles in the Treaties of Versailles, articles agreed to with great reluctance by the Dutch, provided for this.

CHAPTER V.

THE ENGLISH IN INDIA.

IT was on the last day of the year 1600 that a *Company of merchants* received a charter for trade to the East Indies under conditions as to laws and monopoly and international relations, very similar to those inserted in Sir Humphrey Gilbert's charter for Newfoundland (p. 23); and in imitation of the Dutch we more or less persistently endeavoured to set up commercial establishments on the coast of Hindostan. Little could it be foreseen that the various European Factories set up by treaty with neighbouring potentates were the roots of the first power which should rule the whole Peninsula, and still less could it be surmised that the change would come, not from long established Portuguese Goa or the wealthy and numerous Dutch settlements, but from the modest British Company with a capital of £30,000, established to do some trade in pepper and spices, which had succeeded in settling itself at Fort William, Fort George, and Bombay. The story of the conquest of India is too complicated to be narrated here; for full comprehension an elaborate study of geography and ethnology and history is necessary. But some features can be delineated which are of singular significance and interest to the student of modern history.

India: what it is.

It must not be forgotten that the term 'INDIA' is neither an ethnological nor a national expression, but rather a geographical term: it describes peoples only by their dwelling-place—the peninsula from the Himalayas to Cape Comorin. The number of 'peoples' and their relationships cannot be shown in any simple way. A population of some 280 millions is composed of peoples differing from one another more than Prussians and Scotchmen differ from Spaniards and Italians. There are one hundred living languages, at least, of which twenty are 'cultivated' ones. To put the facts very succinctly, there are (1) aboriginal inhabitants, especially in the hill and forest regions and diffused elsewhere as the low castes, (2) a vast population of non-Aryan descent speaking Tamil, Telugu, and kindred tongues ; (3) the results of waves of early Aryan immigration which came down the Ganges and Indus valleys; succeeded later (4) by streams of Mohammedan Aryans, both Persian and Afghan. And so it comes about that neither religion nor language is more than a general clue to classification to be most carefully used, for many of the earlier races were won over to the religion of their conquerors, and more or less completely to their languages. At the same time it must be remembered that these races have now lived together for centuries, and that there is a single religious system predominant, Hinduism or Brahmanism, which includes 200 millions of the population. And there has been a very considerable reduction of such differences as arise from Race by the intimacy with which the Hindu Religion enters into the ordering of daily life and the formation of habits of mind. Natives of India declare themselves sensible of a more close affinity with one another throughout the peninsula than English writers have usually supposed [1].

[1] 'This much can be said without contradiction, that the Hindus from all parts of India have manners, customs, sentiments, likes and dislikes, very much alike, differing now and then in minor particulars owing to local exigencies. If any one wishes to see these facts for himself, let him go to Benares, or to Haridwar near the Himalayas, or to Rames'varam in the extreme south, and he will find what a vivifying power the Hindu Religion is. The Gurkhas that come from Nepaul, the Sheikhs of Panjab, the Telagu and Tamil-speaking communities in the south, meet on the common ground of one religion, one nation, sharing the same feelings and sentiments.'—(*Private letter from a Brahman student at Cambridge, April*, 1891.)

Our Establishment of Rule.

The history of the gradual establishment of our rule may be divided into the following periods:—

(1) THE PERIOD OF FACTORIES, 1612–1746, when we had only trading settlements on equal terms with other European nations.

(2) THE STRUGGLE WITH FRANCE for paramount influence in the Carnatic district (S. E. India), 1746–1759.

Macaulay's essay on Clive gives full credit to the vigour of the French attempt. M. Duruy's History of France shows how it is regarded by Frenchmen of to-day. In India, he writes, France had two eminent men, *La Bourdonnais* and *Dupleix*; had they been able to work together, and had they been supported, they would have gained Hindostan for France. The former had given prosperity to the islands of Bourbon and Mauritius, and made France supreme in the south of the Indian Ocean. Dupleix was forming great projects for driving us from India; he desired that the French Company, of which he was the administrator in India, should be aggrandized not only by commerce but by territory. But these two leaders disagreed: the former was recalled and put in the Bastille; the latter, supplied, as he complained, not with money and good soldiers, but with 'la plus vile canaille,' failed against Clive, was in his turn recalled, and died in misery in Paris. *Lally*, an Irishman in the French service, of unconquerable courage if not of large ideas, but without resources behind him, had to make war on the Indian rajahs, and could not prevent Clive from carrying all before him. His soldiers refused to enter the open breach of Madras because they were unpaid. He himself with 700 men defended Pondicherry against 22,000 for nine months. It was taken and razed, and 'ce fut le coup de mort pour la domination française dans l'Inde. Elle ne s'y est pas relevée.' Or as another Frenchman puts it—Louis Blanc—'By whom was France vanquished in India? By France herself: by the rivalry between Dupleix and La Bourdonnais.' In considering what a despotic monarchy can do in the way of making use of great men, we must note that the colonial history of France records the sad fact that the two most distinguished men who promoted her imperial interests beyond the seas, and gave her a temporary promise of colonial greatness, both died in the bitterness of undeserved disgrace. The grand services of Colbert earned him a dismissal, with reproach, from the king on the one hand, and on the other a secret burial by night for fear of the populace. One hundred years later, Dupleix, the inventor of the method of conquering India for Europe, found neither king nor people more appreciative or more just.

(3) THE PERIOD OF CLIVE, 1751-1767.—Our firm establishment in the Carnatic and our mastery of Bengal.

(4) THE PERIOD OF WARREN HASTINGS, 1772-1785.—The first Governor-General, the extension of dominion by means of the Subsidiary system.

(5) LORD CORNWALLIS and ADMINISTRATIVE REFORM, 1786-1798.—A non-intervention policy towards the Native States.

(6) LORDS WELLESLEY and HASTINGS and the SUBSIDIARY SYSTEM resumed, 1798-1828: dominion greatly extended.

(7) LORD WILLIAM BENTINCK and ECONOMIC AND SOCIAL REFORMS, 1828-1848.

(8) LORD DALHOUSIE, EXTENSION, ANNEXATION, and INDUSTRIAL IMPROVEMENT (RAILWAYS), 1848-1857.

(9) THE MUTINY, and ABOLITION OF THE COMPANY *as an intermediary in administration*, 1857.—The Company was at first a body of traders protected in certain trade privileges by royal charter. But powers of another kind had soon to be applied for and they were granted; in 1624 the Company was empowered to punish its servants while out of England either by application of civil law or by martial law; in 1664 it was empowered to levy war on any prince or nation 'not Christian.' This allowed it to raise and employ troops and to become in effect a belligerent power. Afterwards an independent High Court of Justice was set up. The India Bill of Mr. Pitt (1784) established a *Board of Control* as a Government Department to aid and control the Company in

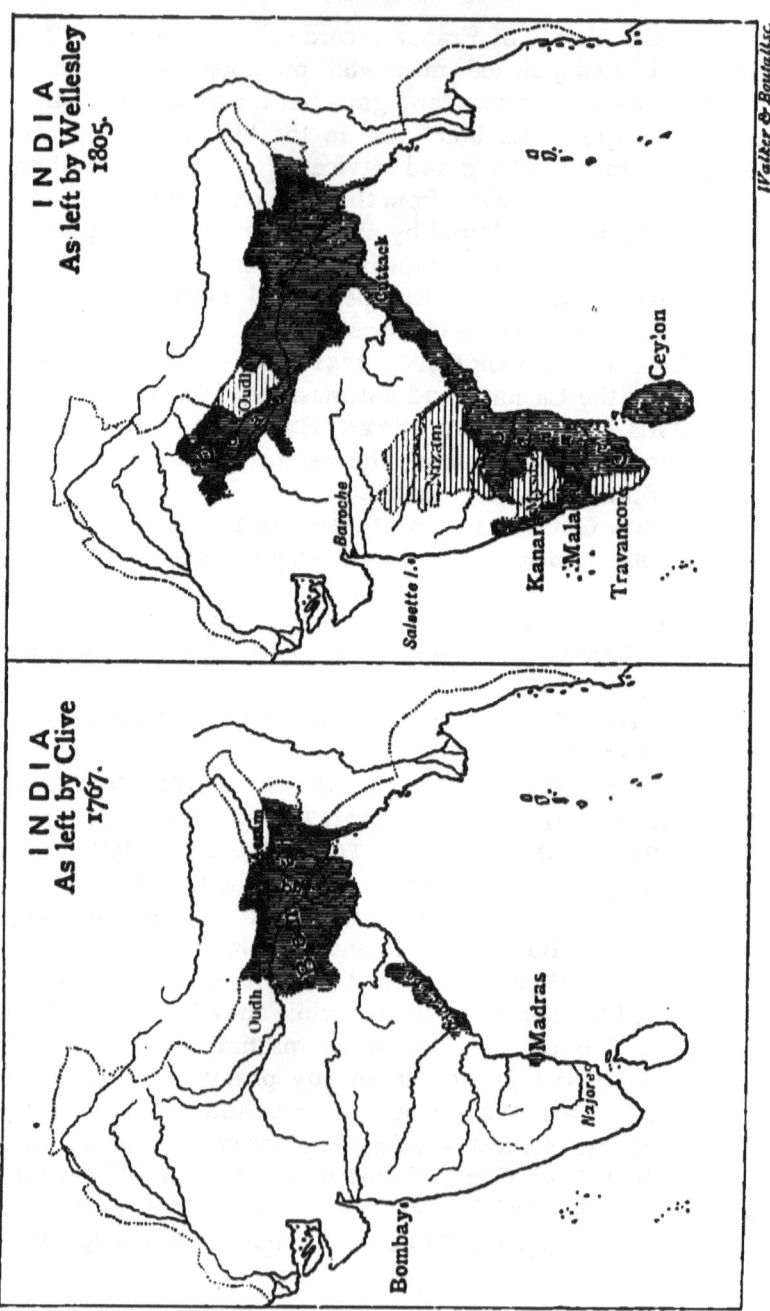

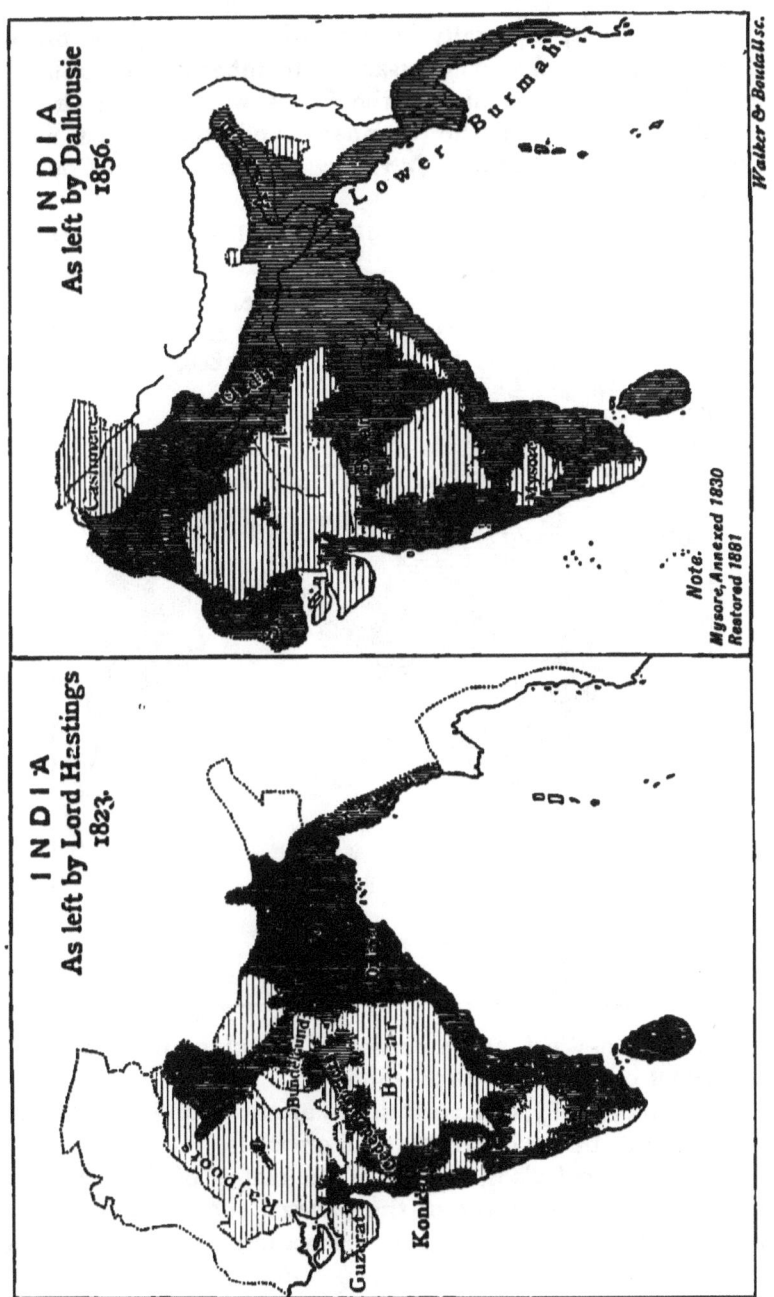

its government, especially in territorial matters; the president of this Board was necessarily a member of the Cabinet; and the commandership of the forces was made a Crown appointment. Both the Company and the Board were abolished in 1858 and a *Secretary of State* with a Council instituted.

(10) ATTEMPTS TO DETERMINE A SCIENTIFIC FRONTIER

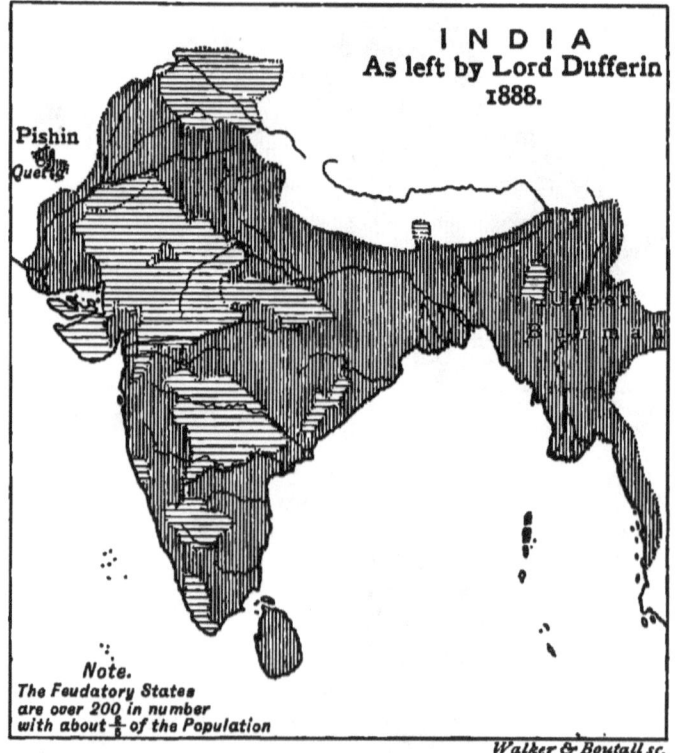

on the North-West, and inclusion of the kingdom of UPPER BURMAH on the East, 1858–1886.

(11) And, finally, concentration of attention on INDUSTRIAL AND SOCIAL DEVELOPMENT, 1886 onwards.

Professor Seeley's indication of the stages of development by means of the dates of the *renewal of the Company's charter* is very convenient and instructive. In 1773 was instituted the *Governor-Generalship* and a Supreme Court of Justice; in 1793 the *Settlement of Bengal* was made, and public expressions of Anglo-Indian opinion that India ought not to be either Anglicized or Christianized were put forward; in 1813, when the *monopoly began to be withdrawn*, and the country to be thrown open[1]; in 1833, the *monopoly in trade was at an end*, and legislative labour began in a systematic way—Macaulay's share in Indian Government was from 1834 to 1838; in 1853 the constitution of the *Civil Service* by competition was introduced; then came the *convulsion of* 1857, and the series of changes ends.

The deepest impression upon the reflecting mind is a simple one—that made by the astonishing fact itself *that England rules India*. As an illustration of the function of Mind in the movement of the world it is of singular force. We see a 'conquest' achieved by a nation not populous relatively, and far away from contact—Henry Martyn was eighteen months in getting to the scene of his labours—and, while it was going on, England fought America and France, continued to found colonies, and was taking her place at the head of the manufactures and trade of the world. Mahmud of Ghazni was next neighbour to India; Timour had no other pursuits than that of leading his immense hordes; but European civilization gave us greater advantage than either contiguity or numbers. Reading the history of the past centuries of India we feel that our establishment as its undisputed rulers is a historical fact which has hardly a parallel.

To the student of history, and to the student of politics especially, our position in India suggests certain specific questions of great interest. In endeavouring to answer them the intention is not to settle them dogmatically, but to suggest where answers may be sought.

[1] Macaulay in 1834 found the new spirit so active in Anglo-Indians that he says of his brother-in-law, Trevelyan, 'He has no small talk. His mind is full of schemes of moral and political improvement, and his zeal boils over in his talk. His topics, even in courtship, are steam navigation, the education of the natives, the equalization of the sugar-duties, the substitution of the Roman for the Arabic alphabet in the Oriental languages.'—(*Life and Letters*, anno 1834.)

I. WHAT RIGHT HAVE THE ENGLISH IN INDIA?

As *owners*, none. This is no case of a territory sparsely inhabited or inadequately cultivated where we may very easily find good reasons for joining in occupation, if not for actually displacing those whom we find in possession. On the face of it, India is in civilized occupation already; the backwardness is not such that the moral right of tenure was forfeited, as may be asserted of New Zealand, for example, where we maintain 600,000 people in a higher state of comfort and convenience than one-eighth of that number could attain before we took possession. So that we distinctly repudiate the idea of ownership, and we speak only with hasty carelessness of India as our 'possession'[1]; the correct style is our 'Dependency.' The cities and villages and lands belong, in the main, to the same owners as they did before we went there; we have not entered upon possession as the Israelites did in Canaan, or the Normans in England. Estates have been acquired by companies and individuals, e. g. in Assam and Ceylon, but on terms of purchase. The famous Permanent Settlement of Bengal does certainly appear to have been a blunder of the first magnitude. The fortunate zemindars or revenue agents who happened to be in office one hundred years ago were treated as if they were proprietors. The Government was to receive revenue from them as a tax might be taken from English landowners. As it is, the twelve million ryot-holdings in the Province pay some £13,000,000 a year rent to these zemindars, of which the Government receives £5,600,000. But even so, the intention was sound enough; knowledge of the real relations of Government and zemindars and ryots under the old States was what was lacking; there was in no sense any appropriation on the part of Englishmen.

---

[1] How wholesome has been the effect of abolishing the East India Company is shown in the change of *idea* of our relationship to India. Even Wilberforce, when working hard for an opening for Christian effort in 1813, speaks of the Hindus not only as our fellow-subjects, but as our 'tenants'; evidently thinking that we did, through the Company, *possess* India.

Again, as *conquerors*, no right is claimed by us. We do not hold India by the title of conquerors in the sense that the Spaniards held Mexico; we subject it to no tribute; we impose upon it no restrictions in order that profit should be artificially diverted for our own benefit. We are there now as *rulers*[1]. The right upon which we rely as a reasonable justification for being there is the right of doing good by ruling. We challenge the judgment of the world on the issue that we are doing better for the nations of India than any rulers of whom we have heard, or than any that would come forward if we retired. True, we are acting as judges of our own case; but it is a situation in which no higher court is known than our consciousness of the responsibility of nations to the Righteous Ruler of the universe. In proof that our decision is due to no merely private bias of our own, competent foreign observers can be quoted. Baron von Hübner, formerly Austrian Ambassador in Paris and Rome, thus sums up his impression of English influence in India (*Through the British Empire*, 1886, vol. ii. p. 250):—

'No one can deny that the British India of our days presents a spectacle which is unique and without a parallel in the history of the world. What do we see? Instead of periodical if not permanent wars, profound peace firmly established throughout the whole empire; moderate taxes; the tribunals already beginning to make their influence felt on native morality and notions of right; perfect security in all the cities as well as in the country districts and on the roads; materially, an unexampled bound of prosperity... And what has wrought all these miracles? The wisdom and courage of a few directing statesmen, the bravery and discipline of an army composed of a small number of Englishmen and a large number of natives, led by heroes; and last, and I will venture to say prin-

---

[1] In asserting this view it is not meant that this was the original position taken up by the British, or by any other European nations, in the East. Certainly the natives of India are far from allowing us any such motives. They think that it was the climate alone which prevented us from proceeding in India as the Normans did in England. And, indeed, they are not even now willing to recognise the distinction drawn in the text. They regard our 'ruling' as based upon 'possession.'

cipally, the devotion and intelligence, the courage, the perseverance, and the skill, combined with an integrity proof against all temptation, of a handful of officials and magistrates who govern and administer the Indian Empire.'

Dr. Geffcken, the eminent German publicist (*The British Empire*, 1889), says :—

'There is not the shadow of doubt that, after the fall of English authority, the ancient anarchy would assert itself once more.' (p. 31.)

'English rule has been cheerfully borne because India has never been so well governed before.' (p. 31.)

'The acts of Clive and Warren Hastings are not to be palliated; but from the beginning of the present century the English government of India has been so good that India has never before known the like of it.' (p. 17.)

We have said above that we subject India to no *tribute*. This is denied by many, whose opinions are vigorously and with great array of statistics expressed by Mr. Dadabhai Naoroji (*Essays, Speeches, and Addresses*, Bombay, 1887). Whatever might be the value of his figures, we should still maintain that they cannot now be used to sustain the position that we exact tribute as such. We certainly wish now to receive nothing from India for which we do not give a *quid pro quo*. We fondly, but we hope not foolishly, trust that we offer services in return for all that we receive. If it can be shown that we exaggerate their value, we hope that we are willing to consider the charge. But the British State makes no claim whatever to receive revenue from the provinces of India, and we are hoodwinked by those in authority if any such revenue is levied. A considerable yearly sum is certainly received by us, but the corresponding services can be plainly indicated. Our countrymen in the Military and the Civil Services spend but a portion of their income in India because most of them have domestic expenses in England, where their children are educated; they retire on pensions, after service in a tropical country, and India has to remit these pensions, but this is only instead of paying higher salaries during active employment. Heavy remittances are made as interest on the loans by which Railways and Public Works were constructed, and as profits on trading operations carried on by English capitalists. There has been some 'booty,' not to say 'plunder,' in the days gone by, but, the era of conquest being past, such consequence of the régime of war has, we trust, finally disappeared, and whatever we receive henceforth will be on purely economic principles—interest on capital lent, wages for services rendered, or profits on legitimate trade. We can now claim that the principle laid down by John Bright, not as the highest, but as the lowest that we can accept, is generally operative: .'You may govern India, if you like, for the good of England; but the good of England must come through the channel of the good of India.'

II. CAN IT EVER BE RIGHT TO SEIZE AND KEEP THE REINS OF AUTHORITY BY FORCE?

If one thing stands out more vividly than another in Professor Seeley's brilliant chapters on India, it is the striking fact that it was not by force, in the sense of the overbearing of moral energy by superior physical might, that we either acquired or maintained our position in India. We have won our way, not by weight of physical might, but by moral energy. If we read over the accounts of the defence of Arcot,—the battle of Plassey,—the defence of Lucknow; or consider the relative numbers, and the fact that we were in hostile regions, our opponents in the heart of their own territories; or note how many of our soldiers were not European, but Sepoys, and how these Sepoys seemed in crises to count for very nearly as much as Europeans, it begins to seem as if a handful of civil servants and officers had conquered India! The mistake is in supposing that the Indian populations were homogeneous, and that there was any sentiment of disloyalty to a fatherland in the minds of Indian princes who joined with us in alliance against other Indian potentates, or of Indian soldiers who entered our conquering legions. Because Vortigern called in the roving sea-pirates to help him against his fellow-countrymen, we despise him for his selfish lack of patriotism and of sense of kinship; but had those pirates been used by Saxons to keep out Normans, or by Normans to help to conquer Saxons, we should have thought it quite natural. True, had Saxons called in Saracens, or the Normans landed with a contingent of Tartars, we should have condemned the intrusion; and to a similar extent we do condemn the Hindoo Rajahs who thought that they could use French or English help for their internecine feuds. At the time of the mutiny the Sikhs rallied to our banner because to them 'Delhi was the accursed city of the Mogul, the centre of Mussulman arrogance, the place of martyrdom of the great Sikh prophets, devoted by their predictions to the vengeance of their disciples.' Whether we condemn the natives or not, their rulers, at least, showed no signs of condemning themselves, but, to their own ultimate confusion, presented themselves as ready instruments of empire to Dupleix and Clive and Hastings. By means of a system of alliances and a sagacious use of their rivalries, our capacity for direction and organization achieved the great result.

In the days of Clive there were not 10,000 of us in India: now we are only some 200,000. In the army in 1884, the Natives were exactly double the number of Europeans, 126,000 to 63,000. The police and frontier services are performed by 144,000 Native Police, mainly under European officers. Of course there is other force in reserve. The home Army and the whole British Navy would be called upon to support the Army in India if need were: but, after all, not many men could be spared in any case, and perhaps none at all if England were engaged in war at the time.

The true situation is described with great clearness by Professor Seeley. No great display or exercise of *force* has been required, or is required, because the counter *force* is so slight. If there were such a force against us as the united will of a large proportion of the Indian nations, we could not have gained supremacy and could not resist expulsion. If a flock of sheep has no moral determination to go northward when the shepherd desires it to proceed southward, southward his determination will make it go. If a panic gives them a combined determination, their physical force will be called into play, and they will stampede without possibility of his successful resistance. The peoples of India had no such united will, and the determination of a Commercial Company in an advanced stage of intelligence and discipline succeeded, because it was the only strong force in operation: but the force was the force of mind and character and will. Whether strong wills should rule weak wills, or should supply the place of will when absent, is one moral question; whether physical might should overbear physical weakness is another. And when the End of action is not the good of the stronger alone, but the common good of both, on what ground is a policy to be arraigned which has issued in the placing of rule and control where superior moral and mental strength are found?

III. SHOULD NOT ALL GOVERNMENT BE SELF-GOVERNMENT? IS NOT A BAD NATIVE GOVERNMENT BETTER THAN THE BEST FOREIGN RULE?

We acknowledge the force of the appeal of Byron's Greek to the degenerate modern Greek when under Turkey:—

> Dash down yon cup of Samian wine,
>   We may not think on themes like these;
> They made Anacreon's song divine:
>   He served, but served Polycrates—
> A tyrant—but our tyrants then
> Were still at least our countrymen!

In British minds trained to admire the Greeks at Marathon, and Bruce at Bannockburn, and William the Silent behind the dykes of Holland, there is a natural objection to being now called upon to approve of ourselves playing the Persian, the Southron, and the Spaniard. It would seem as if we must re-read much history, and give up much cherished poetry, before we can thoroughly approve of our position.

In the first place, we must insist on the distinction, the vital distinction, between *subjection* and *education*. The paramount purpose of our rule in India being once declared to be the EDUCATION OF INDIA, the situation differs entirely from those mentioned above. Could it be reasonably maintained that the Persian wanted to subject Greece for its own good, or that the Spaniard desired to retain the Netherlands for the sake of fostering the prosperity of those provinces, our sympathies would be at once affected, and the question we should ask would be whether the Persians and Spaniards possessed the means of training Greeks and Dutchmen for higher things.

Secondly, we must keep in mind that the nations of India have long lived under foreign yokes: conqueror succeeded conqueror; few indigenous governments are found, and the mixture of populations within the same areas has been both effect and cause of successive waves of conquest. If we turn over the pages of a history of India, it soon becomes plain that instead of imposing a tyranny on free peoples, or peoples struggling to be free, we have *substituted one government for many*, a lasting government for incessant changes, with all the turmoil, waste, and misery which fell upon the masses as hordes of new conquerors came upon the scene, or as their own unstable tyrannies rose and fell.

As to *permanence*, that is a relative quality. A thousand years would hardly seem a permanence to a Chinese historian. And what if it be our lot to be of all the tyrannies of India the one for which all these had prepared? the final stage of all tyranny, under which new peoples are to be fostered until they, by acquiring the conditions which make independence stable and beneficent, secure independence itself? This is our hope and aim. And one thing is sure—when their day of Marathon arrives they will have their freedom; and the battle will have been fought finally, not with sword and shield, or rifle and artillery, but by force of opinion and intelligence, rendering our continuance in India an anomaly and an intrusion. There is here a prospect of a strife of a new kind; and in the development of the peoples of India we are cheerfully educating them to do without us. Against the idea of foreign tyranny we oppose our claim to be upholding the idea of Education; for the schooling of these nations we believe that we have been appointed—for the purpose was not in our own minds at first; it was brought out only after we found ourselves charged with this high duty.

Thirdly, we maintain that we are not, to the Indian peoples, altogether an alien and outside government. To a considerable extent we are working upon the idea of *admitting them into a community of nations*. The British Empire is a quasi-federation, of which India is a chief member, though not a sharer in the supreme authority. It is by rising within this group of connected nationalities that its progress towards self-rule is almost certain to proceed. A gradual increase of the sphere of its local authorities will at length lead up to a share in the supreme control of the empire, and eventually, no doubt, to final independence: possibly not as a single nation, but as several. This is only conjecture, but we think there is good reason for regarding it as the line of progress. Every effort is made to awaken and to strengthen the idea that Hindus, Maories, and Yorkshiremen are fellow-subjects of a common empire. The path of constitutional advance for all will be determined as a problem of internal, not of international, policy.

This leads to our next question.

IV. IS IT NOT ENTIRELY INCONSISTENT WITH ENGLISH NOTIONS OF CONSTITUTIONAL GOVERNMENT TO RULE A COUNTRY WITHOUT A CONSTITUTION IN WHICH THE PEOPLE THEMSELVES HAVE GOVERNMENTAL FUNCTIONS, or at least in which provision is made for the expression of their will? Are we not proud of our record in history as a pioneer and a model of constitutional government?

In answer to this it may confidently be asserted that whatever be our present method, *we have destroyed no liberties*, we have taken no popular constitutions away. We found no parliaments and have destroyed no representative assemblies. Institutions that we did find of that kind we ignorantly interfered with in early stages, with the idea that they were blocking the path to freedom; but they were only village councils, and there is no reason whatever why we should not now make every endeavour to use them as instruments of government. But we found no parliamentary institutions at all. Nor, in the second place, are we to be blamed for not having immediately set about creating some of these. The whole teaching of history is against paper-constitutions. Even Locke, an Englishman, could not, even with the good will of the people, devise one that would work for an English colony—South Carolina ; nor had the French theorists of the Revolution any better success ; their constitutions would not 'march.' The growth of the English Constitution is a result of long and detailed struggle, and no one but the most optimistic of doctrinaires would waste time in endeavouring to transplant it to Asia. When we take into account the popular sympathies and principles advocated for us at home by John Stuart Mill, and when we remember that he spent his official life in Indian affairs, we may fairly say that in his book on *Representative Government* we have not only a defence of our present position by a thoroughly Radical politician, but a warning against taking up any other. At the same time there is an aspect of the British rule in India not to be summarily disposed of. We found no *constitutions* of a representative kind, but it is not true to say that we found no organized governments at all. The peninsula was full of States governed after the manner of Orientals, by despotic princes. And it is undoubtedly an open question *whether we have sufficiently employed these native governments* as instruments of popular well-being. The methods of Lord Cornwallis and Lord Wellesley in the earlier period stand contrasted in this respect, as do those of Lord William Bentinck and Lord Dalhousie in the later. Lord Dalhousie, for example, decided against the Native rulers, and annexed several States, notably the Punjab, believing that the princes and their courts were obstacles to progress. Other distinguished administrators objected to this view : Sir Henry Lawrence, Resident in the Punjab, for example, offered to resign when the change was made. And a review of the Governor-Generalship of Lord Dalhousie leads some men to regard him as one of our most enlightened representatives, others as arbitrary and narrow-minded, despising established and well-tried agencies for good such as cannot possibly be replaced by our own direct action as rulers in every department of every State. Popular government we could not give, but it is not certain that we might not have made the Native rulers effective, by transforming them from irresponsible despots to responsible princes. In industrial organization we find Sir James Caird, the eminent agriculturalist, at the close of his report to the British public on India and its people [1], making a strong appeal that we should commit to each province the responsibility of its own operations, and enlist in the work the native landowners, officials, and municipal bodies. We shall see farther on that in another Oriental country the Dutch have applied this method with success to a people very much lower in civilization and intelligence than most of the peoples of India.

V. BUT IS IT NOT SOMETHING OF AN INTRUSION FOR A EUROPEAN NATION TO UNDERTAKE THE CONTROL OF A GROUP OF ASIATIC NATIONS? Do not the ethnological differences which certainly exist, as the effect of past centuries and different experiences, render our attempt, however well meant, *artificial* to a degree which must be pernicious and lead to disappointment and eventual disaster both to them and to ourselves?

Our reply is that history exhibits the unity of the human race as having an influence sufficiently powerful to offer some counteraction to the differences between nations. *The generic elements of our nature are as real as the differentiae*, and it is upon them that we now rely. And an analysis of these differences leads us to think that we have here a genuine case of natural adaptation for the status of TUTELAGE or EDUCATION. It is trifling with the terms *natural* and *artificial* to speak in a condemnatory sense of a school as an artificial institution. Man is natural: and schools for children are natural organizations for bringing the generations, as they come successively into being, to a level with those which are successively passing away. That Asia is comparatively in childhood in intelligence, though not in years, and is susceptible of the training and teaching of school, is our contention. A group of nations, civilized yet unable to withstand a few determined merchants and adventurers, Portuguese, Dutch, French, and English, must be in a

---

[1] *India: the Land and the People.* By Sir James Caird, 1883.

condition of comparative weakness proceeding either from immaturity or from senile decay. Our presumption is that it is the former, and that education is the remedy; and we believe that differences of character, far-reaching as they are, do not alter the hearts of men, but that our common humanity in its essence is there, offering a solid basis for an education towards a progress akin to ours, but rich also with variations of its own. That the life of long centuries already past should rather compel us to take the view that the Indian nations are beyond education, being weak through decay of their organic mental and bodily structure, is another view which may be held, and used for the conclusion that they ought to be left to govern themselves. These alternatives must here be left to the judgment of our readers.

There is one remarkable sign that our rule in India is not an interfering despotism of a kind that must be opposed by all defenders of the liberty of peoples. One of the marks of tyranny is that it inflicts evil, not only on the victims, but on the tyrant himself, who is spoken of by poets as really the most to be pitied of all. Now a mark of the true schoolmaster is exactly the opposite of this: by the exercise of his craft he is himself taught and disciplined. Which of these is true in our case? We can refer to the writings of Mill, the lectures of Max Müller, and the works of Sir Henry Maine, for some illustrations of the effect upon ourselves of our being in India. There are indications within everyone's reach, that the discharge of this great responsibility is enlightening the conscience and widening the sympathies of Englishmen, and so preparing for Asiatic peoples a union with the European divisions of the race.

VI. BUT IS NOT GREAT PREJUDICE WIDELY FELT IN INDIA, WHICH IS IN ITSELF REASONABLE AND WHOLESOME?

It is. A Mohammedan student from India when being guided through a book so considerate and liberal as Mill on *Representative Government* was found to be very indignant over many passages, and his copy was scored and dashed with notes of ejaculation and interrogation, with 'What about so and so?' 'Why not apply this to India?' and so on. And every one is conscious that our presence in India is to some extent resented. But that it is so in the main, or largely, there is no evidence. The actual voices heard are not those of the masses of the Indian peoples. The Parsees, for example, who impress us as people whom it is rather hard to keep in a political position subordinate to the Suffolk labourer or the Irish cottier, are themselves almost foreigners —'colonists' in fact—and would have little place in any popular government in India. The Bengalese peasantry, on the other hand, never had a voice in their own government, and would be surprised beyond measure at being asked to look beyond their village interests. The great Tamil-speaking peoples make no complaint. *The voices heard are those of dispossessed rulers, not of the masses of the ruled.* The Mohammedan aristocracies desire a return to power, of course. But we remember that the failures and blunders and disloyalties of Stuarts and Bourbons did not prevent them from finding in their exile voices lifted and swords drawn for their return to power and privilege: it would indeed be against nature for privileged classes to be philosophically acquiescent in their own displacement simply because increase of prosperity in the way of peace and industry had followed their ejection as rulers of the people. Again, the academically trained graduates of Calcutta, Madras, Bombay, Lahore and Allahabad, naturally feel themselves competent for a share in government, and lack neither voices nor pens for the statement of their ambitions. Their appeals must be heard, and indeed are being heard: from such men a civil service and a magistracy are being organized; but slowly and by steps. This is as it should be, and is what has been formally promised; although it is not to be forgotten that this is not exactly a reform demanded by the people at large. 'The Native,' says a German authority, Dr. Geffcken, 'invariably prefers to take his law from an English magistrate, because he implicitly relies on English impartiality.' The infusion of Native elements into the political and judicial system without injury to the English element is the task before all who would be considered statesmen in their treatment of India.

VII. IS NOT OUR RECORD STAINED?

Undoubtedly. Deeds of discredit and disgrace are on the pages of our Indian record. The proceedings of Clive and Hastings receive at the hands of foreign historians a condemnatory treatment which we are not at liberty to set aside by attributing it to national envy or jealousy, and it is useless for us to attempt to take high ground on those records. Many deeds done in the name of the great Company, and with the power of England supporting the doers, are to be recorded with sorrow and shame. Annexations carried out with subtilty[1], or with open violence, spoliations unjustifiable and not to be forgotten, have been part of public policy. And of greater mischievousness still are harshness and inconsiderateness on the part of Anglo-Indians to Natives in private life, amounting to unpardonable levity and even to actual disregard of common politeness and kindly humanity. Even where no positive causes of alienation can be alleged, *distance* as between mind and mind still operates terribly to prevent wholesome relations. Sir James Caird has to note that even as late as in 1883, 'Though the people have for six generations known no other rulers, we are still strangers among them. Our representatives come and go, now faster than ever, and we and they look on each other with distrust.' Of the public wrongs we may fairly claim that they sprang from one or other of two causes: either, because for at least fifty years the existence of the Company gave a *commercial character* to our rule, and the idea of profits and dividends was never wholly absent from the minds of our Indian administrators, if not of the Governor-Generals themselves, at

---

[1] For example, the refusal by Lord Dalhousie to continue the semi-independence of a Native State when the ruler had no direct heir, by not allowing him to adopt an heir in the usual Hindu way, could only proceed from a plan in which Native opinion was counted as of little value, and hardly gave ground for any great admiration for straightforward equity on our part. That the annexation of Sinde in 1843, as described by a Director of the Company, is painful reading, can hardly be seriously denied.

least of the rank and file of officials: or else, because of the disposition at one time to proceed upon the method *of dealing Orientally with Orientals*; assimilating downwards, that is to say, instead of upwards. But the gradual diminution of the Company's share in the administration diminished the former cause of evil, and the increase of intercourse with India of Englishmen, other than Government officials and officers of the army, and of Natives with England, is reducing the latter. And since the steam and telegraph services have brought the Government in India effectively into contact with the Indian Department at home, and therefore with Parliament and the constituencies, public policy will proceed upon principles at least as high as Englishmen, who, after all, are mortals not angels, are guided by at home. Mill's defence of the Company is plainly due to his own successful connexion with an honourable service: the abolition has certainly modified in an upward direction the *idea* of the relationship between India and ourselves. If the roll of British statesmen in India contains some names of dubious reputation, nothing but national pride is felt when we pass down the roll and read the blameless names of such high-souled rulers as Bentinck, Elphinstone, Macaulay, Lawrence, Hobart, Mayo.

Summary of Benefits.

As material for thought and reflection on this great problem of cosmopolitan history, a brief summary may be given of the benefits accruing, at this end of the nineteenth century, to the peoples of India from British rule.

(i) PUBLIC PEACE. The *Pax Britannica* effects for India what the *Pax Romana* did for the peoples round the Mediterranean basin at the close of the 'Classic' period of history. The invasions from the North-West[1], the contests

---

[1] The scientific frontier problem is of primary importance; but, unfortunately, there are divided opinions upon it at present. The mountain chain which at first might be thought a rampart has never proved to be so; it can be forced in too many places: and important outposts beyond it seem indispensable; e.g. Quetta and

of rival dynasties and confederacies, the invasions from the sea by Portuguese, Dutch, and French, have all ceased: by the establishment of one invader there is rest from all others. The fear of one—again on the open North-West—Russia, is still a strong determinant of warlike policy; from all others without, and, still more important for India, from all within, there is—Peace.

(ii) SECURITY OF LIFE AND LIBERTY TO PRIVATE PERSONS such as was never known before in Oriental nations, except possibly in China and Japan, certainly never in India. Every man can now follow his trade, and conduct his life according to his own ideas and the customs of his family and nation.

(iii) SECURITY OF PROPERTY. Every man now looks with confidence to reaping the fruits of his labour, according to the custom of his trade and locality, the operation of the seasons, and the working of commercial markets.

These three securities are the foundation-stones of social life; and Englishmen have been privileged, like architects restoring a grand cathedral by insertion of new foundations, to give new strength to the structure of Indian society.

(iv) THE ORGANIZATION OF INDUSTRY AND TRADE by means of English capital and English science. The great value of this assistance becomes manifest when we remember that two English public men who were always deeply interested in India, John Bright and Henry Fawcett, incessantly pleaded for India as a poor country. They considered it proved that the masses of India had only just a bare margin of living. And, indeed, the India Office estimated the whole annual produce of Indian industrial effort as about one-twentieth of that of the United Kingdom. To this country, where labour was already abundant, a stream of capital has flowed under the flag of England. It has been applied to supplying India with a main arterial system of

---

Candahar. If the fear of Russia adds three millions a year to the expense of government in India, as is said, no trifling on this point is permissible. Dr. Geffcken strongly advises the maintenance of the advance-posts.

railways, and to developing her own irrigation machinery. By direct Government loans, or by means of English companies backed by Government, the savings of Englishmen are industrially developing Indian provinces. The widows of British officers, clergy, merchants, and tradesmen, receive their dividends from their investments unconscious of their co-operation in industry with the rice-growing peasants of Bengal and Madras. The amount of English capital now employed in India cannot be much less than 200 millions sterling, and after taking the toll of interest to the shareholders in Britain a substantial net return is in the hands of Indian peoples already, and the mechanism of an improved industrial system, with still greater advantages in store, is being constructed at the same time [1]. The point of a very important paper by Sir William Hunter [2] is that a revolution has taken place which is bringing India well within the central circle of commercial nations, and he adds that 'India, having had conquering viceroys and consolidating viceroys, is now waiting for a commercial viceroy, to deal with a whole series of economic questions of the first magnitude.' Her development in exporting power, from 69 million tens of rupees in 1879, to 98 millions in 1888, has meant also development of importing capacity from 51 millions in 1879, to 80 millions in 1888 [3]. The

---

[1] It is alleged by Native critics that it is England alone that reaps the benefits of this. She finds employment for spare capital and for many of her sons in these enterprises, where they occupy the chief posts of profit and credit. But the objection is analogous to that of those advocates of the Labour-interest at home who are unable to discriminate between Labour unassisted and Labour assisted by Capital and directed by organizing talent. They do not see that by the latter method Labour receives more net reward, after all that Capital has appropriated is deducted from the gross produce, than it could possibly receive without the assistance of Capital.

[2] Royal Colonial Institute Proceedings, vol. xix.

[3] As the value of the rupee has changed, the actual development is best seen in comparing some quantities: e.g., from 1879 to 1889 import of woollen piece-goods increased from 7 million yards to 11 millions; of kerosine oil from 6 million gallons to 38 millions; export of tea from 38 million lbs. to 99 millions; of wheat from 2 million cwt. to 17 millions; of jute cloth from 5 million yards to 15 millions.

G

change has also carried with it the beginning of *a revolution in the relative positions of agriculture and manufacture in India*. The new methods of manufacture have proved well adapted to some of her cities with their teeming populations. At first the change was not to their advantage. English machine-goods came in, and native products could not hold their own; and at the same time Indian food and raw material were more easily carried to the ports by the new railway system, and the city populations in India had to bear a rise of prices. But from the rise of prices producers of agricultural commodities reaped great benefit; and when the town-populations began themselves to use machinery and to find that the railways carried their products cheaply to the markets, their turn, too, had come. How far the substitution of factory-work for hand-work need cause deterioration in the artistic qualities of Indian work can hardly be determined: the change is inevitable, and the really helpful course is not idle lamentation, but bringing art to bear on the new methods. For India the full entrance into the commercial circle of nations is a change of the first magnitude already, and still greater effects have to come.

(v) EUROPEAN SCIENCE, LITERATURE, AND RELIGION.

Soon after we took up our place in India there was a period of considerable hesitation. Our Indian officials and our Anglo-Indian merchants assumed for a time the responsibility of closing the doors of India to European civilization. This was not altogether from commercial motives, but was, in some minds at least, based on a conviction that any change was neither necessary nor desirable. On one hand, Englishmen were not satisfied with their own moral and religious condition at the close of last century and in the early years of this. At a time when the poor of Great Britain were uneducated, and when religious zeal was absent from the classes who supplied the officials, the officers of the army, and the merchants, there was no strong feeling that we had anything to teach others. And, on the other hand, there were some minds really affected with admiration for the treasures of philosophy and poetry and religious aspiration which the study of Indian literatures was disclosing. 'The new and mysterious world of Sanscrit learning was revealing itself to those first generations of Anglo-Indians. They were under the charm of a remote philosophy and a fantastic history. They were, as it was said, Brahmanized, and would not hear of admitting into their enchanted Oriental enclosure either the Christianity or any of the learning of the West[1].'

The necessity for the renewal of the Company's charter in 1813 was the opportunity for the critical struggle. The enthusiasm of the Evangelical Christians working for the abolition of slavery in our Western Empire proved sufficient also to carry their principles to victory in the East. 'I have long been looking forward to the period of the renewal of the East India Company's charter,' *William Wilberforce* wrote to a friend, 'as to a great era when I hoped that it would please God to enable the friends of Christianity to wipe away what I have long thought, next to the slave trade, the foulest blot on the moral character of our countrymen, the suffering of our fellow-subjects in the East Indies to remain, without any effort on our part to enlighten them and reform them, under the grossest, the darkest, the most depraving system of superstition that almost ever existed on earth.' These were strong words, and expressed convictions based on imperfect information, no doubt; but Wilberforce was thinking of the practices reported, while the Anglo-Indians were thinking of the poetry and philosophy. Throughout the churches the result of the final division in the House of Commons, on the proposal to insert in the charter a clause allowing missionaries free scope, was awaited with the greatest anxiety. Wilberforce wrote, 'I heard afterwards that many good men were praying for us all night.' The clause was carried and became law, and from that time India was made accessible to the missionaries of every Christian church.

Another crisis is associated with the name of *Lord Macaulay*, himself the son of a leading Evangelical Churchman: he determined that what education was to

---

[1] Professor Seeley, *Expansion of England*, p. 251.

be given should be given in the English language, and should be of English character. For a long time this sufficed; a theory of 'filtering' was in vogue; a small learned class was to study, at the expense of the State, and its influence was to be left to work downwards. In 1854 the principle of popular education was asserted; and since then, while higher education is almost self-supporting, the chief duty of Government is considered to be 'the spreading of sound elementary education among the masses of the people.' We must not forget that a similar struggle has been waged for popular education in England, and with a similar issue; so that, after all, our policy in India has kept pace with our own policy at home.

No small part of the work of education has been discharged by the *Missionaries*, the Presbyterian church being honourably distinguished for its enterprise in this direction. On the religious work of the missionary societies we have the following official Government report: 'No mere statistical statement can give a correct idea of all that the missionaries have accomplished. The moral value of what they preach is acknowledged by hundreds who do not join them. Their doctrinal system has given the people new ideas, not only on purely religious questions, but upon the nature and existence of evil, the obligatory character of the law, and the motives which should govern and direct human life. The Indian Government cannot avoid expressing how much it owes to the benevolent exertions of those six hundred missionaries, whose blameless lives and self-denying labours have inspired with a new vital force the great communities living under British rule.' The lives of Schwartz, Carey, Martyn, Heber, and Duff, and of such lay supporters of missions as Outram, Edwardes, and Havelock, are imperishable monuments of high Christian character and energy manifested plainly among the Brahmans and Mohammedans of Hindostan.

In concluding these broad reflections, is it a mere fancy to suggest that in India under British rule we have in partial realization Plato's conception of a GOOD STATE? and that, without his extremes? We have (*a*) the GOVERNING CLASS, and we trust that we may say that they are free from private interest, and that they are *Wise*; we have (*b*) THE AUXILIARIES in the shape of a trained magistracy, a disciplined army of Englishmen and Natives, and a well-organized civil service under Civil Servants of the first rank, who, we hope, are entitled to be reckoned as possessing their proper virtue, *Courage* in the discharge of their functions; we have (*c*) THE MASSES OF THE PEOPLE, *Temperate* in the sense of pursuing in orderly manner their industrial functions; and (*d*) all three working in that combined harmony which Plato called *Justice*. Only, Plato had to pass on to assume that such a State, if ever existent, would not be stable, but would be presently corrupted; we are sanguine enough, for the present at least, to believe that the virtues of the Indian State are preparing for consolidation and progress.

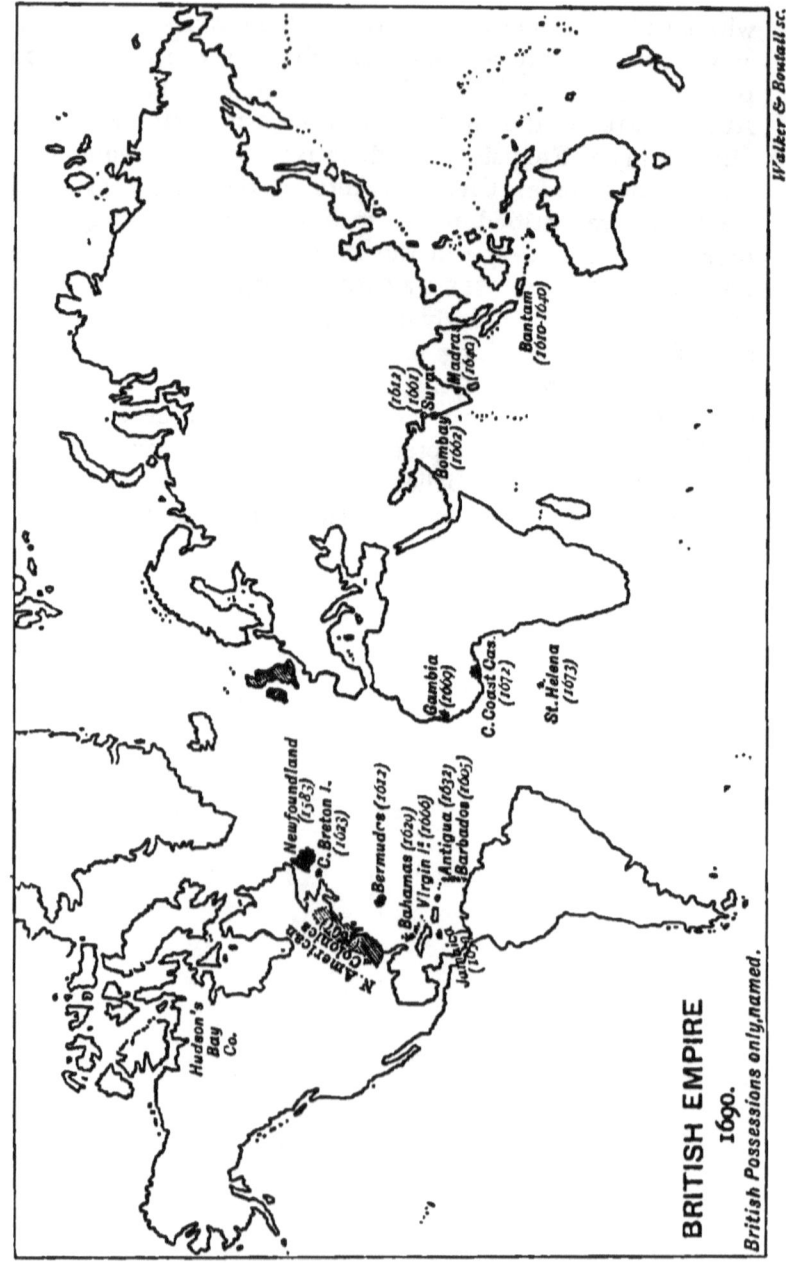

CHAPTER VI.

RECONSTRUCTION AND FRESH EXTENSION.

IN 1783 the colonial empire of England underwent a violent disruption, which on the face of it seemed to show that the expansion of Europe was not to proceed much longer by way of extension of imperial dominions. It certainly appeared to indicate that however successful a nation might be in raising up daughter-communities, it was not to be expected that *political* ties would be long maintained; and if statesmen laid great stress on the maintenance of such ties as essential to the object for which colonization was entered upon, there was nothing to be done but to abandon imperial and colonial ambitions. But this view did not attract much attention in Great Britain. The impelling power of commerce was in operation, and on our imperial mission we proceeded with marvellous success. In India, as we have seen, we never paused until some three-quarters of a century afterwards we became undisputed rulers of the whole peninsula. And in three other directions our work went on, either by filling up and developing territories already in occupation, or by adding new ones from time to time. The four chief lines of reconstruction and fresh development form the topic of this chapter; namely, in the West Indies, in Australia, in Canada, and in Africa.

§ 1. THE WEST INDIES.

Numbers are not everything, but they do count, and it is at first almost with a sense of easy irresponsibility and relaxation of attention that we turn from the vast and intricate problems of India to the history of our share of the group

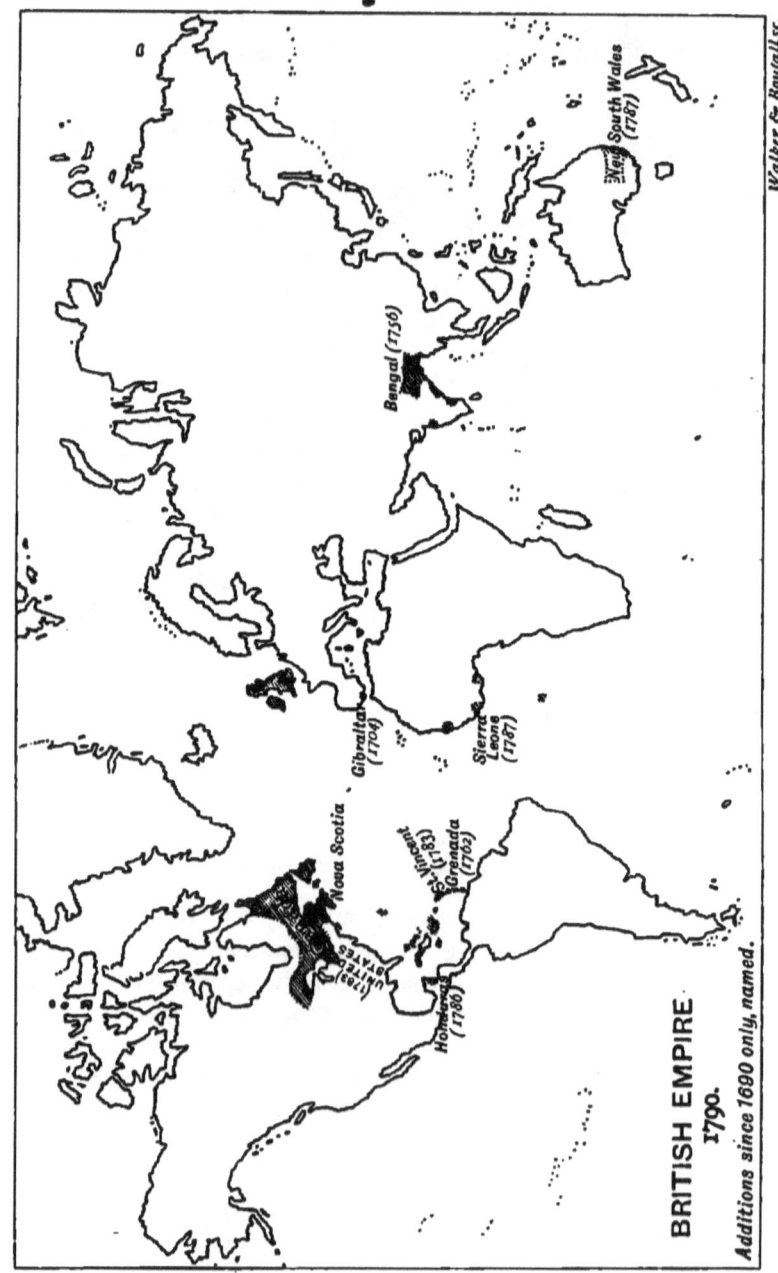

of islands in the Caribbean Sea. We have been dealing with people in such millions that we feel comparatively unmoved when considering the million and a quarter of our fellow-subjects there, a population less than one-fiftieth of that under the Lieutenant-Governor of Bengal alone, about half of that of the single island of Ceylon. But this group of colonies, although on so small a scale, possesses a history which has many attractions and is very instructive. Three features of interest can easily be perceived :—

(*a*) These islands are the connecting link between our colonization and the romantic history of Spanish discovery and colonization. In them we made *our first effort after tropical or sub-tropical colonization* in competition with Spain.

(*b*) They were *for a time the centre of our colonial interest.* After the shock of the separation of our thirteen colonies, although we still had Canada, we were despoiled of our possessions as sources of wealth under our own trade-regulation, retaining only these fiercely-contested sugar-islands. The securing of them by Rodney's great victory was to us the great consolation of the war which ended in 1783. And they rapidly became a source of constant and increasing wealth. At the close of last century the West Indian interest in the city of London and in Bristol was one of the chief elements in politics as well as in commerce. To have a plantation in Jamaica was to be an object of envy; it was much the same as being an Indian 'Nabob.'

But (*c*) of more permanent interest still, it has been in the field of our West Indian colonization that *the great battle of Slavery* has been fought and won—a moral contest of singular interest and singular significance: the protest of modern ideas of morality against classical and mediaeval carried to an issue that presently involved, not only England, but Europe, and eventually the whole world of nations. The chief heroes of West Indian history are men who never saw the islands, but who took up the cause of human liberty as there outraged, and thus initiated the abolition for all peoples of the status of serfdom and chattelage.

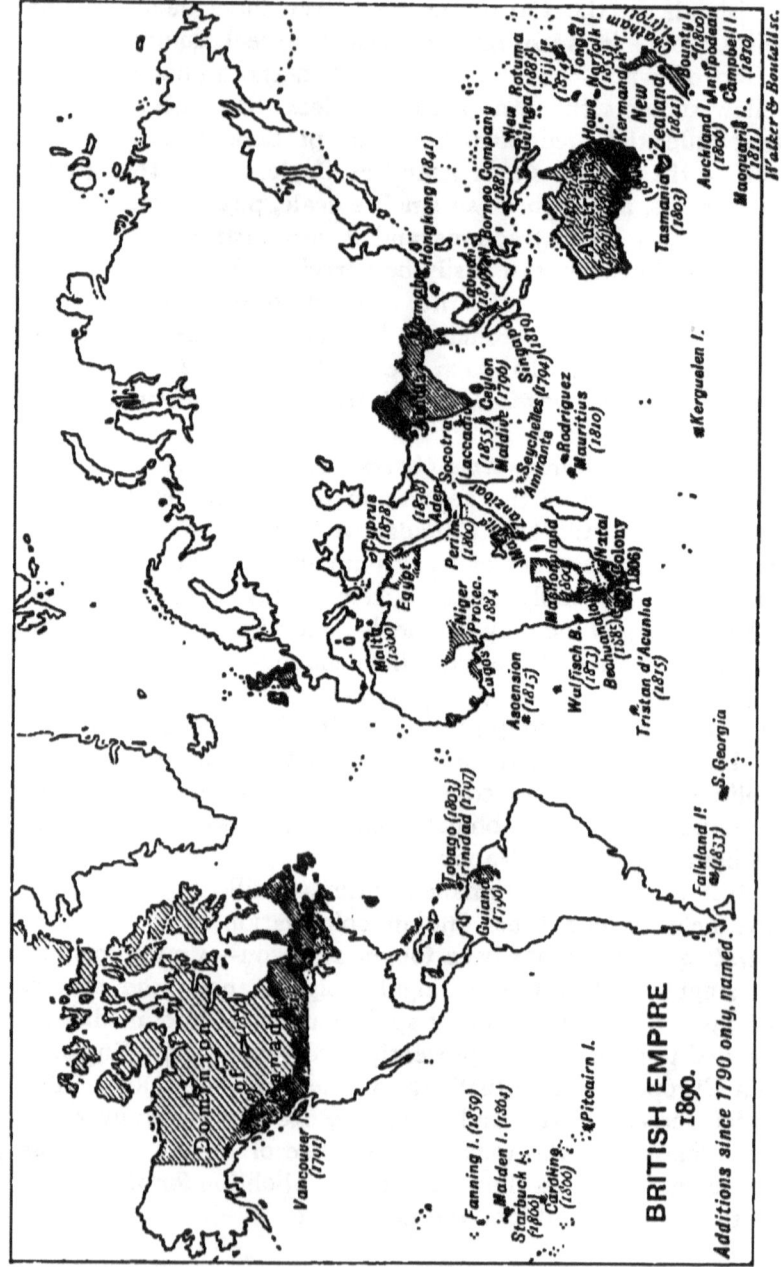

History of our West Indies.

We soon secured a nominal footing in the Caribbean Archipelago, appropriating Barbados in 1605, when some Englishmen touched at the island and carved on a tree the inscription, 'James, King of England, and of this island.' The occupation of the island began in 1625, and settlers soon proceeded there in considerable numbers, cultivating tobacco, indigo, cotton, and a certain plant from which they brewed a refreshing drink, ignorant then of its future as the source of great good fortune for that part of the world—the sugar-cane. It was not until 1640 that a Dutchman from Brazil taught the Barbadians the secret of boiling the juice of the fully ripened cane. But the avidity with which the new industry was taken up soon made up for any lost time. In twenty years the whole of the leeward coast was covered with plantations, and the little island—about the same size as the Isle of Wight—had 50,000 settlers. Men of some wealth left England on account of the civil wars, and a constitutional government under a charter was established. The island was called 'Little England,' and Mr. Payne calls the Barbadians 'the earliest type of the true English colonists,' and says that before the Act of Navigation restricted its trade to the mother-country, and Jamaica had come into competition, Barbados was 'the most populous, rich, and industrious spot on the earth.' Many of Cromwell's prisoners were sent out there as slave-labourers, and the colony early took part in the employment of West African negro-slaves as well. Jamaica was taken from the Spaniards in 1655 on the failure of an expedition against St. Domingo. Settlements were made in St. Kitts and the Bahamas, while the Spanish kept Cuba, most of St. Domingo, and Porto Rico; the French were occupying Martinique and Guadeloupe and part of St. Domingo, the Dutch St. Eustatius and Curaçao, and the Danes St. Thomas and the Virgin Islands. In the eighteenth century wars there was a good deal of taking and retaking of the smaller islands between the British, French, and Spanish, but the final war ended in our being secured in the possession of

Dominica, St. Lucia, Antigua, St. Vincent, Tobago, and Trinidad, besides some smaller islands. At the close of that century we took part of Guiana from Holland, and of that portion—usually included under the term 'West Indies' —we have made the most prosperous of all our possessions in that quarter of the world. By the Treaties of Versailles we secured a place for our mahogany-cutters in Central America (Honduras), and have since made it into a regular colony, though a very small one. The most important members of the group now are *Jamaica, Trinidad, British Guiana,* and *Barbados,* and their development has until recently been bound up with the *Sugar-industry.* Each of these colonies has some points of peculiar interest, but our object will be adequately gained by noticing some of the chief points of the history of Jamaica.

Jamaica.

This typical *English plantation-colony* when taken over by us in 1655 offered us quite an open field, for the Spanish cruelties had cleared it of its native inhabitants. We found no one except some negro slaves, who ran away to the mountains when the Spaniards were ousted, and gave the newcomers trouble for more than a hundred years, being known as 'Maroons,' often furnishing a grim kind of sport to the planters when their thefts and murders became intolerable, and regular 'hunts' were set on foot. The sugar-cane was soon introduced, as Barbados had shown how congenial a soil these islands offered, and sugar, molasses, and rum became the staples of the island. The trade was limited by law, but as the markets included both Great Britain and the American colonies the restriction was not much felt, as France and other European markets were at that time being supplied from their own sugar colonies. By means of our factories in West Africa a continuous supply of negro slaves was secured, and the large-scale plantation system was in full operation, Jamaican prosperity reaching a height which is surprising until its causes are examined; incomes of £75,000, and even £100,000, a year, from single estates being known, at a time when probably none of the landed nobility or gentry of England had revenues anything like so large. So important an element in British commerce was the West Indian trade that it is recorded that Burke desisted from some plans which he was forming for the mitigation and eventually the abolition of the trade, because he perceived that the West Indian merchants could get up an opposition that would ruin the Whig party if it ventured to follow him. Gradually, however, the situation was examined, and the more it was considered the less it was liked by those who had no private complications with the wealth it produced. Some men of high character and indomitable energy made up their minds that Slavery and the Slave Trade were abominable, and after fifty years of agitation they procured their abolition. The Trade was abolished first (1807): the institution itself not until 1833. But, important though this change was in its effect upon Jamaican industry, it is not accurate to speak of the abolition of slavery as the only cause of the rapid decline of value in Jamaican estates; nor indeed is it certain that it was the chief cause. There are facts which show that the decay had really begun before slavery terminated. The other cause in operation was the gradual *breakdown* of Jamaican and Barbadian *monopoly* of the British sugar market. This came about partly by the *admission of fresh competitors* within the charmed circle of privilege. Trinidad and Guiana became British territory, and so had access to Bristol and London, in 1798; Mauritius, taken in 1810, was admitted on the same terms as the West Indies in 1825; and Ceylon in 1836. As hitherto these countries had been foreign, they had paid a duty of three guineas a hundredweight, while Jamaica paid about twenty-five shillings, they now entered for the first time as competitors on equal terms. Jamaica and the older island were placed at a peculiar disadvantage by this. Trinidad and Guiana were almost untouched; they abounded in fine virgin soil, and both the sugar-cane itself and the method of slave labour were well adapted for yielding immense returns to early outlays on unexhausted land.

In Jamaica the wasteful character of slave labour had gradually exhausted much soil, so that Jamaica had naturally passed her zenith. But in 1846 there was a complete revolution. When Lord John Russell effected the complete equalization of the sugar duties, the rich sugar lands of Cuba, Porto Rico, and Brazil, a hundred times as extensive as Jamaica, came into competition, and the heyday passed completely away. The equitableness of this sudden equalization is a question of great interest. On the one side Free Trade required it; but on the other, the planters of Jamaica and the abolitionists of slavery were led to join hands in protesting strongly together against it, for it placed the slave-grown sugar of Cuba and Brazil on a level with the free-labour sugar of our own colonies. Freedom's name was invoked on both sides—freedom of trade on the one, and freedom of labour on the other. As our own colonies were still suffering from the dislocation of their labour-organization it was hardly considerate of the mother-country to decline to give them a little more breathing time. But freedom of trade was the moving principle of that day; and it bore all along with it, so far as British policy was concerned.

The revolution in its labour system and the loss of its monopoly might have sufficed to ruin the prosperity of Jamaica; but it was to be exposed to a third attack. It was discovered that sugar could be profitably extracted from *beetroot*, a plant which Europe could grow for itself. That this plant contained a kind of sugar had been known for some time; it was grown in small quantities from the beginning of the century, but it is only since 1860 that it has been largely grown for the production of sugar. By 1850 it had reached the ratio of one to ten, by weight, of the sugar produced in the world. Since then it has crept up; in 1866, one to four; in 1885, four to five; in 1890 it is ahead, five to three [1].

[1] 1849: Beet 95,000 tons.   1885: Beet 2,100,000 tons.
    Cane 930,000   Cane 2,500,000
    1860: Beet 336,000   1890: Beet 3,630,000
    Cane 1,500,000   Cane 2,118,000

And a still further obstacle was to be placed in the path of our West Indian sugar colonies; for the beet-growing nations of Europe set up a *Bounty-system* for the fostering of that crop, amounting in some cases to £2 a ton. Hence it has come about that our own colonies, compelled by us to remain within the Free Trade circle, had to see their rival industry becoming prosperous under a Protective system. *All these causes* operated to bring Jamaica's already reduced production from £2,800,000 in 1857 to £1,400,000 in 1885; and of this sugar was only half, for fruits for the United States were taking its place as the more profitable business. So that the prosperity of Jamaica was affected by three causes: (1) by the compulsory abandonment of its industrial method, (2) by the advent of one competitor after another into the market, and competitors who had slave labour applied to fresh soils, and (3) by the competition of another plant for which its own soil was unfitted. And so the prosperity of the plantation period was over, and Jamaica is now being transformed into a market garden and orchard for tropical fruits and vegetables. This will not lead to great incomes for large proprietors as of old, but the recent official reports show that it is leading to considerable prosperity, in which the labouring or peasant classes have the chief share.

In other West Indian colonies the pinch has not been quite so severe; in *Barbados* the freed negroes had no unoccupied lands upon which they might squat and set up as peasant cultivators; they remained at work on the sugar plantations, and the colony has, on the whole, made progress in many respects, although the gentry are not so wealthy as before, nor are absentee proprietors who draw large incomes from the island now numerous. In *Trinidad* cocoa is largely grown in addition to sugar, and both there and in Guiana the coolie system is in vogue (see Chapter ix). But if we remember that exports are not the only measure of industrial activity, that a country is neither a farm nor a shop, but may be in part self-supplying, there is little ground for complaint. And if we take the broad test of the number of comfortable homes which the colonies support we cannot but feel satisfied, for it becomes plain that if there is no longer opportunity for amassing great fortunes, the whole level of comfort has been raised throughout the islands. In Jamaica the whites are diminishing in both numbers, wealth, and preponderance of influence; hence the restriction of franchise became unjustifiable[1], and yet its extension led to the serious riots in which Governor Eyre lost his place—though with Carlyle on one side and Mill on the other it is not possible to pass either absolute acquittal or sweeping condemnation on moral grounds—and the island passed from the standing of a colony to that of a dependency.

Our colonies in the West Indies are, however, in a somewhat critical position. There is reason for holding that these colonies are just now so placed as to be *far from deriving unmixed advantage from remaining within the empire at all.* They owe their position to the imperial relationship, no doubt, and this leads to important commercial ties. But commerce, like politics, must not reckon on gratitude as a motive power; and the commercial position of the islands is affected adversely by their subordination to England. First, because of the sugar bounties given by the beet-root-growing countries to that form of sugar, handicapping our cane-growing colonies in our market. And, secondly, they are kept within our commercial circle, and therefore are not able to treat with outside nations on any reciprocity plan, however advantageous to themselves it might be proved to be. The United States is a natural market for their sugar, but the United States Government has to deal with these islands as part of the British Empire, and therefore it can enter into no arrangement of the kind dear to the American mind such as giving West Indian sugar free access in return for the West Indian colonies giving them some advantage in return. The position is a trying one, and cannot be permanent. More than one West Indian

---

[1] The population at the last census was 14,432 whites (there used to be 30,000); coloured (i.e. of mixed race), 109,946; blacks, 444,186; coolies and Chinese, 13,000. The black and coloured population increased nearly 12 per cent. in the last ten years.

has spoken in public of the possibility of separation from the empire unless Great Britain allows them fiscal independence, such as has long ago been granted to the colonies of Australia, Canada, and the Cape. Sentiment is wholly against separation from England, with either independence, or admission to the 'Union' of North America; but the demand for liberty to negotiate treaties must grow as Guiana increases in importance and Jamaica continues to find the relative weight of its external trade increase in favour of the United States in comparison with Great Britain [1]. The interests of this million and a quarter of people do not occupy much of our attention, nor ought they to do so. But to themselves it is of prime importance that an equitable solution be sought without delay.

§ 2. Emigration Colonies: Australia.

Few empires have suffered the shock of such a loss as that of our thirteen prosperous colonies in 1776-83 without the shattering of their system. But the actual hindrance to the course of England's imperial progress was much less than appears on the surface. It has been pointed out that we found compensations; and, further, for a long period the trade connexion was not seriously injured, as the United States continued to deal with us very much as before owing to the essentially natural course which, in many respects, trade had already taken. Our attention was soon drawn to other regions, and for a quarter of a century we went on picking up old colonies here and there: the Cape of Good Hope (1806), Guiana (1803), and Ceylon (1795), all from the Dutch; Mauritius from France (1810); and Trinidad from Spain (1797); and we enlarged our hold on West Africa, while all this time our dominion in India was rapidly extending. But there were places also being quietly prepared in different quarters of the globe which were to become the seats of

---

[1] The trade of Jamaica was in 1875 with Great Britain £2,100,000, with U.S.A. £700,000; in 1889 it was, with Great Britain £1,500,000, with U.S.A. £1,300,000; with us it steadily declines, with U.S.A. it steadily grows.

colonies in the full sense of the term, new homes for the British people in temperate regions.

The name of CAPTAIN JAMES COOK stands at the head of the Englishmen who prepared for this new movement. Travelling very largely in the interest of general science and discovery—so much so that special orders were given by the French Government that he was not to be interfered with by their navy—he was at the same time preparing for our appearance in the Southern Seas. In 1787 our first settlement was made on the shores of Australia in *Port Jackson*, a short way to the north of Captain Cook's 'Botany Bay.' It was very far indeed from displaying any manifest promise of being the first of a peculiarly free and industrious group of communities. The first motive for its foundation was of an opposite kind, namely, to found *a prison beyond the seas*. This was the actual origin of the first Australian colony, New South Wales, and for a long time the system was more or less in operation—in Victoria, then in Tasmania, then in Western Australia (see Chapter ix). But the need for emigration of freemen became pressing, and colonization of this kind became a serious subject with some very thoughtful men. The projector who made most impression in the new movement was Edward Gibbon Wakefield, who laid down as a principle that a new colony should set aside a certain part of the proceeds of the sale of its lands for the conveyance of fresh immigrants and for their assistance in starting their colonial life. His plan had its most effective trial in the division called South Australia and in New Zealand; and although the new colonies in no case carried it out continuously and strictly, it had considerable influence.

In 1851 came a great and sudden attraction in the shape of the discovery of the BALLARAT GOLD-FIELDS, and a stream of men, mostly of adventurous and energetic character, poured over: some to get rich in the way they aimed at, others to turn from disappointment in that direction to other employments of a more ordinary kind.

As the colonies grew, the despatch of convicts from England began to be opposed, and at home men like Archbishop Whately, who were convinced that the system was pernicious, as not attaining the reformatory effect which they considered that all punishment should have, joined in the opposition. When at length the colonists of Victoria declared their intention of sending some of their malefactors to England, the Government at home took the hint, and changed the place of transportation to other parts of Australia, and they presently abandoned the system entirely.

The original colony, New South Wales, was in Australia something what Virginia was in America; as people came out and occupied land at vast distances, the new colonies of Victoria (1851) and Queensland (1859) were marked off, while South Australia earlier still received a separate government, the Swan River Settlement was changed into Western Australia, and Tasmania was constituted a separate colony so early as in 1804. For New Zealand we had a race with the French in 1840, gaining first formal occupation by only three days. This group of islands had passed through a series of informal connexions with British people; whaling ships resorted to its coast, deserters from the ships took up their abode there, traders with the natives often called there, and some missionaries had been despatched from Australia. A New Zealand Company was formed, and a Government connexion made by the appointment of Captain Hobson as Governor in 1840.

The history of the Australian colonies has been almost purely industrial. New Zealand, for example, is almost a simple case of a *purely industrial emigration colony* of British people. It was not sought as a refuge from religious or political oppression like New England, or founded as a convict settlement, like New South Wales, or stimulated into sudden prosperity by a rush for gold like Victoria; it never knew any slavery or coolie system like the West Indies, nor does it contain an appreciably important foreign element like the Cape Colony and Canada, and it has not now, like the last-named important member of the empire, to live in constant necessity of considering everything in relation to a powerful neighbour. Its history has been as peaceful and serene as that of an English county, save for one considerable difficulty, that of finding a stable basis of relationship with the native race, in which justice to them should be harmonized with our own colonial development.

But in this way Australian progress has proved somewhat unexpectedly brilliant. How difficult prophecy is in matters of such a scale is evident from the following opinion of one of our ablest statisticians of the last generation. Porter, in his *Progress of the Nation* (p. 133), written up to 1851, thus looked out on Australia's future:—'According to present appearances and the knowledge we have obtained concerning the nature of the country, it does not appear probable that Australia can ever become an agricultural country. . . . It seems impossible that the colony can ever assume anything approaching the importance of our North American possessions—(then Canada only)—either in regard to productiveness or to population.' Certainly Australia has not caught Canada yet, but it has nearly three million people to Canada's five; but in 1889 the external trade of the Australian group (not including New Zealand, of which Porter was not thinking) was 116 millions sterling to the 42 millions of Canada.

In their history, therefore, these colonies cannot be said to offer any considerable elements of romance; they need for their historians not bards or minstrels, but political economists or students of natural science. The old convict days and the later period of life in the gold-fields offered, no doubt, a scope for the portrayal of life and character in certain rough and picturesque aspects, but they have not, as a fact, found either a Defoe or a Bret Harte to give them a hold on the imaginations of the English people. And, again, the wild unfettered life of the bush, and the escapades of the bushrangers, have failed to win the favour of any powerful Muse, and they remain mostly unhonoured and unsung[1].

---

[1] *Robbery under Arms* (Bush-ranging), *The Miner's Right* (Gold Mining), and *The Squatter's Dream* (Squatting-life) by Rolf Boldrewood, an Australian writer (English publisher, Macmillan), deserve attention from English boys.

Perhaps we must take it that the absorption of energy in the making of fortunes has prevented the formation of any such leisured class as is the matrix, so to speak, of poets and novelists, and also that the overpowering attractions of home literature have prevented the growth of Art of their own. However it may be, the fact remains that English boys, who make bosom friends of imaginary buccaneers and pirates, of backwoodsmen and Red Indian chiefs, have formed little personal acquaintance with the whalers or kidnappers or bushrangers of Australia. The tragic story of Burke and Wills and Wright, in their brave but ill-managed endeavour to make a track across the Australian continent, stands almost alone among the enterprises of adventure in that quarter of the world in having won a permanent place in the memories of ordinary Britons at home.

Accordingly we refer to the chapters on Trade and Government and the Supply of Labour for some glimpses of the elements of Australian history which offer the most important material for the student of the colonial phase of English history.

§ 3. CANADA.

The War of Independence, which removed from the empire the bulk of our own colonists, proved no obstacle to our still retaining a very powerful grip on the continent of North America. Our own early colony of *Newfoundland*—practically ours for colonizing purposes since the days of Elizabeth, although the great cod-fisheries were by treaties kept open for general resort—remained unaffected, as did the territory called *Nova Scotia* and *New Brunswick*, on the south side of the St. Lawrence estuary. But the nucleus of the new British North America was beyond the St. Lawrence, the province of QUEBEC, acquired from France in 1763. At the outset of the War of Independence we very nearly lost this foothold too. A very unstatesmanlike measure in 1774 (the Quebec Act[1]) had disgusted both the

[1] This Act made the provinces into one royal government under

English and the French colonists, and, in fact, all Canada was occupied by the friends of the thirteen revolted colonies, except the keystone, Quebec. But, on the whole, the French inhabitants of these provinces had but little sympathy with their New England neighbours, either in personal character or in political principles, and the few British subjects who had already settled there were joined in considerable numbers by English people from the separated colonies, who, under the name of Royalists, had sided with the English Government in the war. The French population was some 65,000 when we took over the province; and it is a singular fact that we find growing here, under British government and under British political institutions, *the most successful 'colony' which has ever issued from the French nation.* Besides about a quarter of a million people of French origin in other parts of the present Dominion, there is a compact community of over a million people of French birth or French descent in the neighbourhood of Quebec, a number twice as great as that of French people in the whole of the colonies and dependencies of the French Republic to-day. It is not with any foolish self-complacency that we claim that the exchange of French rule for British was a distinct gain even for the French colonists in 1763. They themselves are the best judges, and their contentment is their verdict. Our rule freed them from a number of oppressive feudal burdens which had been carried over the water and were insisted upon by the seigneurs recognised by the French Government. In fact, we may fairly say that we saved them the trouble of either taking sides in the great Revolution which was soon to come upon their native country, or of effecting a revolution for themselves. They could at once benefit by the advance of English constitutional and social ideas, and they accepted it as a deliverance. And it further happened that our appearance on that side of the river soon gave rise to dissatisfaction among

the name of Quebec; it ignored the representative principle, placing all power in the hands of a royal council; it re-established the French legal system and the Roman Catholic Church.

the Red Indians, which came to a head in a thrilling tragedy, the conspiracy of Pontiac. The necessity of meeting this vigorously put the Red Indian difficulty on a footing which was peaceful and secure in comparison with the harassing and discouraging condition in which we found them. From time to time troubles arose, and there was some friction between the French element and the British, but all this did not prove sufficient to prevent the French province of Quebec from agreeing to the formation of the Federation which unified Canada in 1858, nor sufficient to prevent that Federation from being on the whole a great success. We have therefore achieved successfully the incorporation of a foreign colony within a British one, not only with their consent, but without depriving them of the qualities which distinguish them, and without checking their prosperity, which makes it all the more surprising that our nation has not found six centuries sufficient to effect similar results in Ireland.

The original province was divided into two, Upper and Lower Canada, in 1791. In the former the settlers were mainly British; and their first legislative assembly not only placed the province on a line with the mother-country as to laws regulating property and civil rights, but had the honour of passing in its very first session an Act abolishing slavery, even for the negro. By 1812 the colony was so well satisfied that its interest lay in remaining within the British Empire that, in spite of some very trying experiences, both French and English elements united in opposing the attempts of the United States—then at war with Great Britain —to draw them into union with themselves. And just as these attempts failed with the English element, so the long hostilities between Great Britain and France did not alienate the French element; a striking instance of the power of proved interest to override divergence of sentiment and religion and nationality. There was, however, a constitutional revolution in 1837, due to a lack of full representation in the Government and some soreness between the two colonies. The revolt was quelled, and a governor, Lord

Durham, sent out specially to report. The result of that report eventually was a *union of the colonies as 'provinces' of a single colony*, and a completely REPRESENTATIVE GOVERNMENT so far as their internal affairs are concerned. (See Chapter vii.)

In 1867 the idea of union was carried farther: the colonies of Nova Scotia and New Brunswick—hitherto quite separate from each other, hanging each by its own stem to the parent-tree — were united with Canada proper, and the whole group were formed into a single federation as the 'DOMINION OF CANADA.' Newfoundland declined to join, and is still outside the Dominion. Later on, divisions of the vast territory to the west and north-west of the older settlements were made, and one by one created 'provinces' of the Dominion on the same terms as their older colonies: Manitoba, British Columbia, and the North-West Territories (including Assiniboia, Saskatchewan, Alberta, Athabasca, and an unnamed region), are the separate provinces to-day. Prince Edward Island, near Nova Scotia, is the latest member of the Dominion. The seat of central government is at a town virtually created for the purpose, Ottawa. The proportionate importance of the various provinces is shown by the composition of the Lower House of the Dominion Parliament:— Ontario (formerly 'Upper Canada'), 88 members; Quebec, 65; Nova Scotia, 21; New Brunswick, 16; British Columbia, 6; Prince Edward Island, 6; Manitoba, 5. The North-West Territory has not yet a population sufficiently concentrated to be formed into electoral districts.

A connecting link of no small importance within the Dominion, and a bond between Europe and Asia, has been constructed in the *Canadian Pacific Railway* from Quebec to Vancouver, along which trains have run since 1885. This line is 3000 miles long, running chiefly over vast prairies, but with 300 miles of tunnelling through solid stone in the Rocky Mountains. It forms a route between China and Liverpool shorter by 1000 miles than the earlier trans-American route, the Central Pacific by San Francisco. Its importance in the development of Canada and in the linking together of Europe's western shores with Asia's eastern is beyond adequate estimation. Lines of steamers between Vancouver and China, Japan, and Australia, are being organized, and an English traveller may reach Sydney, or Shanghai, or Yokohama, without having seen any but the British flag on his route; and, so far from having turned a mile out of his way, he will have saved ten days by having seen no other land than British territory.

There is over all human things of any compass at least one shadow; the shadow of Canadian destiny, so far as its position as a British colony is concerned, lies in its having a *long border of* 3000 *miles*, with no physical boundary along a very large part of it, and no natural bulwark anywhere, and with *the most rapidly growing nation in the world stretched mile for mile along the other side of that border*. The possibility of annexation being demanded from across the St. Lawrence and the lakes must be in every Canadian mind; and circumstances will from time to time force it into flame or leave it smouldering. For the present we may claim liberty to leave it, but we are bound not to ignore its possibility, or to refrain from indicating the manifest probability that the question will ultimately find its solution in the minds of the 60,000,000 of the United States, who have three courses from which to choose: *Compulsory Federation* by gradually but persistently drawing Canada towards themselves, or by *violent measures* in some crisis, or *acquiescence in the manifest preference of the Canadians for the present régime*.

§ 4. AFRICA.

When we took charge of the Dutch possessions at the Cape of Good Hope[1], in the brief period when Holland was under the power of France at the close of last century, the Dutch had not made any extensive settlement themselves:

[1] The English took forcible possession of the Cape in 1795, but the Peace of Amiens restored it to the Netherlands in 1803. In 1806 we resumed possession, and at the Peace of 1815 it was finally ceded to us.

a century and a half had not carried them beyond some 10,000 white people, and these were so far from being helped by their home government that their trade was hampered, and they themselves dispersed to an absurd extent about the vast territory. So little of promise was there that the last of the Dutch governors saw no chance for more European immigrants finding a living: and so little was trade organized that some wool brought down to the beach was unsold, and lay there until the winds scattered it. In contrast with this, the white population in 1885 was estimated at 340,000, and the value of the wool exported in 1884 was a million and three quarters sterling. England at first took the colony as a protectorate, as there was great danger of its falling under French influence when Holland had to succumb to France, and whilst the French navy was still strong. We evacuated the country at the Peace of Amiens in 1802, but re-occupied it when war was resumed, and insisted on retaining it at the settlement of affairs in 1815. It was an important naval position, and we felt also that it would be of service for colonizing purposes. But we had little idea of the complicated problem which we were undertaking to deal with. We were at once making a fresh outlet for British capital and labour, and incorporating a group of foreign European settlers of stiffer mould than the French group in Canada, and, besides this, were laying the foundation of an interest in Africa which was to prove that on that continent too our nationality was to be the chief instrument of European influence.

The *Northern* coast of Africa was naturally a colonizing ground for the Mediterranean nations, but France has proved the only one to take advantage of it. Spain has some connexion with Morocco, and Italy has interests in Tunis, while Egypt was regarded for years as of international concern. The *West* of Africa was open to all; France has long had some territory there, and she has recently considerably extended it; we have enlarged ours; and in 1884 Germany took up a position. Further south on the same coast Portugal retained a hold; and on the marking out of the river

Congo an *International State* was formed under the protection of Belgium immediately, of France in reversion, recognised by agreement of the nations assembled at the Berlin Conference of 1885[1]. At this Conference an understanding was arrived at which has been at the basis of the negotiations of 1890–91 between the European powers. It was decided that any nation desirous of taking an interest in any of the newly-opened-out regions of Africa should notify this desire to the other powers of Europe. The CONGO STATE was the first-fruit of this, *Belgium*, by the activity of her king, taking the place that Holland might rather have been expected to secure. On the *East* side Portugal retains another tract, and Germany has appeared again; while even Italy has made a beginning for external dominion. But all these possessions and occupations and sovereignties are of less importance than the permanent and progressive colonies settled by England in the south (to say nothing of her protectorates on the east, in the centre, and in the lower parts of the basin of River Niger). They are nearly all comparatively recent and unformed, and are not of the physical character required for colonies of the most valuable type; while in the *South* England is *filling up large colonies*, and *constantly pushing their boundaries* farther and farther into the interior. Our peculiar advantages are two: (1) the very obvious one that we have established in the South *a solid basis* of operations in an almost European climate; and, in spite of the facilities of navigation common to all the nations colonizing in Africa, we have the advantage in that we are extending colonies already formed; and (2) the physical conditions of the African coast. This coast at Delagoa Bay and onward to the Zambesi mouth is too malarious for Europeans to be able to take their families there and establish permanent homes by forming great seaports. Much the same thing is true of the western

---

[1] This Conference is called the *International Congo Conference of Berlin*, 1885, to distinguish it from the Congress at Berlin in 1878, which dealt with the affairs of South-Eastern Europe after the Russo-Turkish War.

coast between Cape Colony and Benguela (in the hands of Germany). The *ports will therefore be on the southern curve* of the continent, even for the territories far inland, and this curve is in our hands. These advantages give us the foremost place now and the greatest promise for the future.

The problems before our South African colonies are: (1) (*a*) to arrive at a thoroughly workable understanding with our *Dutch fellow-colonists*, and (*b*) with such Dutchmen as are still *independent neighbours*; and (2) to do the best for the *native races*, especially by training these to take their place at our side in the formation of a mixed community.

The Dutch in South Africa.

In solving the former of these the English and the Dutch have managed to live on, but in a hand-to-mouth fashion, and the Boer war of 1879 showed how far we were from real and effective harmony after eighty years' dwelling together. The inclusion in our empire of a large territory to which dissatisfied Dutchmen had moved across the Vaal river, proved to be premature; we had to fight, and the Boers had the best of it; and then we decided not to bring our strength to bear, but to give way. They occupy accordingly two very extensive regions, one quite independent, under the name of the *Orange Free State*; the other, the relinquished Transvaal, or *South African Republic*, internally independent, but under our control so far as relations with other States are concerned. But although the actual settlement of this part of the problem is still to be worked out, we can have no doubt what the result will be when we look at the problem in a really comprehensive way. The incorporation of these countries is only a question of time. The Boers, though in the majority in South Africa at present, are not increasing so fast as the English colonists, and no stream of emigration can be directed from Holland of anything like the volume of the stream from the British Isles. Already indeed the English element is becoming unmanageable by the Boer Governments, and such men as go out there are of a temper not to be trifled with whenever they take their affairs heartily into their own hands. Another imperial war is not likely: it would be exceedingly unpopular at home, even for the support of our fellow-countrymen, and if it came to be an actual conflict our colonists would be all the better for depending on themselves. That British supremacy within the older portions of the Cape Colony will be settled eventually on a peaceful and recognised basis there is no reason for doubting. We have come to terms with French Canadians; Germans in great numbers find satisfaction in the constitutional liberties of Australian colonies and American States, where, though strong in numbers and wealth, they live contented amongst Englishmen or men of English race: and no cause can be discovered to be at work which permanently threatens to prevent a sound *modus vivendi* being reached at the Cape, with thorough harmony eventually. At present the extensive areas of the Transvaal and the Orange Free State are occupied chiefly for pasture, but their rich mineral resources will soon be tapped. A network of railways is being laid down which will develop a community of interest that must go far to make concord among all Europeans in South Africa both easy and indispensable.

The Kaffirs and other Natives.

Nor is the second problem one likely to be of insuperable difficulty. The condition of the *native inhabitants* of the colony of Natal under our rule has proved indeed to be so satisfactory to the natives themselves that the difficulty that had to be faced there was to keep them from pressing into the colony in unmanageable and undesirable numbers. Numerous and costly wars have been waged with tribes of Kaffirs as our colonies grew, but perhaps the great Zulu war of 1879-80 was the last on a large scale: disturbances may occur in the future, and border warfare may have again to be faced; but we have already included many of the most vigorous tribes within our dominion, and are working out relations with those dwelling immediately beyond our borders.

Government in South Africa.

There has been at times in South African history a serious *want of accord between the Imperial Government and the Government of the Colony* in relation to the acquisition and administration of native territories. The Imperial Government has intervened to an extent which the colonists have resented as contrary to their own rights, and as interfering with their free development, and therefore as detrimental to the English cause in South Africa. The position of affairs is one of transitional character. The Home Government has not set up the Cape Colony as Suzerain over several newly-added territories, but has reserved the sovereignty. For this purpose a High Commissionership for South Africa has been established, but the pre-eminence of the Cape Colony is recognised by the appointment of the Governor of that colony to the High Commissionership. In discharging his commission, however, he is not in any way bound to act upon the advice of the Cape Ministry, as he is in the affairs of the Cape Colony itself: for other districts he acts in direct responsibility to the Crown. Accordingly, South Africa in 1891 presents a variety of relationship between a mother-country and outlying dependencies which is quite unique in the number of its grades. A glance at the accompanying map shows the territories; the varieties of political status are as follows:—

i. Under RESPONSIBLE Government [1]—Cape Colony: including Griqualand West, and the isolated patch at Walfisch Bay.

ii. Under SEMI-RESPONSIBLE Government—Natal.

iii. Under the GOVERNOR OF CAPE COLONY—

(*a*) As *High Commissioner for S. Africa:* Basutoland, Pondoland, the British *Protectorate,* the British *Sphere of Influence.*

(*b*) As *Governor of Cape Colony:* The Crown Colony of British Bechuanaland.

(*c*) As *High Commissioner for S. E. Africa,* with the

---

[1] See chapter on *Government.*

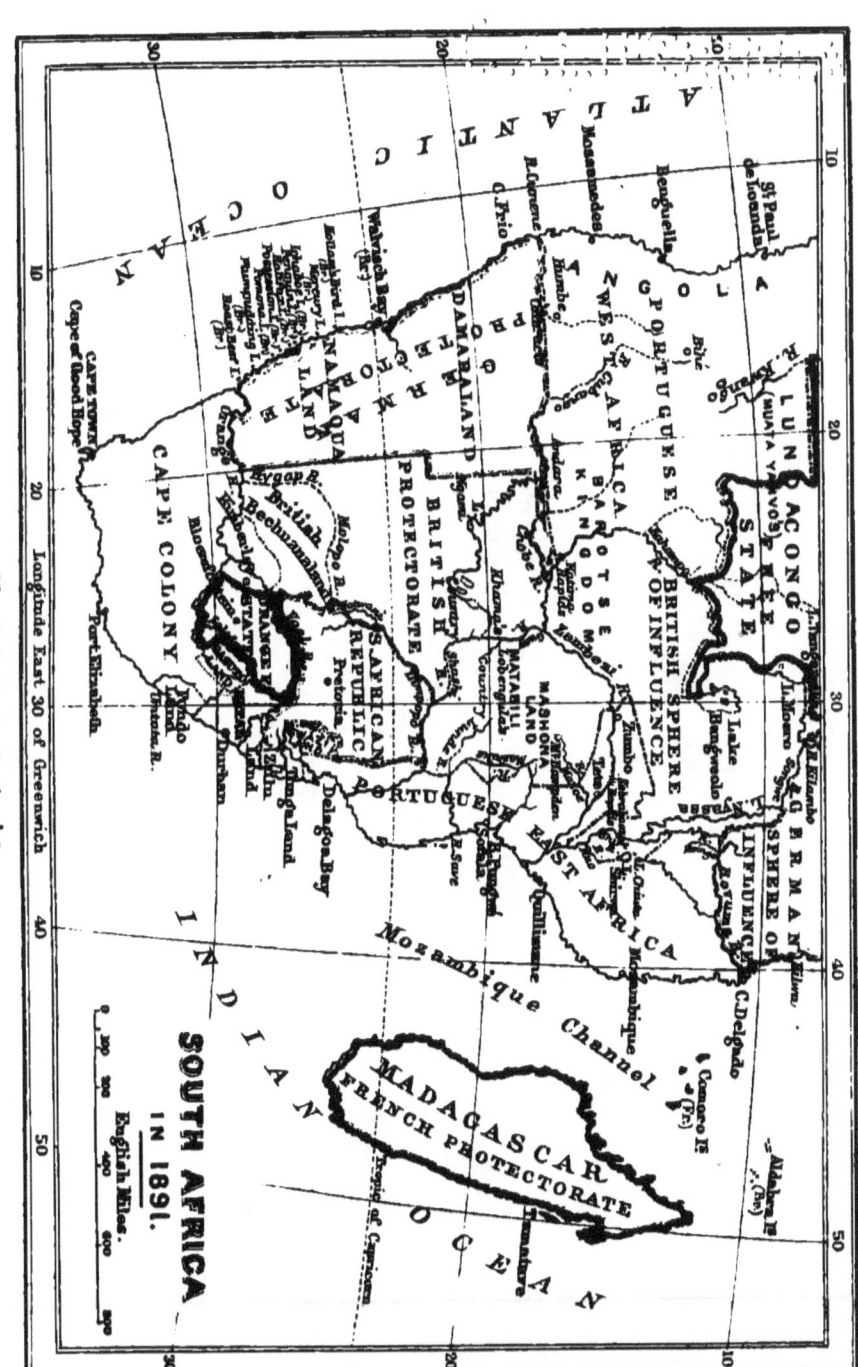

Governor of Natal as Special Commissioner: Zululand, Amatongaland.

iv. Under *a British and Boer* COMMITTEE OF CONTROL—Swaziland.

v. Under British SUZERAINTY as regards foreign relations—Transvaal (the S. African Republic).

vi. INDEPENDENT—The Orange Free State.

Trade.

The trade of our South African colonies has been much assisted by the discovery of *Diamonds* in profitable quantities, amounting to something like three million pounds' worth a year for some years, and the towns of Kimberley and Johannesberg are entirely supported by a mining population. Another article of luxury, *Ostrich feathers*, has proved a source of profit, nearly a million pounds' worth annually being exported. The industry of *Natal* (a separate colony since 1856) shows an inclination towards a semi-tropical industrial character in the form of sugar-planting, and more than 30,000 coolies imported from India are now at work on the plantations.

The extension of our interest inland is proceeding by means of the old method of a *Chartered Company*—the British South African. This charter, like the old ones, confers a certain amount of quasi-political authority, but this is so guarded as not to commit the British Government to all that the Company may do. By means of an expeditionary force of volunteers the Company surveys land in the territory under our 'Influence,' makes preliminary treaties with native chiefs, and lays foundations for future advance. A Bishop of one of the South African dioceses made a special journey in 1889 and reported to his friends at home on the opening for missionary work in these regions, beyond even where Moffat laboured for so long.

The Partition of Africa of 1890.

The year 1890 will be a memorable one in history for both Europe and Africa. It has seen the carrying out of the policy of which the lines were laid down at the Berlin Conference of 1885. By this on the one hand Africa is drawn into the vortex of civilization, and on the other the spheres of the various European nations are marked out, so far as assignment of territory by mutual agreement can do it.

This partition is in many ways remarkable, and not least in that it has been arranged without war: diplomacy has had a real triumph. Opportunities for dispute abounded, but no one would fight, and terms were promptly settled, except between Britain and Portugal, and Britain and Italy, which required longer deliberation.

Our first treaty was with the *Germans*; and, as croakers of both nations denounced their respective Foreign Offices, there is probability that something like equity has been attained. Englishmen have been especially gratified by being at last established at Zanzibar, the emporium of general trade, and in Uganda, so important for interior communication. It is well to remember that our position here is really *imperial*, not purely national, as a large portion of the trade of that region is carried on by our Indian fellow-subjects, not by English people.

In April 1891 negotiations were still proceeding with the *Portuguese*, in the south-east, and with the *Italians*, on the extreme north of this central district; but it is plain that England can agree to no delimitation as final which prevents an open road being kept from her southern colonies right up to the valley of the Nile—not because any traffic would go all the way from one extreme to the other, but because an open track through the heart of Africa will revolutionize the continent. She has not claimed to control all this tract, but insists that it be kept open.

The praise of railways as means of effecting the advance of civilization is sounded so loudly that sometimes we feel sure there is exaggeration which can lead only to disappointment. Still, at some stages of progress railways have certainly worked wonderful changes, and we may at any rate hope that for Central Africa we shall find truth in what an African traveller (Mr. H. H. Johnston) has written:

THE PARTITION OF AFRICA
Up to 1880
Up to 1891

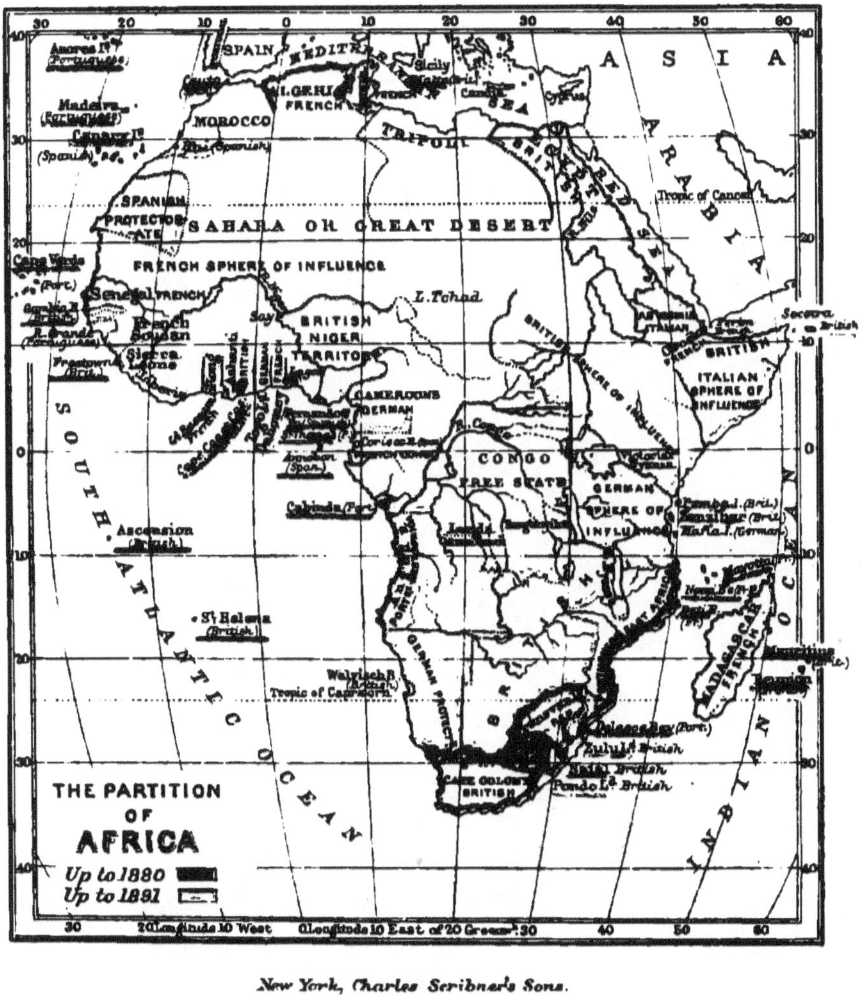

New York, Charles Scribner's Sons.

Callgirl

'There is no civilizer like the railway; and to build a railway through an uncivilized country is to centiple its existing trade, or to create commerce if none exists: the railway saps race prejudices, and dissolves fanaticism.' The railways and lakes of Africa may become the finest highway in the world.

WEST AFRICA.

The Coast Settlements.

The events of the nineteenth century have diverted us from our earliest African settlements, the Gambia and the Gold Coast. The development of these has not been striking, even with the addition of Sierra Leone and Lagos. The obstacles are twofold—(1) The coast is so deadly for white people that the English element has always been very scanty in amount, and, it must be confessed, meagre in moral fibre. These colonies have been a refuge for men who have failed in legal and medical and mercantile pursuits, tempted by high salary to hope for success not attainable at home, or frankly going out to an 'honourable suicide,' and there was a time when slave-traders and 'palm-oil ruffians' represented Christendom to the negro tribes. It is satisfactory to know that the abolition of the Slave Trade, the increase of steam-ship communication, and the strengthening of the authority of the Government, have much improved the quality of our influence, especially since the Ashanti war, and competent observers report that the improvement continues. The whole white population is but a few hundred people, and a few years ago there were only two European ladies in Sierra Leone, the wife of the Bishop and the wife of a medical man. And (2) the character of the neighbouring Negro tribes has proved much less tractable than that of the tribes of the great Bantu family in the east and south. The potentates of West Africa, such as the kings of Dahomey and Ashanti, remain much as they were before they knew us; and the tribes on the coast do not impress observers with any confidence in their hold on either religion or civilization. The prosperity of Free

Town and of Lagos is very considerable, especially that of the latter, but it is the prosperity of seaports, not of indigenous peoples engaged in their own occupations.

The new Niger Territory.

But here, too, a change has come over the prospect. Hitherto by West Africa we have understood the coast-line from the Gambia to the Congo, and it is the unhealthiness of the coast, arising from the combination of extreme dampness and heat, which has been in the way of any very successful colonization or influence. But now we are moving upon the *Interior plateau*, between the Niger and Lake Tchad, where we have secured a considerable territory as a Protectorate. Here there are large and vigorous Negro tribes, Mohammedans tinged with Arab blood, and, if they will co-operate with us, a very different future opens out. It is a land of grassy tracts, breezy and dry, a land of large game, and it may become, what indeed it already is to some extent, a great feeding district for cattle and horses; and there are not wanting signs of great mineral resources. International arrangements with France and Germany have been made here also. The French had a settlement at Senegal in 1637, just after we began ours on the Gambia, and since 1857 they have been extending at the back of Sierra Leone, besides adding to detached territories along the coast; and the Germans have taken up a district around the Cameroons. But M. de Vogüé considers that our fan-shaped territory, spreading out from its basis on the sea, is perhaps the most enviable situation in all Africa.

Here, too, we find the *Company method* again in vogue, a *British Niger Company* having been established in 1884 for developing our influence in this region. Taken altogether, there is every prospect that British West Africa will some day develop into something more important than the small colonies hitherto distinguished by their unhealthiness of climate, the inferiority of their European element, and the secondhand character of the civilization acquired by the natives. In this future the great native tribes will be called upon to take their part. Judging by the success of the French administration, so far as it has extended, there is no reason to doubt that a policy of friendliness and upright dealing on our part will be responded to by the Negro tribes, who show great readiness to seize upon tangible advantages, and at the same time to be influenced by noble sentiment.

The consideration of Africa has introduced us to two new adventurers in the region of colonization: Germany and Italy. The advent of Germany dates from the Conference at Berlin of 1885. She had furnished some of the most distinguished of African travellers, notably Dr. Barth and others who opened the way to Lake Tchad, and was feeling that she ought not to be open to the reproach that she could supply discoverers and colonists but could not herself colonize or administer. Accordingly she took up three separate positions in Africa: on the East coast opposite Zanzibar; on the South-West coast at Angra Pequena, to the north of the Orange River; and in the Gulf of Guinea at the Cameroon Mountains. Great interest was roused in Germany, and a map published at Berlin in 1886 was freely coloured to show dominion stretching from these coast-districts to the far interior, and hinting at a broad band of German territory across Africa from West to East. The late treaty has definitely given her what almost amounts to this, and although her territories do not meet in the centre, which is occupied by the neutral Congo State, there is truth in the Frenchman's statement that, while England wanted to cut Africa from north to south, and Germany from east to west, it is 'the German knife which has remained in the fruit.' We have not secured a British line from Cairo to Cape Town; still, we have certain rights of traffic, the Congo State is neutral, and we have marked out a highway for European action against the slave trade.

In 1882 Italy took up a position at Assab on the Red Sea, and in 1885 at Massowah, and in 1890 she assumed a protectorate over Abyssinia; but her claim on Kassala has not been recognised by England (as guardian of Egypt). This Italian movement was begun by a steamship company director, who bought some land for £1800; then followed the flag; Egypt, backed by England, protested, but Italy persisted: she has won a territory larger than Italy, but costing £800,000 a year; and all this has taken place in a decade.

§5. SCATTERED ACQUISITIONS.

In addition to the extensive territories already mentioned, some important additions to the empire have been made in various parts of the world since 1783.

Malta.

Malta was acquired in 1801 from Napoleon. We were (by the Treaty of Amiens) to give it back to the Knights of St. John, under protection of Russia, but as we did not consider that other conditions were fulfilled, and we consequently refused to retire, our refusal became the occasion of the renewal of war: in 1814 Malta was formally annexed. The military government of the island was exchanged for a constitution of the representative kind in 1887.

Aden.

In 1838 we added Aden as another post on our route to India, and placed it under the Government of Bombay.

Mauritius.

The beautiful and fertile island of Mauritius was taken from France in 1810. There is something to be regretted in our having permanently deprived our neighbour of a spot where her colonizing efforts had been rewarded with success, where her character was so amiably shown, and which her genius has fixed, like the island of Robinson Crusoe, firm in the regard of the youth of both countries as the scene of the imperishable idyll, *Paul et Virginie*. But the island—the Isle of France, as it was lovingly named—was used as a naval resort, and even more injuriously to us as a refuge for privateers and pirates, and we were obliged to take it and to keep it. It is still French in character, but its prosperity has not suffered at our hands, and it now resembles our own peculiarly English island, Barbados, as a spot in the ocean which is singularly dense in population, abounds in wealth, and is almost ideal in contentment.

The Straits Settlements.

In 1819 we purchased the island of Singapore, in the Straits of Malacca. Malacca itself (Portuguese) was captured from the Dutch; Penang was ceded to the East India Company. Of Singapore we made a free port, and it is a great mart for tropical produce on the one hand, and British and Indian goods on the other, for distribution in the neighbouring countries. The great bulk of its trade has fallen into the hands of Chinese merchants.

Hong Kong.

The years 1841-2 saw us engaged in a war with China in connexion with the opium traffic. This war, and our whole conduct in dealing with the production of opium and its forcible importation into China, many Englishmen regard with strong disapproval. The war ended in an easy victory: we exacted a heavy subsidy for expenses incurred, and the island of Hong Kong. Of this we made another free port, and it is the main centre for our commerce with China: its total trade, 20 millions sterling, although very great, is not more than half that of Singapore.

Labuan and Sarawak.

In 1847 we acquired the island of Labuan, near Borneo. In Borneo itself there was an unusual spectacle, a principality, Sarawak, independent of our dominion, but ruled by a British subject, 'Rajah Brooke': the principality came formally under our 'protection' in 1888. Through the British North Borneo Company (chartered in 1881) our influence is now supreme over the north and north-west of this great island.

A Pause.

For some years it was a matter of general opinion and consent that our empire should be no farther extended.

In India, indeed, no doubt something might have to be done for India's sake. But for ourselves it was considered that the era of territorial expansion should stop. Dominion was becoming unnecessary to merchants, in an age when Free Trade was dawning, and it was becoming incapable of justification in the light of the principles of constitutional liberty which were in the ascendant in the minds of public men. This was the time when Sir Henry Barkly tells us that as he started out for a Governorship he was told in the very Colonial Office itself that he would in all probability be one of the last to be sent out.

Both political parties shared in the opinion, but with one it was due to political principle, in the other to acquiescence in the inevitable. During its prevalence a Conservative Government refused to take up the newly-discovered Congo region, and the point of vantage at the head of the Bight of Benin where the Cameroon Mountains stand; and a Liberal Government refused to undertake a protectorate over Zanzibar, and reproached Queensland for intervening when other nations began to parcel out New Guinea.

The Fresh Departure of 1880-90.

The movement was felt first on the continent, and the *French* themselves ascribe it, for their own part, to a desire to turn attention away from the yearning to recover the Rhine Provinces.

The *Germans*, on the other hand, felt that they had strength to spare now that the question of superiority between France and themselves was decided in their own favour, and they were naturally jealous of England's world-wide empire, especially as our colonies attracted and absorbed considerable numbers of German subjects. *Italy* presently began also to look abroad in her turn. The first to move, however, was neither of these, but an entirely new candidate for imperial honours, the treaty-formed State of *Belgium*. The newly-opened Congo river-basin was accepted by the King of the Belgians as a field of enterprise, and as was natural from him, a neutral and international character was given to a society called the Congo International Association, afterwards recognised as a State, with Belgium the predominant influence, and France the reversionary legatee. This was in 1876. Our acquisition of Cyprus in 1878 was due to 'foreign' policy; in order to compensate for Russia's acquisition of Batoum after the war with Turkey we established ourselves at another strategic point. A serious step was taken in 1881 when France assumed the protection of *Tunis*, giving her over 600 miles of Mediterranean shore: Great Britain undertook to restore peace and order in *Egypt* in 1882, and as France left us to settle the difficulty, we control that country for the present. And soon a real scramble for unappropriated territories almost all over the world took place. In Africa we have seen what took place, the most notable action being the vigorous movement of the Germans in three directions. And as Madagascar was brought under France by a final treaty with its potentates in 1885 (recognised by Great Britain in 1890), and as the Sultanates of the Western Soudan are parcelled out, the movement has issued, in less than ten years, in leaving Africa but three independent kingdoms of any note, Morocco, Tripoli, and Dahomey, except that Mahdism has won back from Egyptian supervision some regions of the Eastern Soudan.

The rage for appropriation has extended also to the PACIFIC OCEAN. New Guinea was coveted by Germany, and had it not been for the assertiveness of Queensland and some well-timed and resolute objection on her part to the inaction of the Colonial Office, we might have been shut out and have had a foreign shore stretching opposite the coast of N. E. Australia. We agreed, however, with the Germans upon a division, and the Dutch also secured a share, the part lying nearest to their own existing possessions. The Americans have too much influence in the Sandwich Isles to make European occupation possible, and they also have succeeded in securing a quasi-international position for Samoa; but most of the other Pacific Islands are either 'protected' or 'possessed' by European powers. The important group of Fiji came under our protection almost in spite of ourselves in the time of our lethargy, 1874: the reasons why the Empire which included New Zealand and Australia should undertake to protect the islands were so strong that the dread of aggrandizement was overcome, and Fiji was annexed. The threatened development of New Caledonia as a convict-refuge at the very gates of Australia gave rise to warm feelings among our colonists, and the French have consented to be careful, though without formally altering their plans.

The last step on our part is an apparent act of retrogression—the cession of Heligoland to Germany. To lose territory, said Jules Favre, is to lose self-respect. This instance proves the contrary, for no thoughtful Englishman thinks any the less of the British Empire in consequence. On the other hand, scrupulousness for other people's opinions has been asserted as a motive for international action. The island was not British but German; and we have shown that we no longer mean by 'Empire' one European nation ruling over the home-soil of another.

CHAPTER VII.

THE GOVERNMENT OF THE EMPIRE.

THE British Empire exhibits forms and methods of Government in almost exuberant *variety*. The several colonies at different periods of their history have passed through various stages of Government, and in 1891 there are some thirty or forty different forms operative simultaneously within our empire alone. At this moment there are regions where Government of a purely despotic kind is in full exercise, and the empire includes also colonies where the subordination of the Colonial Government has become so slight as to be almost impalpable. We find one reflection rising in our minds, however, when we survey the history of this complicated variety, namely, that we are looking at the natural growth of an organism, which in its development has taken differing forms in adaptation to differing needs. No cast-iron mechanism is before us, but a living society, exhibiting vital principles both in what it continues to retain and what it drops or adds by way of alteration. The Briton is supposed to be of rigid character; but in Government he has proved himself in this respect to be the most elastic of all Europeans.

In the Government relations existing within an empire, the prominent question is that of the *partition of power* as between the *central authority* and *the new communities*. A colony must be to some extent under despotic government. It is subject to an outside authority in which it has itself no share. True, the colonies of France are excluded from this category, by reason of their having representatives in the central Legislature of the French Republic. But this gives them the character of normal French Departments; their inhabitants are *citizens* of the Republic in the fullest sense of the term, and *colonists* only by their previous history and present geographical distance. The endeavour so to neglect this history and to overlook this distance is a logical outcome of Revolution principles, which produces no ill effect because in effective working it is ignored, as the Legislature can overrule at its own good pleasure the minute fraction of itself which directly represents the colonies, and in effect their presence is a sign of good-will and a maintenance of principle rather than the actual means of securing good government for the islands and districts concerned. They contribute advice, of course, and most valuable advice, but they do not control.

Within our empire no such thoroughgoing abolition of the state of dependency has yet been achieved or attempted, although it is a favourite topic of discussion in some quarters. In our Crown colonies the inhabitants have no share in the control of their own affairs, or only so slight a share as to amount but to an official manner of uttering a protest or expressing an approval. That our despotism is always of the benevolent kind we may certainly claim to be the intention if not the fact: our success varies both in time and place, and indeed it must be estimated by several standards before a final judgment can be attained.

The student of the philosophy of government would very probably find in this field a more really serviceable series of examples of *Parental Despotism* than in those countries where the 'despot' has been a single person. An individual ruler interferes with government in a way which is more disturbing than is the case when a nation is the irresponsible authority; unless it is a mistake for us to think that a nation is unlikely to be influenced by whims and caprices of so volatile and incongruous a character as those which may rise in the breast of an individual ruler, or to be subject to such violent changes of disposition as are found in any succession of personal rulers. Again, in the constitutional history of the colonies the working of *cause and effect in human history* is forcibly displayed. A survey of the whole of the European colonies in respect to their governments shows how far from being either accidental in nature or inexplicable to us are the varieties of their constitutions. There is perhaps no single case in which we may not fully expect to be able to put our finger upon the causes of the variation if we turn to the history of the case and consider it in its known circumstances and conditions.

The Original Methods of Government.

It is to be observed that the government of each of the European colonies bore from the outset the unmistakable impress of the constitution of its mother-country. The simple idea of a *colony* was at first that of a number of men of any nation who had gone abroad; if Spaniards, they were Spaniards still: and the territory to which they went was, by one kind of title or another, a portion of the soil of their now extended native-land. Indeed, even if they went to live within another Christian nation there was an endeavour to acquire a separate status, if not always a separate local habitation. Treaties were entered into by which such people were withdrawn from the authority of the country where they sojourned under promise of obedience to their own Government, and respect for the laws of their new place of abode. More complete, however, was the continuance of citizenship when the colonists went outside Christendom, to regions uninhabited or in the hands of 'savages.' There full allegiance was retained as a matter of course, and the old laws were maintained, unaffected by the emigration. In the case of emigrants from countries where there was no participation in 'government' by the people at large, there was little hankering in the colonies after government, as distinct from management; and as few members of the home governments—no princes or princesses, and but few people of rank or high office, if any—ever emigrated, men accustomed to be ruled easily acquiesced in government being carried on for them at home, or by delegates despatched for the very purpose of ruling over them. But in cases where there was a popular constitution at home there were sure to be among the emigrants some who had the franchise or had held some office; such men were not at all disposed to admit that they were disfranchised by their change. In short, the existence or the absence of a constitution in the home countries determined the position in the new colonies.

In Spanish Colonies.

In the Spanish colonies the arbitrary monarchy of Spain was reflected in this way, and the copy was fatally close to the original. The Viceroys at Mexico, Lima, Bogota, and Buenos Ayres, and their leading officials, received their authority from their monarch, in no wise from the colonists; and they were, as a matter of fact, Spaniards going out to exercise government functions, and not emigrants or colonists raised up from among their brethren. Of 170 Viceroys who ruled the various provinces of Spanish America in the course of three centuries, only 4 were born there; of 610 Captains-General and Governors, only 14. Spaniards were sent out for all posts of profit, even down to the clerkships in the Government offices. This, of course, was nothing less than a caricature of the state of affairs at home, for, after all, if Spanish offices were in the hands of a few, it was the whole Spanish aristocracy, not a limited class that was privileged; and it was their own aristocracy, and not another. But when the colonies had been for years in existence, and a colonial aristocracy had grown up, it was a gross neglect to continue to resort to Europe for all officials, and yet this was what was done. The colonial aristocracy included men of good stock—rich, ennobled even—but they were not considered to be within the select circle of those privileged to be delegates of the royal authority. The Spanish governors wielded power chiefly by complicated checks and intrigues; keeping a gap between the whites and the coloured people, for example, in order to play off one class against the other; using the clergy as spies over the laity, the poor over the rich. The colonists suffered lamentable deterioration from this short-sighted policy. They lived in a sub-tropical climate, and were surrounded by populations of inferior mental type, and thus were sure to lose ground; and yet, in addition to this, they had to bear the loss of not having their energies evoked by having to undertake the control of their affairs. All this led straight to revolution; the situation was instability itself. As soon as the centre of the Spanish empire—the sole heart of authority—was shaken by the French revolutionary attacks under Napoleon, the body politic was ruined as then constituted, and a reorganization round new centres became a necessity. In the entire lack of preparation for this reorganization we find the cause of the unstable and turbulent political histories of the republics into which the Spanish dominion in America became divided.

Had Spain chosen to make a proper use of the colonial aristocracies, with here and there princes of the blood, or grandees of the first class, as viceroys, she might have had a number of dependent kingdoms that would not only have remained within her empire, but have been stirred with all the force of patriotism to assist her at the gloomy time when she had to appeal to her former foe, and depend upon England to lead her in expelling the French from her soil. The disgrace of the Armada was not greater than the degradation of being unable to maintain her own integrity against Napoleon; and this might have been spared her, if loyal aristocracies in Mexico and Venezuela had been in existence to furnish her with both money and men. As it was, the rich classes were alienated, and looked on with indifference, and when they found that their opportunity was come they broke loose, and after a wasteful and useless struggle on the part of the home country the empire was broken up. The new states have had to pass through a severe training; and it is not surprising that they are still unsettled. They are all now republics or confederations of republics.

Portuguese.

The Portuguese system offers no important point of difference. Its one great colony, Brazil, followed the Spanish colonies in declaring its independence, and in 1890 it cast off the last fragment of sentimental allegiance.

The other Spanish and Portuguese possessions are still

governed from home; but, with the exception of Cuba, there is no reason for any other course being taken, as they are not emigrant colonies to any considerable extent, but places where a handful of white people reside among masses of people of colour; their position is not different, in short, from that of our own Crown colonies.

Dutch.

Holland has had only two colonies to which any considerable number of Dutchmen have gone out, Java and the Cape; and only in the latter has there been opportunity for local government, as they have been settlers, rather than merchants or planters, in no other. Even here they had only a qualified success, as we have seen, and a revolution was in progress at the time when the British took possession of the colony. In the brief period of its separate existence the Dutch settlement at New Amsterdam (now New York) reproduced very closely the republican type of government of the Netherlands. The Dutch have established a method of rule in Java, however, which well deserves the attention of Englishmen. Its principle is the assignment to native chiefs of certain functions of a subordinate kind; some reference to it will be found in Chapter x.

French.

The French system of governing their colonies has received high praise in many quarters, at least for the theory which guided it. There was a genuine attempt to provide a method which should bring to bear on the colonies as combined forces the wisdom and experience of home statesmen, and the energy and local knowledge of the best of the colonists themselves. (1) At home there was constituted a *Council*, comprised of twelve officials of the Government and twelve delegates from the chief commercial cities of France; each colony had a Governor and an Intendant sent out from home, and a council of planters, honoured with the dignity of being denominated a Royal Council. (2) Salaries and not fees were the reward of the functionaries. (3) The cost of government was defrayed almost wholly from home.

From this thoughtful and liberal plan greater results might have been expected. But there was a defect beyond the remedy of theory: the condition of the Government at home was hopeless: when for 'Government' we have to substitute 'Court' we can see how it came that the fortunes of the colonies were hampered, and the well-laid scheme rendered useless. The best posts in the colonies were bestowed upon Court favourites who for any private reason desired to go for a time into exile, and the infant colonies derived no assistance from them; while at the same time they were not encouraged, or, indeed, permitted, to manage their own affairs in their own way, even if the idea of such a thing had occurred to their patriotic French minds. The high mark of their prosperity was reached just before the Revolution. Hayti was then at the very climax of wealth-producing activity. But what a farther trial would have effected we have no opportunity of knowing, for the bewildered white people, who had become citizens of a free, equal, and fraternal Republic, endeavoured to retain the negroes in subjection, but were overborne; and, through terrific scenes of fire and blood, Toussaint l'Ouverture—as fine a hero as a nationality need desire—led his black brethren to an independence which was presently to take form in a thoroughly-established Negro Republic.

As the absorption of France in continental wars led to her being deprived by Great Britain of her possessions in America and India, she has had no further opportunity of working out her methods on a large scale. Her islands of Martinique, Guadeloupe, and Réunion are treated as parts of the soil of France, and the people are flourishing and contented. Her other dominions are too full of natives to allow of any government other than parental. Representation by Senators and Deputies is still in force, and the Council for the Colonies is again being remodelled (1891), but on the old lines. Algeria has a distinctly military character, not having attracted immigration from France to the extent that was hoped. The army of occupation is 50,000 strong, and the colony is a heavy charge on the national revenue.

In British Colonies.

Plenty of good land, and *liberty to manage their own affairs*, are enumerated by Adam Smith as the chief causes of prosperity in all new colonies. So far as 'good land' is concerned, England was not, at first, as he says, so fortunate as Spain and Portugal, or even as France; but he considered that our *political institutions* were more favourable than those of any of the other three nations to the improvement and cultivation of such land as we had, and that for that reason there were no colonies in his day in so prosperous a condition as the English settlements in America.

The fundamental idea that substantial heads of families have a right to be regarded as units of the State was carried over the seas by the groups of emigrating Englishmen in the seventeenth century, and upon it rose colonies in which, as Adam Smith says, 'the liberty to manage their own affairs in their own way' was complete in everything except foreign trade, and was in every respect equal to that of their fellow-citizens at home, and secured in the same manner, namely, by assemblies of the representatives of the people. The early charters had, indeed, an aristocratic character, and there was something of a monarchical impress upon them as well. The land was often granted in a mass to a company or a person at home, and a share in government, either directly or through delegates, went with it. But this was not in any way directed against the principle of liberty. In order to start new colonies men of influence and wealth were indispensable, and it was only just and reasonable that they should have a voice in the management of affairs. In some of the colonies the settlers were merely auxiliaries and dependents working with other men's capital, and therefore not entitled to independence. In such colonies as were founded by the wealth of the settlers themselves, in Massachusetts, for example, no such subordination ever had place; even the Governor was elected by the people: in the others, as Pennsylvania and Maryland, it continued until the settlers became their own masters in industry, and worked with their own capital.

For these reasons we are not surprised to find that as early as 1619 a House of Assembly 'broke out' in the colony of Virginia, then just twelve years old. In that Assembly we see the *first-born child of the British Parliament*, the eldest brother, so to speak, of the legislatures of the United States and of the English colonies of to-day. This Assembly was composed of a council and a body of twenty-two representatives from the eleven plantations, elected by the freeholders, imposing taxes and passing laws, meeting either annually or at frequent intervals.

In the various colonies there was a period of struggle against the privileges conferred by the original charters; but there could be only one issue: gradually the proprietors withdrew or were bought out as the diminution of their commercial interest rendered their control an unjustifiable interference, and eventually in some of them even the Crown had no delegates, and after the revolution of 1688 it had very limited authority in any. Still, when the influence of the *Crown*, after 1649, had almost entirely changed into that of *Crown and Parliament*, authority by Acts of Parliament was asserted where the mother-country thought it essential to her own interests to do so; this was almost exclusively in matters of trade. The Navigation Acts were in force in America, and the various regulations constituting the monopoly or colonial system were imposed by imperial authority throughout the colonies.

Crises.

Two crises occurred in the history of Colonial Government relations:—

(i) When the legislatures of the thirteen colonies in North America claimed the sole right of taxation, even for imperial purposes, and preferred the severance of all political ties to the surrender of this right. This has been dealt with in its place in Chapter iv.

(ii) When in Canada the unreformed Parliament of Great Britain persisted in endeavours to rule the colony in matters of social and even domestic character, such as had never been controlled in the Atlantic settlements. Canada was a conquered possession, not a settlement, it is true; but the attempt to treat it as a conquest nearly ended in another catastrophe. What eventually occurred, however, was the establishment of a relationship between that colony and Great Britain which has proved to be the type for all subsequent colonies in which the English people are settled in numbers sufficient to form self-governing communities.

The First Modern Colonial Constitution.

Canada was in 1763 in character as well as in history a conquered country: its population of 65,000 was mostly French. The introduction of British rule was so great a benefit that the colonists never really faltered in their preference for the new régime. Feudal rights which had been brought over the Atlantic were abolished, and many a burdensome hindrance to colonial industry disappeared with them, after the enquiry in France into the conduct of the officials had led another colonial administrator to the Bastille, but in this case with a fate that was deserved. The inability of the British Government to allow an oath of allegiance for members of the local Government which the French Canadians could in conscience take produced the chief difficulty. As at that time Ireland was under a Protestant Parliament and Romanists in England were disfranchised, how else could we have acted in Canada? Lord North's *Quebec Act* of 1774 made things worse, as it altered what was good, reviving the old French laws, which the inhabitants did not desire, and left unaltered what they wished to see changed, their exclusion from participation in the government. Chatham denounced this Act; and its enactment alarmed the colonists on the Atlantic coast, and showed what might be feared. In the war of Secession the Canadians were divided in sympathy: a sagacious Governor, Sir Guy Carleton, afterwards Lord Dorchester, saved the colony, after all had been lost except Quebec itself. After the secession of their southern neighbours, the Canadians again asked for a

House of Assembly, and also asked for the restoration of the Habeas Corpus Act. This latter request was granted, but it was not until 1791 that the Quebec Act was repealed, and representative Assemblies granted. At that time the colony was divided into two provinces, Upper Canada, mainly British, and Lower Canada, mainly French, each with a Lieutenant-Governor and a legislature. Very liberal powers were granted; no taxation was claimed by the Imperial Parliament, except in connexion with commerce. The first proceeding of the legislature of Upper Canada was to declare English law of property, civil right, and trial by jury to be law of the province, and to abolish slavery. This would appear to be a very fair treatment, but it did not satisfy Charles James Fox, who, during the passing of this constitutional Act, anticipated the policy of the Manchester School of fifty years later by urging that the colonies should govern themselves altogether. And the event proved that the colonists were only partially satisfied. The official element—the Executive department of government—remained responsible to the Imperial Parliament, and unfortunately did not lead the Canadians to entire contentment and tranquillity. There was, however, satisfaction sufficient to keep even the French province loyal during the great war between Great Britain and France, although it must have been with strangely mixed feelings that a citizen of Quebec heard the news of victories which shattered the French navy and drove the French armies out of Spain; and they were also rendered proof against the enticements of the United States to join them in their war against us in 1812–15. Indeed, in this last struggle the Canadians maintained their own cause along their borders with a valiant and capable militia.

Utilitarian Doctrine in Practice.

By 1837, however, the discontent had grown into disaffection, and in Lower Canada there was open rebellion. The settlement of the difficulty was effected by means not very commonly in high favour. For once *systematic thought was brought to bear upon politics*. That group of thinkers, writers, and public men, hard-headed and clear-minded, if not exactly profoundly philosophical, who are best described as *the Benthamite school*—James and John Mill, the Austins, George Grote, Charles Buller, and others—had their opportunity. A young peer of considerable promise, Lord Durham, was sent out as Governor in 1838; he issued a famous report, due to the pen of Charles Buller, in which the Radical philosophers' principles were vigorously applied. Lord Durham himself made some mistakes which caused his recall and led to his premature death; but his successor was of the same mind, and in 1840 Parliament was persuaded to give effect to the proposals made in the report. The colony was united again, with a single Legislature, to meet alternately at Quebec and Toronto; but the main point was that *the Executive branch of government was brought under the control of the colonists*. The principle that all officials must be responsible to the Legislature, which had long been the keystone of the British constitution, at once gave self-government to Canada, and ended the effective control of the mother-country. The Governor alone was excepted, and for a time he retained the appointment of some *officials*; but in 1845 Governor Metcalfe yielded this point also, and the Governor alone represented the suzerainty of Britain. The official regulation (No. 57 of Rules and Regulations) now runs thus: 'In colonies possessing what is called Responsible Government, the Governor is empowered by his Instructions to appoint and remove Members of the Executive Council, it being understood that Councillors who have lost the confidence of the local Legislature will tender their resignation to the Governor, or discontinue the practical exercise of their functions, in analogy with the usage prevailing in the United Kingdom.' In certain matters he refers home for instructions whether or not to veto measures of the colonial Legislature, but in *all* that are of purely local effect he is bound to take the advice of his Cabinet, which is entirely dependent upon the colonial Legislature. The obstructive effect of the previous condition of things was proved by the increase of vigour and enterprise which ensued immediately upon the change. Various restrictions on commerce were removed; municipal bodies were created for the towns; the railway enterprise of England was emulated; education was reorganized; and the legal code was consolidated. *The year 1841 is therefore the year of the inauguration of modern Colonial Government.*

It is worthy of notice that the constitution adopted is of *the old British form*. So much is this the case that it is assumed that any legal or political procedure not specifically provided for will be the same as in England. It has been decided by the highest Law Court that the Upper House of Queensland—and the same applies to Canada—has not equal rights with the Lower House because the Upper House in England has not. The constitution is not of the form which the Canadians saw in operation in the United States. There the Executive and the Legislature are kept quite distinct. Both are elected by the people, but independently of one another, the Executive being elected once in every four years, and having power for that period whatever amount of dissatisfaction may arise on the part of the Legislature. But in Canada the English constitution has been transplanted; the Ministry is a committee of the Legislature. The success of this first experiment practically decided which of the two forms of Representative Government evolved by the Anglo-Saxon race should be generally adopted in our colonies, and the solution has been accepted by such Latin nations as France and Italy[1].

[1] The ground of Canadian preference for their present political position to incorporation with the United States was thus analysed by Lord Dufferin at Toronto in 1874.

    Canada has its Executive and its Legislature bound together, and so is able to follow out English habit and practice.

    Canada has in its Governor-General a means of preventing deadlocks between branches of the Legislature, or between local and central authority.

    Canada has its Judiciary appointed, as in all countries except the U.S.A., by the Government, not by incompetent popular election.

    Canada has its Civil Service permanent, not changing with party successes.

    Canada has its electoral system, as a matter of fact, pure.

Extension of Responsible Government.

The granting of Responsible Government to our other colonies has, so far, extended to the following nine—Newfoundland, New South Wales, Victoria, South Australia, Queensland, Tasmania, New Zealand, Cape Colony, and (in 1890) Western Australia. In all of these the Governor is the only link between the Home Government and the Colonial, and in all of them his powers are limited to the exercise of the veto. Even this is circumscribed. It is tacitly understood that the *veto* will be resorted to only when the *foreign relations* of the empire are affected, or when some Act is passed which the Secretary of State decides to be incompatible with existent Imperial legislation. For example, even in Canada, which has a certain treaty power, no Treaty of Commerce which placed French goods at a disadvantage relatively to those of other countries would be allowed on the first ground; none which put English goods at a disadvantage, on the second. Attempts have been made to invoke the veto in other cases, notably when there was a deadlock in Victoria between the Upper and Lower Houses, but Parliament decided that the colonists must settle the matter for themselves. It was in the course of a debate during this conflict that the Attorney-General of the colony, speaking in the Lower House, alluded to the possibility of inviting the Governor to embark on an Imperial man-of-war in the harbour if he should attempt to take the settlement of the dispute out of the hands of the colonists. On the other hand Lord Dufferin said in a speech in British Columbia in 1876 that had Mr. Mackenzie, then the Premier of Canada, been really guilty of charges levelled against him of surreptitiously defeating a measure of his own, either he would by the Governor-General's intervention have ceased to be Premier, or he (Lord Dufferin) would have left the country. He points out how the Governor is a first-rate arbitrator, and secures a more really democratic government than that of the United States.

The official statements are thus worded [1]:—

'Article 54. In Colonies possessing Representative Assemblies Laws purport to be made by the Queen, or by the Governor on Her Majesty's behalf, or sometimes by the Governor alone (omitting any express reference to Her Majesty), with the advice and consent of the Council and Assembly. They are almost invariably designated as Acts. In Colonies not having such Assemblies, Laws are designated Ordinances, and purport to be made by the Governor with the advice and consent of the Legislative Council.'

'Article 48. In every Colony the Governor has authority either to give or to withhold his assent to laws passed by the other branches or members of the Legislature, and until that assent is given no such law is valid or binding.'

'Article 50. Every law which has received the Governor's assent (unless it contains a suspending clause specially reserving it for Her Majesty's confirmation) comes into operation immediately or at the time specified in the Law itself. But the Crown retains power to disallow the Law; and if such power be exercised at any time afterwards, the Law ceases to have operation from the date at which such disallowance is published in the Colony.'

Legislation on social and even moral questions is completely under local control. Not only is marriage with a deceased wife's sister *allowed* by the Crown, but the idea of intervention was abandoned—in spite of some appeals by powerful local bodies—when Divorce Bills greatly extending facilities for divorce were recently passed in Victoria and another in New South Wales. Even trade, which has so often been the chief object of British policy, has been handed over to the control of the colonies.

The constitutions of the colonies are frankly *democratic* in character. The franchise is manhood suffrage in some, household suffrage in others. The position of the Cape Colony is very anomalous: there the native majority must be

[1] Rules and Regulations of the Colonial Service, compiled by the Secretary of State's directions, *Colonial Office List*, published annually.

excluded, and an income of £50 from property or salary or wages is the basis, giving 86,000 electors where manhood suffrage would give about a quarter of a million. It is with the object of preventing the occasion for so oligarchical a constitution that in one colony, Queensland, a strong party vehemently protests against the importation of coolie labour into the colony. But on one point conservative feeling seems to be strong. In no colony is a women's franchise in force, except for municipal and other local boards.

Voting is by ballot: Parliaments are dissolved either every five years or every three. In some colonies members of Parliament receive a moderate stipend in order to prevent the monopoly of representation by men of property.

Law.

The whole province of Law in both the Personal and the Property departments is within colonial control. There is, indeed, an appeal from the Supreme Court in each colony to the Queen in Council, i.e. to the Queen as advised by certain paid members of a 'Judicial Committee of the Privy Council'; but even here it is not an appeal to English law. Colonial law is placed on the same footing as the law of Scotland, and the Judicial Committee has only to decide in any case what the law of the colony is in reference to the matter in dispute. The affairs of Quebec and Mauritius are decided by the old French law, of Guiana by the Dutch law, of the Straits Settlements by the Koran, unless there are distinct colonial enactments bearing on the case.

Defence.

For defence against foreign nations the colonies have been accustomed to depend mainly upon the forces and the exchequer of Great Britain; but now they are beginning to provide for their own protection by adding to their militia some small regular forces, and by building a few ships and some fortifications. The expenses of Government are no longer borne by Great Britain: even the Governor and his personal staff are paid out of the colonial exchequer. On the other hand we exact no contributions whatever from them for the protection which they continue to enjoy, from our navy especially, nor any contribution towards the heavy annual charges in the shape of interest on our National Debt, although without that debt the territories of all of them possibly—of some of them very probably—might now be in the hands of the French or Germans. The organization of Imperial defence was one of the chief matters taken in hand at the Imperial Conference in London in 1887, and certain measures were agreed upon[1].

Semi-Responsible Governments.

If all our colonies were of the simple type of those which enjoy Responsible Government the constitutions might be identical throughout. But a fresh feature appears in most of them, namely, the presence within the colonies of people of other races who were already in possession when we went there. Where these are European no overpowering difficulty has been felt: in Canada all that remains is slight occasional friction; and although at the Cape the friction amounts to irritation and frequent disturbance between the Dutch and British elements, there is every prospect that harmony will eventually be attained. But where there is *a large number of inhabitants not of European race who bear an overwhelming proportion to the white settlers* it has not been a part of our policy to hand over a colony either to the narrow circle of the whites or to impose a franchise which should include natives as well as white people. Some *modus vivendi* must be found, and it is in this situation especially that the existence of an Imperial authority outside the colony is of the utmost value. In West Australia 40,000 white people may have Responsible Government because the aboriginal inhabitants are so few

---

[1] The annual expenditure for defence of the empire, as stated by Sir C. Dilke before the Royal Colonial Institute, in May, 1890, is £60,000,000: divided into—Great Britain, £38,000,000; India, £20,000,000; the Colonies, £2,000,000.

in number as to be a negligable quantity; but in Natal the 40,000 Europeans are in a different position, with 360,000 Zulus and other Africans and 30,000 coolies from India and China around them. Accordingly the sagacity of our statesmen has produced a modified form of government which is denominated 'representative' in the official documents of the Colonial Office[1]. The general principle is that *legislation* should be largely in the hands of the colonists, but *administration* directed from home through a Governor advised by officials of his own appointment. Legislation is not left freely in the hands of the colonists, as the Governor's veto is much more freely used than in the responsibly-governed colonies. In Barbados we see a good type of government of this intermediate or representative class. The Governor, the Chief Justice, the Attorney-General, the Solicitor-General, the Colonial Secretary, the Auditor-General, and the Inspector-General of Police are appointed by the Secretary of State at home. Of these seven chief officials, four are Englishmen sent out, three are old residents in the colony. There is a Legislative Council (or Upper House) to which members are nominated by the Governor 'during pleasure,' and an Assembly to which members are elected by the eleven 'parishes' of the island. The Colonial Treasurer is the highest official whom the colonists, through their Assembly, appoint: this was a wise conces-

---

[1] It is not necessary to attribute very much of the organization to political sagacity: (i) The Crown colonies were most of them conquests, and the early character of their government was coloured by their origin, being often of a military type; and (ii) there was not within the colonies a sufficient number of intelligent and disinterested persons from whom members of a Government could be chosen. The exercise of government from home was therefore quite natural; where sagacity has been shown has been in the modifications introduced in response to differences in the circumstances of the several colonies, and to the changes taking place as progress went on. At the Cape, for example, there is a Responsible Government, although it is a conquest or cession: at Barbados there is not, although it is an original settlement of our own. In one case the situation has led to a special treatment in the direction of liberty, in the other in the direction of parentalism.

sion to the radical objection of English people to relinquish control of money-matters. The Executive consists of an Executive Committee, chiefly official, and so far responsible to the Imperial Government, but partly representative of the Assembly: the Governor, the Officer commanding the troops, the Colonial Secretary, the Attorney-General, one nominated member, one member of the Legislative Council, and four members of Assembly, all of these chosen by the Governor. All money-votes and all Government measures are initiated by this Committee. The veto is frequently employed, and the hand of the Imperial Government is constantly felt. The Assembly, though called representative, is not based on either household or manhood suffrage; a limit of property is placed just above the point which would admit the day-labourers who form the numerical majority of the population. How an agitation for manhood suffrage would be dealt with if pressed upon the British Parliament or British Political Associations it is not easy to forecast. It would have some educational effect, as it would put before the English people the practical question whether (1) all men are equally fit to be entrusted with government—in which case where would the 18,000 white people of Barbados be with 160,000 as the coloured party?—or (2) whether some solid advantage may not be gained by human beings from *being governed* thoughtfully and with sincere intention to secure the general welfare of the community.

In this class of Representative governments each separate colony has some difference of detail, but the main features are the same; they are Barbados, Bahamas, Leeward Islands, Windward Islands, British Guiana, Bermuda, Malta, and Natal.

Crown Colonies.

The third class consists of the CROWN COLONIES. In these the principle of *Imperial control* is resolutely carried out: there is no pretence of popular government, but an open declaration that the white inhabitants are *not* in the eyes of

Great Britain the natural rulers. The *great military and naval stations*, of course, fall at once into this category; except Malta, which has lately received a constitution (1887). The welfare of the inhabitants of these possessions is subordinate to the strategic or commercial purpose for which they are held. In this category we place Gibraltar, Aden, Singapore, Labuan, Hong Kong, The Falklands, St. Helena.

In other colonies *the welfare of the native inhabitants* in harmony with that of the British residents is the purpose of our rule, and we have therefore to undertake the responsibility of governing them. The most important are Ceylon, Jamaica, Trinidad, Honduras, Mauritius, Sierra Leone, Gold Coast, Lagos, and Fiji. In a Crown colony the Governor and his officials govern; some provision for *advice* from residents is usual by means of the introduction of a few residents or unofficial members into his council, but these are appointed by the Governor himself or by the Secretary of State on his recommendation, and he is not bound to take their advice. Few posts exist in modern times where a man of administrative ability can be more effective than as Governor of a Crown colony. He can have ample scope for his talents in these important communities, and if he can win the confidence of those whom he governs the confidence of his chief in Downing Street is fairly certain to follow. He can do much towards gratifying reasonable hopes of the white people to enjoy a profitable trade, and the equally reasonable hopes of the coloured people to be raised in the scale of civilization by the kindly and considerate influence of capable and upright officials. And since the Colonial Office has almost satisfied itself that its prime duty in selecting Governors and in promoting officials is good government and not merely the bestowal of lucrative offices, a succession of able men have conferred real and substantial benefit on the native populations of the Crown colonies, and upon the Europeans who have shared in their general prosperity.

The Secretary of State.

In relation to the Representative and the Crown colonies the importance of the SECRETARYSHIP OF STATE for the COLONIES at home comes out strongly. As a matter of fact this Secretary exercises powers of singular variety. He is the *de facto* ruler of some twenty countries situated in various parts of the world. Although responsible to the other members of the Cabinet, and with them responsible to Parliament, he always has a wide field of action in which his procedure is left to himself. There is no case in this century in which a Colonial Secretary has been compelled to withdraw from a Cabinet, nor any in which a Cabinet has lost office, through disapproval of Parliament on a colonial question. It is, however, only since 1854 that the department has been a separate one. For many years the colonies were under the care of the Home Secretary, but in 1854 they were attached to the Secretaryship of State for War. In that year the Colonial department was constituted, and Sir George Grey was the first Secretary. The department consists of a Parliamentary Under-Secretary, a Permanent Under-Secretary, three Assistant Under-Secretaries, each with a division of colonies allotted to him, and a large staff of clerks. There is a single service for the Representative and Crown colonies, and officials are promoted in it from one colony to another. In some cases it is deemed expedient to send out men of some distinction in other spheres as Governors, as General Sir Henry Norman, who was sent to establish the Crown system in Jamaica in place of the Representative system after the disturbances during the administration of Governor Eyre in 1865.

Protectorates.

The events of recent years have brought within the empire territories where *an elaborate system of government would be premature*. What has been wanted has been a provisional supervision of affairs. Thus we have now a number of territories called *Protectorates*, each directed by a Chief Commissioner and a staff. Such are the portions of New Guinea allotted to Great Britain in 1888; the Somali coast in North-East Africa; Zanzibar and Pemba in 1890; Perak and other small native states in the Malay Peninsula; Sarawak and Bruncei in Borneo; and various scattered islands in the Pacific.

In a Protectorate a native potentate is maintained in power, and a British official, designated either Commissioner or Resident, is placed at the capital in sole charge of foreign relations, and with varied and undefined powers in internal affairs.

And beyond these there are some territories within which no authority is as yet exercised, but which are *reserved* for us by treaty with other European powers whenever we choose to move forward into them—the 'SPHERES OF INFLUENCE' in Eastern, Southern and Western Africa.

Subordinate Colonies.

We should also note that there are places which are directed from other colonies, the officials being responsible to the Governors of these and not directly to the Secretary of State. Aden is thus governed by a Resident acting under the Governor of Bombay, while Perim Island and Socotra Island are under subordinates of the Resident of Aden. The Seychelles are subordinated to Mauritius; Norfolk Island to New South Wales; Rotumah to Fiji.

Chartered Companies.

In Africa we find once more in extensive operation the principle which proved so effective in the early days of colonization, GOVERNMENT THROUGH CHARTERED COMPANIES. These companies have certain responsibilities in exchange for certain privileges, as the East India Company once had. They can raise a military police, enrolling natives under European officers, can issue a coinage, maintain a river fleet, and under certain restrictions regulate trade. The *British East Africa Company* (1888), capital Mombassa; the *Royal Niger Company* (1886), capital Asaba; the *British North Borneo Company* (1877); and others, are thus continuing the old policy. Besides the signal example of the International Congo Association, there is also a *German* East African Company, a German New Guinea Company, and a German Company for Damaraland (S. W. Africa); and *Frenchmen* are considering whether it is not time to adopt this method by establishing a company for the Niger and Soudan.

These companies have been constituted hitherto by large capitalists without any appeal for general support, but there seems to be no good reason why they should not be more widely based. Public subscription-lists might be opened, and the shares made of small amount. This would secure for them a wide range of popular interest and sympathy. For a contrast of judgments as to the 'company' method, Adam Smith's chap. vii. may be compared with J. S. Mill's defence of the East India Company in his *Representative Government*. The method seems to be a sound one in cases where the Imperial Government is unwilling to assume direct government of regions and yet desires to encourage and regulate British enterprise. It is stated by men who know Africa that intermittent journeys and expeditions can be of little effect, and that philanthropy therefore does not supply the kind of motive power required. Popular interest fluctuates, and must do so in the great variety of human affairs brought from time to time before the attention of a world-people like the English. As in religious enterprises the Missionary Societies, so in general affairs a Chartered Company, supplies *a permanent activity*, and when *regulated by principles approved by Parliament*, and embodied in their charter as the condition of State countenance, offers an admirable agency for extending European influence. The method may prove of very great effect in developing Africa, especially if a broad popular basis by means of small shares were laid. Its practicability, its elasticity, its combination of freedom and responsibility, and the success already achieved, have attracted the attention of all the European nations concerned with Africa.

FEDERATION.

In the sphere of government there are in our day two great tendencies working in opposing directions: a tendency towards the *aggregation* of communities where the strength that comes from union is the primary necessity, and a tendency towards *separation* where good government can be best secured by that full use of the knowledge and sentiments of communities which is possible only to the smaller groups into which geographical and racial conditions have separated men. On the continent of Europe the unification of Italy and of Germany have at last followed upon the unification of Britain and France and Spain, and centralization has been the predominant tendency. But in the British dominions the separative tendency has, as we have seen, prevailed. The result has been that our empire is much weaker than the other great empires. We may rejoice at the liberties acquired by our great responsible colonies, but the reform has hardly strengthened the empire as a unit, in relation to the empires of Germany and Russia and the republics of France and America. From this has arisen a more earnest attention to the question whether there are no means by which the disintegrating forces might be counteracted; whether the empire might not become more really a single State than it is.

There was a method of union well known in the Greek world of 2000 years ago, and revived with some signal successes since the mediaeval period,—the method of FEDERATION. The combination of local with national strength which stands before us in the great federation of thirty-eight States into which our own former thirteen colonies in America have developed, strikes the attention of all men, especially since the Union triumphed in the War of Secession of 1861-65. And as Englishmen and Colonists look at their own empire, the question arises whether the time has not come for us to work in the opposite direction to that in which 'progress' has been made in the two generations just passed, and to seek in federation a means of reunion. The general acceptance of the term *federation* is itself an indication of the length to which the movement towards separation has hitherto proceeded. Federation is union by *foedus*, that is by *treaty* or *compact*, and implies persons or bodies otherwise independent; it does not strictly apply to the union of the members of a single body. The 'States' of America are sovereign states acting under a compact. To speak of 'federating' Great Britain and her colonies is to acknowledge the virtual independence of the latter.

CONFEDERATION.

But before this is applied to the widely-scattered members of our empire it is reasonable to ask whether anything has been done in the way of forming groups within the empire. Such groups have been formed. It is convenient to speak of them—in distinction from groups of communities which by their union form a sovereign power—as CONFEDERATIONS, and we have already had before us one successful example of confederation, and in several cases steps towards forming others are being taken.

(a) In Canada.

The growth of population in our North American territory led to the formation of 'colonies' which were not merely extensions of Upper and Lower Canada but of distinct status, directly related to the United Kingdom. In 1867 the important step was taken of unifying all these as a confederation under the title of the DOMINION OF CANADA. One after another all the colonies in that region, including the old East Coast colonies, Nova Scotia, Prince Edward Island, New Brunswick, and British Columbia, but not Newfoundland, have entered this union, and we have in this Confederation another successful application of the method by the English race. Each colony or 'province,' as it is called, has its own Lieutenant-Governor and Legislature working within defined limits, and there is a Governor-General with a Ministry and a Parliament for the Dominion as a whole. A signal instance of the strength acquired by union has been the construction of the Canadian Pacific Railway, which might indeed have been built by the Canadians if they had remained entirely separated, but could hardly have been built so promptly and so rapidly, if at all. The success of confederation in Canada is undoubted, although occasionally there is some friction, (1) on the part of the French inhabitants of Lower Canada, overborne by the more rapidly progressive provinces to the West; and (2) on the part of the East Coast provinces, not satisfied always that they receive as much from the funds of the Central Exchequer as their contributions entitle them to receive, or as their needs, as estimated by themselves, require.

(b) In the West Indies.

The success of Confederation in Canada led to a somewhat premature judgment on the part of some English statesmen that it might be applied to some other parts of the empire. In 1871 the smaller islands in the West Indies were formed into two groups. Antigua, St. Kitts, Montserrat, Nevis, Dominica, and the Virgin Islands, were formed into a single Government under the title of the LEEWARD ISLANDS, in which there was a central Governor, but separate Councils and Legislatures on the different islands continued as before : Barbados, St. Vincent, Grenada, St. Lucia, and Tobago were grouped as the WINDWARD ISLANDS. But the failure in this latter case is instructive; one member of the group, Barbados, so far excelled the others in wealth, vigour, and prosperity, that a severe struggle arose in that island which resulted in the success of the *anti-confederationists*; the group was constituted without it, and it still possesses a separate Government. Jamaica also is separate, and so is Trinidad, though Tobago was annexed to it in 1889; and the Bahamas constitute another Government still. As within the Windward and Leeward Islands the local legislatures remain, and there is no central legislature at all in the former group, Centralization is not yet far advanced. When we consider that the whole population of the British West Indies is but one million and a quarter, and that there are no great differences in their industrial pursuits or in their populations, we cannot consider that Confederation has made much way in this part of our dominions, while these islands are ranged under six separate Governments.

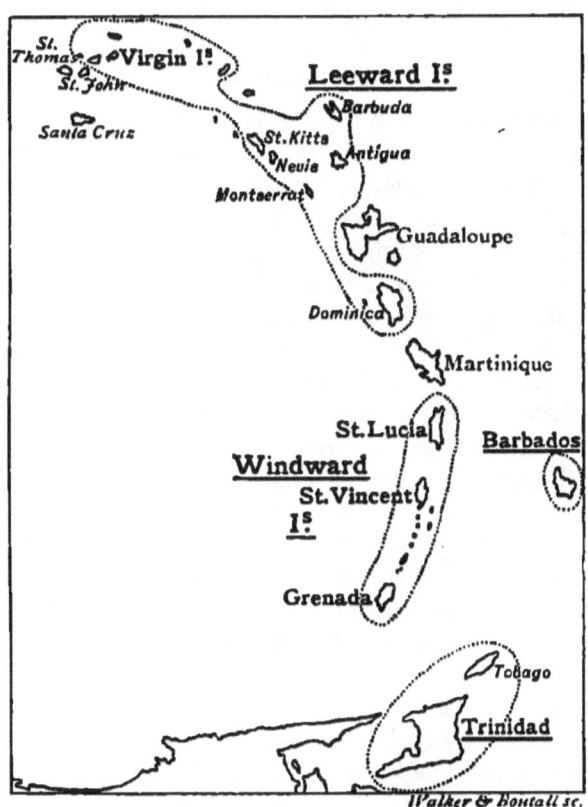

(c) In South Africa.

It was in South Africa that the attempt proved to be quite premature, and considerable irritation and disturbance greeted the proposal of Lord Carnarvon in 1875-77 to establish a South African Confederation. Still, the idea is familiar to our countrymen out there, and though we may readily accept their decision that the time has not yet come for any movement, we all feel that the curious agglomeration of colonies, republics, and protectorates of South Africa is at present in a situation which is only provisional and preparatory. The Dominion idea was not accepted at once by the extreme eastern or extreme western provinces of Canada, yet none of them seriously question its value now.

(d) Australasia.

It has been a common saying in Australia that our fellow-countrymen in that part of the world did not recognise the term 'Australian'; each recognised only his own colony and the empire. But the advocates of combination for certain common purposes achieved a great step forward in the formation of a *Federal Council in* 1885. It was to be only a 'Council,' its decisions having no force over any colony unless accepted afterwards by the colonial Legislature. Victoria, Queensland, Tasmania, and West Australia joined, New South Wales, South Australia, and New Zealand standing out, and, so constituted, it met twice. The results of the deliberations were not unsatisfactory, and the opinion that the move was in the right direction rapidly grew. In February of 1890 a Federation Conference, not private but representative of the different Governments, was called at Melbourne. It adopted an address to the Queen declaring the opinion of the conference to be that the best interests of the Australian colonies require the early formation of a *union under the Crown into one Government, both legislative and executive.*

Events proceed quickly in Colonial History. In the course of 1890 the hesitation of New South Wales was finally overcome; powerful factors being the weakening of the Free Trade position at the election of 1890, the report of General Edwards on the Defences, and the difficulties about Chinese immigration. A *Convention* accordingly assembled at Sydney in March, 1891, which agreed upon a Constitution to be recommended to the several Colonies. The Federation is to be called 'THE COMMONWEALTH OF AUSTRALIA';

it is to have a Federal Legislature and Federal Executive, with the present Colonial Legislatures and Executives in addition. The *Federal Legislature* is to consist of (1) a Senate of 8 members from each 'State,' and (2) a House of Representatives with members according to population. The Governor-General will be the only official appointed by the Crown, and he will be the Commander-in-Chief of the Army and Navy. A *Cabinet* of seven ministers, responsible to the Federal Legislature, will be the Federal Executive. Posts and Telegraphs, Immigration, and Marriage Laws will be amongst the matters placed under Federal authority, and on the specially difficult subject of Trade Regulation there will be common policy. There is to be no Appeal except in Public Law. Some modifications may be made before the Constitution is finally adopted, but it is almost certain that the Confederation will be accomplished before this century closes.

IMPERIAL FEDERATION.

The application of federation to the relationship of the mother-country to the subordinate constituents of the empire is, however, a more complicated problem. It is usually discussed under the title of IMPERIAL FEDERATION, and became a movement in politics when an *Imperial Federation League* was formed in 1884, chiefly by the efforts of an Englishman who had always given great attention to colonial affairs, and had held for a time the office of Parliamentary Under-Secretary, the late William Edward Forster. The unity of the empire as a combination of resources for common interests and common defence, without interfering with the existing rights of 'Local Parliaments' as regards 'local' affairs, is the fundamental principle of the League. It includes in its membership Englishmen at home and in the Colonies, and has succeeded in keeping itself quite clear from the party politics of the United Kingdom.

§ 1. PARTICIPATION IN AN IMPERIAL SOVEREIGNTY.

In the present constitution the Queen and Parliament of the United Kingdom is the sovereign authority for all affairs of the empire, and other 'Parliaments' are delegates and subordinates. The entrance, therefore, of any colonies into a federation with themselves and with Great Britain implies, on the face of it, at once a great responsibility and a great privilege for the colonies. It is a question of their participating in the sovereign power of the empire, and cannot be rightly judged if attention is confined to the purely selfish benefits which any colony may acquire by the change. Increase of efficiency it ought to mean, but for the colonies it must mean increase of responsibility also.

This consideration at once enables us to draw a line among the colonies and so to *limit the field* of our view. For there can be no question of admitting to participation in sovereign power of the empire communities which are not yet entrusted with the government of themselves. The great dependency, India, is at once placed out of court, and all the CROWN COLONIES go with her. They are ruled by the United Kingdom, and so long as they are under this tutelage they are not eligible for admission to the government of other communities. The case of the REPRESENTATIVE COLONIES is not essentially different. So long as the chief officials are not responsible to the colony for their actions, but to the Secretary of State, and so long as legislation is so closely supervised as it is in the case of these colonies, they are not sufficiently self-governing to become members of a federation. This, therefore, limits our field to the RESPONSIBLE COLONIES—Canada, Newfoundland, the Cape, and the colonies of Australasia—ten in all. These are already sufficiently autonomous to render their admission to a compact, on equal terms with the United Kingdom, a matter of great simplicity in itself. If they dispensed with their Governors, and decided to consider themselves in a position to treat independently with foreign countries, they would be independent.

Are these ten colonies, then, by means of imperial federation, to enter *the sovereign body of the British Empire?* Are they prepared to bear a part of the great task we have to discharge in governing India? Are they ready to take their part in controlling the affairs of the West Indies, and Hong Kong, and all our other colonies? For this is our *Imperial* function, and a part which Englishmen have always to bear in mind. The President of the Imperial Federation League, Lord Rosebery, has declared that the title-deeds of the empire belong to these islands; the colonies must perceive that to share in them is to acquire a privilege for which they must be ready to give a return. And why should they not? It may be replied that their own development absorbs all their energies, and must do so for some time to come. This may be so, but on the other side there is much to be said for Englishmen at home having the co-operation of Englishmen in these ten colonies in governing India and our Crown colonies.

Another question is—*Do we in Great Britain wish for their help* in dealing with the other great nations of the world? At present Britain alone controls the foreign relations of the whole empire. Are we ready to admit the colonies? This question must be faced, if not immediately, yet whenever some real emergency arises, war or peace with the United States, for example. And it is plain that the time is rapidly going by when we can ask for help from these colonies *after* a declaration of war, if we have not asked for advice or offered any part in deliberation *before* it. They may *offer* help, but we should not be in a position to request it, much less to demand it.

And further, *are they ready to throw in their lot with us?* are they ready to be committed definitely to imperial policy when they themselves have had a part in shaping it? At present they are so committed without being consulted. On declaration of war by Russia against Great Britain, the wharves of Melbourne may be sacked, and gun-boats make havoc up the St. Lawrence. Federation would involve the continuance of this liability: but it would give them a share in deciding whether or not war should be entered upon.

Again, are the colonies prepared to take *interest in one another's welfare* in relation to foreign nations? If the Norman and Breton fishermen encroach upon Newfoundlanders, are New Zealanders ready to take up the quarrel? Great Britain would have to do so. Will Queensland join us, or would it insist on non-intervention in an affair apparently so remote? On the other hand, would the citizens of Montreal and Toronto be ready to bear their part in supporting the Australian demand for war with France—all over the world as it would have to be—because France persisted in peopling New Caledonia with her irreclaimable convicts, and was unable or unwilling to prevent them sooner or later corrupting Australian towns and counties with their crimes? These are matters of vital concern to inhabitants of the *several* colonies: are *all* the colonies prepared to take them up? It is not easy to see why they should not, if they look at the matter in a broad way. France is more likely to keep hands off Australasian islands if Australia is backed up by Canada and South Africa as well as by England; and in return, each of these other groups would receive support' from the rest in its hour of need. But it must be thoroughly understood that to share England's position is to share a lot in which rights have to be maintained against the aggression of foreign nations in all parts of the world. If these colonies or groups of colonies are yet only in the individualistic or 'selfish' stage, they are not ready for a Federative Union.

Expense of Sovereignty, Present and Past.

Great Britain supports the defensive forces of the empire at great expense. Our Navy costs us about one per cent. of our national income, some twopence-halfpenny in the pound; the Army costs threepence-halfpenny; the debt for past wars, not paid for at the time, fivepence more—a total of, say, tenpence-halfpenny in the pound as our Imperial police rate. What part are the colonies prepared to take in imperial defence? We must not be put off by the plea that they too have debts of their own, as, with some exceptions, their 'Debts' have nothing to do with defence, but are deferred payments for goods received. We in Great Britain have protected the empire, and it is only through us that Canada is autonomous, and that no part of Australia is in occupation by France or Germany. It may be said that these colonies were most of them not born when we incurred this debt; but their territory was in existence, and if that had been occupied by other nations, Victoria, Queensland, and the rest, might never have been born at all. For many years Imperial troops were maintained at the expense of Great Britain in these colonies; in South Africa they were frequently in active service; and in New Zealand they were employed against the Maories. But as Responsible Government was granted it was felt at home that no farther expenditure of this kind was justified, and these colonies undertook their own military defence. In case of invasion they would receive assistance only if it could be spared. In naval affairs also a move has been made in the direction of their undertaking the defence, or partial defence, of their own coasts and harbours as distinct from keeping open the high seas. As, however, they benefit very much as we do from the open highways, this responsibility would be a common one if they shared sovereign power.

The broad question stands thus—Is participation in sovereignty, with all its privileges and all its responsibilities, the 'legitimate' aim for the peoples of these colonies? As Lord Dufferin puts it, 'So long as any colony desires to recognise the supremacy of the Crown and its own civil and military obligations as an integral part of the empire, so long it may safely claim its right to share in the past glory and the future greatness of Great Britain.' Do they anticipate that the next change—for in the Anglo-Saxon world at least change is more normal than fixity—will be a separation of themselves from our empire, leaving Great Britain and Ireland to continue rulers not only of these three kingdoms, but of India and thirty colonies; or will they claim as part of their birthright the sharing with us of the lead in the elevation of whole nations and tribes towards the level of Europe?

§ 2. THE MECHANISM.

If this end were decided upon by them and by us, there would then arise the question of the means of accomplishing it. The chief methods put forward are :—

(i) A reform of the British Parliament in order to give these colonies representation.

(ii) The construction of a new Sovereign Legislature for the empire.

(i) Admission to the Imperial Parliament.

The standing objection to the first method is that the internal affairs of the United Kingdom would be controlled in part by the colonial representatives, whilst Britons would have no control over the affairs in the colonies. A colonial group or party some 150 strong would be present, in a House of Commons of 650, which would utterly *dislocate our domestic legislation*: they would be in respect to it a 'moving cargo,' rendering unworkable parliamentary government as hitherto known. The national affairs of the United Kingdom might perhaps be separated from the affairs of the Empire at large, and the powers of the full Legislature limited to the latter: but this would be not to retain our present Parliament, but to divide it and constitute two Legislatures, and it is therefore a different plan.

(ii) Dividing the Imperial Parliament.

The establishment of two Legislatures: one Imperial, one purely British. This would undoubtedly be to make a great innovation: it would be *inventing* a constitution. One part of this might be a modification of our present Parliament, which might become the Imperial Legislature, local British affairs being removed from its care; or our present Parliament might continue to be British. In either case one *new Legislature* would have to be constructed. We may look to Canada to see how this is accomplished there, and also to the United States; but as these are new countries for which new institutions have been easily constructed, we may learn more from the new constitution at work in old countries. The imperial legislature of the German Empire is composed of a Federal Council of 58 elected by the States, and a Chamber of 397 elected by ballot and universal suffrage by the whole people of Germany, and these in addition to the separate legislatures of the various constituent kingdoms and duchies. Austro-Hungary, again, is working out a federative constitution. It has not achieved success with all its varied groups, but it has succeeded to a considerable degree. By the Beust Constitution of 1867 two National Parliaments were constituted or continued: one for Hungary (a *Diet*); the other called a *Reichsrath*, for all the other constituents of the empire. A third Parliament, composed of *delegations* from these bodies, meets at Vienna and Pesth alternately. There are three executives; one for each part, and one for the Empire. The latter consists of a Chancellorship and three ministries, Foreign Affairs, Defence, Finance, all considered imperially. Commerce was specifically left for the Diet and the Reichsrath to arrange severally; but Hungary has chosen to join the Customs Union adopted by the rest of the empire. The weakness lies in Hungary having received full rights, while the other nationalities were disappointed. Since then the Croatian and Slavonian Diet has received a Cabinet: the proposal to grant one to Bohemia in 1871 was frustrated by the German party. But at least we can see here (1) the subjects chosen as 'Imperial;' (2) a machinery working well, so far as it goes. (*Leger's History*, 1889.)

Such an Imperial Legislature for the British Empire is by no means a chimera—and it may come. If there should be a successful movement in the United Kingdom in the direction of Home Rule for the separate divisions, England, Scotland, Wales, and Ireland, a separate Imperial Legislature would then become indispensable for *us*, and the colonies might at the time of its constitution be admitted. The objection felt by practical English people is, briefly, this. We are one of the great nations of the world; our Parliament is the expression of our public life, our *historical instrument of government*; the welfare of 35,000,000 people, our position among the nations, and the discharge of our duties in India and in our other colonies, all depend upon the efficiency of Parliament: Parliament must therefore gather into itself the nation's wisdom, and wield its resources *to the full*. Could this be done by a Parliament no longer drawing to itself the undivided loyalty and undistracted attention which gives power to our Parliament now? If there is any danger of this, our national and imperial position forbids any risk being run; and it would be an infinitely lesser evil to leave these particular colonies entirely to themselves, and conduct the empire to new developments without them.

It would seem therefore that we must keep in view both these movements—(1) that which aims at bringing the colonies into sovereignty, and (2) that which works within the United Kingdom towards devolution from Parliament of the local affairs of the United Kingdom. If the latter becomes strong, Imperial Federationists may find their objects accomplished independently of their efforts. This would be a reform *within* the constitution, and *naturally* brought about: any other, though no more impossible than the new German constitution, is not likely to be favoured by British statesmen.

§ 3. TEMPORARY REFORMS.

(a) Union for Particular Aims.

Failing the achievement of Parliamentary union, or whilst waiting for it, Imperial Federationists may very well give close attention to the better working out of *certain definite problems within the constitution* of the empire as it stands. There are many reforms which even now are considered to be feasible, some of them urgently necessary. Those set forth by the men most competent to judge are—

DEFENCE OF THE EMPIRE.

INTERCOURSE: including traffic of all kinds, especially the transmission of letters, telegrams, and journals, possibly at rates lower than cost price.

MIGRATION: by which it would be arranged how far Britain might continue to expect a welcome for her emigrants on the part of the colonies.

LEGISLATION ON VARIOUS COMMERCIAL AND SOCIAL MATTERS: e.g. bankruptcy, which would work better if the same laws obtained throughout all parts of the empire where the English race is in the majority.

TRADE POLICY: but this is a knotty problem. To some it is the gist of the whole matter; to others it must at all costs be excluded from consideration. The calmness of many an evening's discussion has changed into heat and acrimony on the introduction of this topic.

(b) Partial Admission to Government.

As provisional and temporary means of closer union, numerous projects for Imperial Councils by which the *voice of the colonies would be heard* at home have been put forward. The most practical of these is a method which is being actually developed, namely, the open and official recognition by the Colonial Office of the AGENTS-GENERAL who are placed by the several colonies in charge of their affairs in London. It is becoming one of the unwritten laws of the constitution that these officials are to be talked with freely, if not exactly consulted, at the Colonial Office in the affairs which concern their colonies. At any time a meeting of the Agents-General, in communication by telegraph with the ministries at Ottawa and Melbourne and other colonial capitals, would constitute a Colonial Council which the Secretary of State would find every inducement to consult, although his responsibility would be to Parliament, not to them.

THE VALUE OF THE POLITICAL BOND.

In conclusion, we have still a question to ask going to the very root of the whole question of Imperial Federation. *What is the value of the political connexion* among the other bonds which by nature subsist between us and our brethren in Canada and Australia? These bonds are many and strong: a common language, a common literature, common science, common social organization, common character, many communities of religion and education; allowing something for German and other 'foreign' elements, we all come of the same stock, we all look back to common ancestors, and we look up to common heroes. What has *unity of government* to give in addition to these sources of fellow-feeling, and others beyond reach of analysis and enumeration?

ADAM SMITH points out (Bk. IV, Chap. vii) in his usual incisive way, and supporting himself with undeniable facts, that Governments had little merit in either 'projecting' or 'effectuating the establishment' of colonies; quite the contrary, so soon as private enterprise had 'effectuated,' then 'Government' stepped in to secure the monopoly of commerce, and otherwise to make profits from the new situation. All this was true of Spain and Portugal; of England, only somewhat less than any of the rest. The debt of the colonies to their mother-countries was not of a political order: it was that Europe bred the *men*. *Magna virum mater*—to Europe they owed the education and enlightened views of their enterprising founders. Nor has England obtained much more solid advantage from them as colonies; they have not followed the analogy of Greek or Roman colonies, by furnishing military forces for our defence, or contributing to our revenues. The monopoly of trade was an advantage which Adam Smith questioned: in any case, it has disappeared. He discusses carefully the possibility of the representation of America in Parliament; and on the whole he is in favour of it. But in the passage in which what seems to be his real judgment is expressed he says of an amicable separation: 'By thus parting good friends the natural affection of the colonies to the mother-country, which, perhaps, our late dissensions (1776) have well-nigh extinguished, would quickly revive. It might dispose them not only to respect, for whole centuries together, that treaty of commerce which they had concluded with us at parting, but to favour us in war as well as in trade, and instead of turbulent and factious subjects, to become our most faithful, effectual, and generous allies; and the same sort of parental affection on the one side, and filial respect on the other, might revive between Great Britain and her colonies, which used to subsist between those of ancient Greece and the mother-city from which they descended.'

EDMUND BURKE, in his speech on conciliation with our American colonies (1775), proposed that our Parliament should accept from America taxes, subsidies, aids, and grants when offered in their own way, namely, through their own Assemblies or Courts, not by imposition of our Parliamentary authority. He did not deny that such Parliamentary authority existed, but he questioned its value as a means of securing the end and purpose of government, and he gave utterance to this memorable declaration: 'My hold of the colonies is in the close affection which grows from common names, from kindred blood, from similar privileges, and equal protection. These are ties which, though light as air, are as strong as links of iron ... Do not entertain so weak an imagination as that your registers and your bonds, your affidavits and your sufferances, your crockets and your clearances, are what form the great securities of your commerce. Do not dream that your letters of office, and your instructions, and your suspending clauses, are the things that hold together the great contexture of this mysterious whole. These things do not make your government. Dead instruments, passive tools as they are, it is the spirit of the English constitution that gives all their life and efficacy to them. Do you imagine that here in England it is the land-tax which raises your revenue? that it is the annual vote in the Committee of Supply which gives you your army? ... No! surely no! It is the love of the people, it is their attachment to their government from the sense of the deep stake they have in such a glorious institution, which gives you your army and your navy, and infuses into both that liberal obedience, without which your army would be a base rabble, and your navy nothing but rotten tinder.'

On January 12, 1887, MR. JOHN BRIGHT expressed as follows his doubts as to the need for Imperial Federation:

'I cannot attend the "federation" meeting, and regret to have to say that I have no sympathy with its object and purpose. Colonies should remain attached to and in perfect friendship with the mother-country, but I am of opinion that any attempt to unite them by political bonds more closely than they are now connected will tend not so much to permanent union as to discord and separation. England will not be governed or in any degree influenced in her policy by Canada or Australia or the Cape. The colonies will not allow of the interference of England with them, with their laws or their tariffs. England's blind foreign policy may involve us in wars with some one or with several of the European powers—wars in which the colonies have interest, but by and through which they may be subjected to serious injury. In such a case what will happen? The federation cord will be strained to the uttermost, it will probably break; the colonies will prefer separation and freedom to the burdens and sufferings which their connexion with a European nation through their mother-country will impose upon them. How would your federation deal with the fisheries dispute between Canada and the United States? If Canada were an independent state the dispute would soon be settled, for she would yield to the arguments of her powerful neighbour; and if there were no Dominion of Canada the dispute would be settled by English concession of the reasonable demands of the Government at Washington. How would a federation composed of delegates or representatives from the colonies of Australia, from South Africa, from Canada, and perhaps from India, deal with this fisheries question? The federation project seems to me to be founded alike on ignorance of history and of geography. I would recommend all sensible men to let the question rest. If we are conciliatory and just to the colonies, and if our foreign policy is less mad than it has been during much of the present century, we may hope that the friendship between Britain and her daughter-states may long continue and may strengthen. If changes come which we cannot now foresee, but from which nations cannot escape, and if separation becomes necessary, let us hope that what will be done will be done in peace and with a general concurrence, and that the lustre of the English name and fame will not be tarnished, but will receive an added glory from the greatness and the prosperity and the wisdom of the states which England has founded.'

The opinion underlying the views of this letter is the same as Burke's: that political ties are not fundamental, not necessary to peace, unity, and concord. There are other bonds superior, and we make a mistake by troubling ourselves about too much 'Government' bonds: they are unnecessary where there is unanimity and fellow-feeling, valueless where interests clash and sentiments are hostile.

It should be remarked, however, that Mr. Bright writes of the empire as it *is*, not as it might be. He allows nothing for the consolidating effects of common government after it has been obtained: his argument supposes that it is a perpetual and unchangeable necessity that England will not in any degree be influenced in her policy by her colonies, nor they by her. Of course if this is so, no more is to be said. Mr. Bright condemned the New South Wales contingent to the Soudan, not only as against his principles of peace, but because the colony took up a cause in which she had no '*interest*.' This narrowness of view as to what may constitute the *interest* of a community must be remembered as part of Mr. Bright's way of regarding politics. But the inability to place much reliance upon Government ties is what makes his letter an echo of Adam Smith and Burke.

On the other hand there is the widespread conviction that *trade does really follow the flag*; that it is not a question of a bit of bunting, or even of a 'live colonial Governor,' but that in the flag there is a magnetic power for trade which cannot be set aside as unreal. In Chapter viii we have shown that this is true, and why it is true.

Sir Henry Barkly, for instance, who has served as Governor of Jamaica, Victoria, and the Cape, points out, as 'benefits of remaining attached to a powerful empire, protection against the ambition of acquiring distant territories at a time when this ambition appears more rife amongst the European powers than at any antecedent period in history; the careers open to colonial youth in the now open character of the civil, military, and naval service of the empire, colonial university degrees recognised, cadetships opened at Sandhurst, and for the navy, and commissions in the army, with examinations in the colonies as well as in England.' If *la carrière ouverte aux talents* is a boon to a country's young blood, it cannot but be stimulating for Canadian and Australian youth to have a common career with youth of the schools and universities of England, and to be eligible for the British army or navy, with all their glorious history behind them, or the civil service with traditions of centuries and worldwide range. These things, by their very nature, appeal to the most ambitious and generous minds.

No one can deny the instability of the present situation. It is acknowledged by colonists that as their colonies are filling up they themselves feel that their patriotic sentiments centre there more and more. And every ten years adds perceptibly to the relative strength of those born in the colonies, to whom England is a place to 'visit,' no longer 'home.' The political bonds of early days have been thrown off: new ones must be such as can be voluntarily entered into and voluntarily maintained.

The Bond of Social Dignity.

The student of the English constitution who neglects to observe the distinction between formal power and political influence will fail to understand its working. Bagehot's work, *The English Constitution*, has made the importance of the distinction clear, and shows how effectively the 'Crown' as a 'source of dignity' and 'fountain of honour' assists in the actual working of government. Of late years this function of the Crown has been applied in the sphere of imperial as distinct from national policy. No list of honours for the Queen's birthday or for New Year's Day is now issued without a large proportion of awards for services in India and the colonies. Ex-colonial Governors are freely called to the PRIVY COUNCIL itself, and colonial Premiers have been similarly honoured; while the order of ST. MICHAEL AND

ST. GEORGE is now very largely conferred for services in colonial affairs, both on Englishmen employed in the higher ranks of the service and on the chief public men in the colonies; and many others have been created KNIGHTS BACHELORS without being on the roll of any order. The order of the STAR OF INDIA was instituted in 1861, and that of the INDIAN EMPIRE in 1878, for services in India or in connexion with India ; and the order of the CROWN OF INDIA was instituted in 1878 for ladies, including the ladies of the Royal Family of England, Princesses of India, and wives and daughters of high officials. It is supposed that this is an age when 'honours' are lightly regarded, and ceremonial a waste of time. But these honours are far from being regarded as 'barren'; not only is cavil disarmed by consideration of the eminent men who bear them, but there is diffused throughout the civil and judicial services of India and the colonies a real esteem for these unmercenary recognitions of service rendered and duties successfully discharged. Their cementing influence will be disregarded only by those in whom psychological observation of men as they are is deficient or distorted. And judging from as high a standard as we may choose to take, can we regard as frivolous or unworthy of seriousness such ambitions as those which, in the days of chivalry, led men to win the 'spurs' of knighthood ? The officials and the public men of an empire of which the foundations were laid by Raleighs and Gilberts and Drakes, gladdened by the smiles and honours bestowed by Queen Elizabeth, are not likely to be unmoved by enrolment in gallant orders instituted for distinguished service by Queen Victoria.

Table of British Colonies classified by their Political Status.

RESPONSIBLE.	REPRESENTATIVE.	CROWN.
Dominion of Canada.	Bahamas.	Ceylon.
Newfoundland.	Barbados.	Mauritius.
New South Wales.	British Guiana.	Straits Settlements.
Victoria.	Leeward Islands.	Hong Kong.
South Australia.	Windward Islands.	Labuan.

RESPONSIBLE.	REPRESENTATIVE.	CROWN.
Tasmania.	Bermuda.	Fiji.
Queensland.	Natal.	Jamaica.
New Zealand.	Malta.	Trinidad.
Western Australia.		Sierra Leone.
Cape of Good Hope.		Gambia.
		Gold Coast.
		Lagos.
		Falkland Isles.
		Honduras.
		Gibraltar (Military).
		St. Helena.
		Ascension (Admiralty).

Subordinate:—Aden, Perim, Socotra.
Rodrigues Island, Seychelles and Amirante Islands, Chagos, and Oil Islands (Mauritius).
Labrador (Newfoundland).
Turks Islands (Jamaica).
Tobago (Trinidad).
South Georgia (Falkland).
Basutoland, British Bechuanaland, Zululand (Cape Colony).

Chartered Companies:—N. Borneo; Br. East Africa; Br. South Africa.
Protectorates:—Niger; New Guinea; Ishore, &c. in Malay Peninsula; Sarawak; Farther Bechuanaland; Transvaal; Somali Coast.
(Special) Foreign Office:—Egypt, Cyprus, Zanzibar.
Sphere of Influence:—In various parts of Africa.

Some idea of the *relative importance of the work of governing the different colonies* may be gathered from the salaries allotted to some Governors, although in Responsible colonies this depends on the colonial government. India, £24,000 (about); Bengal (Lieutenant-Governor), £10,000; Madras, £12,000; Bombay, £12,000; Canada, £10,000; Victoria, £10,000; New Zealand, £7500; N. S. Wales, £7000; the Cape, £6000; Queensland, £5000; Jamaica, £6000; Malta, £5000; Natal, £4000; Trinidad, £4000; Barbados, £3000; Honduras, £1800; Gold Coast, £3500; Falkland Isles, £1000; St. Helena, £900.

CHAPTER VIII.

TRADE AND TRADE POLICY.

IN turning now to Trade, taken generally to designate the production and exchange of wealth, we come, in the opinion of some who consider themselves versed in colonial affairs, to the gist and core of the whole matter. *Of what use are the colonies to us?* it is asked at home, and the meaning is, how do they assist us in relation to the material elements of our national well-being? *Of what use is the mother-country to us?* colonists ask, with the same tangible object before their minds. They acknowledge that empire, influence, the peopling of the world, the extension of civilization, the propagation of religious and moral ideas, may rightly exercise motive-power in some minds; but they take these to be ideals; whereas for real historical interest or for practical future policy they wish to know what has been done mutually between England and her colonies for the material aggrandizement of the one and the material raising up of the other, before they stand on solid ground of universal and abiding interest. Though this opinion may be sometimes felt and expressed in a crude and selfish form, there can be no doubt that in modern European colonies the acquisition of wealth in the mother-countries and the fostering of material progress in the colonies has been the primary and the most prominent operative aim throughout. Other objects have been secondary and obscure, this has been in the front: other objects—religious influence, for example—have been taken in hand by private societies and by notable individuals; this has been more or less an affair of State, affecting profoundly our attitude to the colonies and our policy towards the other nations and races of the world.

Yet Adam Smith begins his chapter—the famous *Chapter vii of Book IV*, 'OF COLONIES,' unequalled in its way as an example of historical and practical study—with this statement:—'The interest which occasioned the first settlement of the different European colonies in America and the West Indies was not altogether so plain and distinct as that which directed the establishment of those of ancient Greece and Rome.' Emigration he shows to have been 'the plain and distinct interest' underlying Greek colonization, and in combination with military occupation, underlying Roman colonization also. But for European colonization there was no such *necessity*; while the *utility*, although it has since become very great, is not altogether so evident; it was not the only motive of their establishment, and was, indeed, only partially understood at the time at which he was writing. He then shows how the Portuguese were in search of a trade similar to that which was enriching Venice, and were not seeking to colonize; while America fell to Spain almost by chance, we might say, and it was only the discovery of its gold and silver that caused her to take much notice of what had happened. Portugal settled down to trade, and Spain, favoured by 'a course of accidents which no human wisdom could foresee,' found herself in the possession of the mines of Mexico and Peru. The English, Dutch, and French joined in the double chase for gold and for Oriental wealth, but so far as America —which became the seat of the most flourishing centres of colonization—is concerned, they found neither of these, but something else.

Whatever the originating motives, the issue, as we have seen, has been the expansion of Europe and the growth of new centres of European industry and new sources of wealth for Europe in the colonies and dependencies of the five European colonizing nations.

Causes of Rapid Economic Development.

In the growth of our colonies signal examples of rapid development of prosperous and well-organized communities are offered to the political economist. Wastes have become inhabited; river-basins and sea-coasts have become the seats of cities, towns, villages, and farmsteads, and all in full view of scientific investigation, their origin known, their progress all recorded. The phenomenon is not new, however—history has repeated itself; the multiplying power of mankind and the productiveness of wealth, when new openings are offered to developed communities, have been demonstrated before. Syracuse and Agrigentum, Tarentum and Ephesus, soon rivalled their mother-cities, and Carthage rose to a population and influence surpassing that of Tyre. Still the *rapidity* of growth of our English colonies—to limit our view to these—is very striking. We see Melbourne, although only forty years old, already larger than Bristol with six centuries of prosperity behind it; Toronto, a village a hundred years ago, a busier and more progressive hive of industry than ancient and not unprosperous cities like Norwich and Nottingham; Montreal richer than Hull, although Hull was a town and port of substance and repute while Indians had wigwams on the island now covered with the buildings and docks of the 'Mount Royal.' And if we look at the virtually colonial cities of Philadelphia, surpassing even Liverpool and Manchester, the pride of Lancashire; Chicago overtopping Glasgow, the wonder of Scotland; and New York, having long passed Venice, Amsterdam, Berlin, and Vienna, already level with Paris, and expected to overtake London in 1920,—we feel that we breathe in a spacious atmosphere, and our political economy should, on this large scale, easily show us the springs and forces of industrial activity. Taking as our basis Adam Smith's summary—*plenty of good land, law and order, agriculture and the arts,* and elaborating the analysis, we may set down as the causes of the rapid prosperity of new colonies :—

Plenty of good land. The timber forests and great wheatfields of Canada; the sheep pastures of Australia and the Cape; the gold-fields of Victoria; the sugar plantations of the West Indies; these have proved good 'land' indeed in the hands of the families of Englishmen, Welshmen, Scotchmen, and Irishmen who have gone out to work them.

Freedom in the employment of land and *absence of diver-*

sion of portions of the produce into quarters where no productive use was made of it. It is not only the amount of wealth, but the hands into which it goes, that affects the *increase* of wealth; and in the colonies the claims and liens of the consumers who—without reproach, be it understood—in Economics are regarded as 'unproductive,' were trivial: in the early days of most colonies the whole of the produce was practically in the hands of the cultivators, and after supporting the cultivators, immense quantities of wealth were available for further employment as capital in the vast regions lying unoccupied over their fences or just outside their towns. This enabled them to offer prodigiously high wages, and the rapid accumulation of savings enabled labourers very quickly to leave the wage-class and themselves to offer wages to new comers; as a consequence the increase of population was stimulated and supported both by increase within and by immigration from without.

The production of monopoly products. This acted either (1) absolutely, as in the case of tobacco which enriched Virginia, as it could not be grown in Europe, or (2) relatively, as the wool of Australia, capable of being grown in Europe, but not in the quantities required. Canada in 1884 exported 76 million dollars' worth of her own products, of which 21 were products of the forest, 40 of the field, and 8 of the sea. Victoria exported 6 million pounds' worth of wool and 4 of gold, out of a total export of 16 millions.

Capital borrowed from home. This cause was always in operation; the original companies supplied capital in the days of the infancy of the American colonies, and emigrants usually took some out with them, either their own or borrowed. The ability of England to supply capital has been a factor of first-rate importance throughout, both for America and Australia. But since the extension of banking and the development of joint-stock enterprise, capital has flowed out freely, from England especially. In New Zealand, for example, in early days in the '40's and '50's settlers borrowed at 20 and 15 per cent.; but the tide has proved so strong that they can now, by means of bank trusts and syndicates, obtain all that they require at 6 and 5, and their local boards and municipalities can borrow freely at about 4. And it is further to be noticed that the colonists have borrowed capital on their *prospective* development. Confidence in colonial stability being firmly secured, they have no difficulty in obtaining loans for thirty years, which they could not repay now, but will be able to discharge when those thirty years have gone. Professor Marshall goes so far as to state that this is the principal cause of their prosperity. 'After all, the chief cause of the modern prosperity of new countries lies in the markets that the old world offers, not for goods delivered on the spot, but for promises to deliver goods at a distant date.... In one form or another they mortgage their new property to the old world at a very high rate of interest ... and a vast stream of capital flows to the new country.'— *Principles of Economics*, p. 713.

Immigration of adult workers. The colonies have not had to rear and educate their population. This has been done for them, very largely, by Great Britain and Ireland. A Registrar-General estimated that it cost £175 to bring up an Englishman to his twenty-first year: on this estimate Australia has received from the mother-country a gift of at least £175,000,000 in thirty years.

Skill and knowledge ready to hand. The whole range of the arts and sciences elaborated slowly during many centuries in Europe is at the disposal of the colonists.

Machinery and tools invented and made. The products of Birmingham and Sheffield are at their disposal; implements of every kind can be had. They have only to pay for them, not to invent them.

Manufacturing and trading done for them. They can devote themselves to their special and particular advantages in their new land. Their clothes are delivered in bales at their doors, ships are waiting in their harbours to carry their produce swiftly to the market.

To these industrial advantages we must not fail to add that advantage upon which Adam Smith so much loves to dwell, LAW AND ORDER AND GOVERNMENT: 'The habit of subordination, some notion of the regular government which takes place in their own country, of the system of laws which supports it, and of a regular administration of justice,'—all at their disposal, he might have added, without battles of Hastings and Bannockburn, and Wars of the Roses, and Nasebys; these privileges had been obtained for them before in blood; barons and retainers, knights' services and freemen's aids, castles frowning over the land, and all the apparatus of feudalism, had done their work in the old islands, and the work had not to be done again. And against foreign foes there were no battles of Creçy to fight, no Armadas to resist, no Blenheims and Fontenoys to draw off their energy and engulf their 'net-returns.' The harassing danger from the Red Indian and the Maori was serious enough where felt, but it was partial and temporary, never severely absorbing or distracting on any great scale. If discipline of this kind is essential to fibre, the Australian colonists, at least, have their schooling yet to come. Is China to be the scourge?

Each of these causes would have gone some way to explain the rapidity of colonial progress; several of them in combination would have gone an incalculably long way; the *combined action of them all*, especially in the case of the Australian colonies, is an explanation adequate even for the progress before our view [1].

Effect on Course of Industry.

For many years the course of industrial development in the colonies was quite simple. They were free to devote themselves

---

[1] The above analysis finds confirmation in the recently published treatise of Professor Marshall, *Principles of Economics*, published 1890. With admirable fulness and succinctness of statement, Mr. Marshall summarizes his view, p. 251:—

'In all ages colonies have been apt to outstrip their mother-countries in vigour and energy. This has been due partly to the abundance of land, and the cheapness of necessaries at their command; partly to that natural selection of the strongest characters for a life of adventure; and partly to physiological causes connected with the mixture of races: but perhaps the most important cause of all is to be found in the hope, the freedom, and the changefulness of their lives.'

to what is known as the agricultural phase of industrial life, the raising of the raw materials required for human needs and comforts. Tropical and sub-tropical colonies found ample market for their special products among the European nations, who learned new wants as these supplies opened out. Not many years were required to raise the consumption of Virginian tobacco and Jamaican sugar, rum, and molasses to a point which gave heavy and increasing profit to the raising of those products; while spices, coffee, cocoa, and tea gradually became regular constituents of the daily meals of Europeans. Timber from Canada was required to make up for the forests cleared away in England, and wool to satisfy the demand for cloth, which had far outgrown the supply from the sheep of these comparatively small islands. Corn, cattle, and fish have been required in constantly increasing quantity. In the colonies Nature offered so liberally and so easily the first-hand produce of her soil that it would have been almost perverse to have turned to the secondary processes. A change however has begun.

On Great Britain the effect was similar, but in the reverse direction. Her colonies, by supplying this raw material, saved her from pressing agriculture to the point of diminishing returns, and gave her free course for development in manufacture and trade. Five great advantages possessed by her were brought out into full effect :—

(i) Her supplies of coal and iron, placed as they are in convenient and economical juxtaposition.
(ii) Her atmosphere, specially suitable for weaving.
(iii) Her seafaring instincts and aptitudes.
(iv) Her aptitude for practical science in all departments of mechanical invention, notably, of course, in the inventions of weaving and spinning machinery and in the application of steam.
(v) Her aptitude for industrial and commercial organization in response to changed needs and opportunities.

Hence it was that just at the close of last century England had finally ceased to be an exporter of corn, and was winning her way into all markets for woollen, cotton, and linen manufactures. And she was on her way to her astonishing pre-eminence in sea-going trade, in which she was to employ half the shipping of the world.

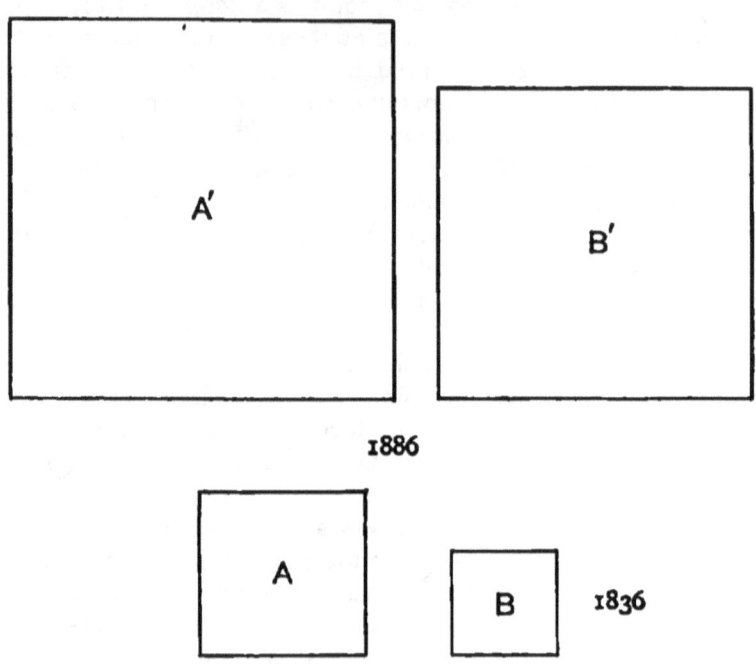

FIFTY YEARS' GROWTH OF THE TRADE OF THE BRITISH EMPIRE.

A represents Trade of U. K. in 1836.
B represents Trade of Colonies, &c., in 1836.
A' represents Trade of U. K. in 1886.
B' represents Trade of Colonies, &c., in 1886.

The closeness of our trade relations with our present colonies and possessions is shown by the fact that their average trade with us (in the years 1880–1883) was 199 millions, out of a gross 429 millions, notwithstanding all counter-influences of distance, convenience, suitableness of products, and competition of commercial rivals. On the other hand, our trade with them was 186 millions out of

715, about *one-fourth*; while French colonies contributed but 21 millions out of the gross French trade of 425, about *one-twentieth* of the whole. Holland's was about the same fraction as that of France, Spain's about *one-tenth*, Portugal's about *one-fiftieth*.

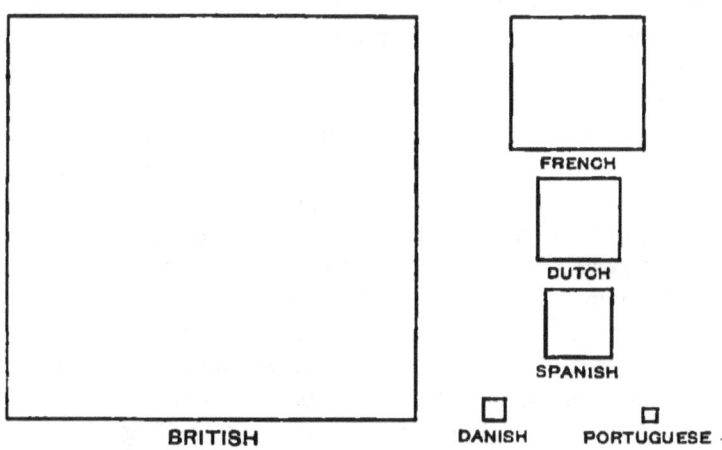

TRADE OF EUROPEAN COUNTRIES WITH THEIR DEPENDENCIES.
AVERAGE ANNUAL VALUE 1880–82. RAWSON,
STATISTICAL SOCIETY, 1884.

TRADE POLICY.

Monopoly Period.

The European nations began colonization with the idea that new countries would be the *possessions* of the old, and their policy in relation to trade was the carrying out of this idea. The Crown of Spain, by its share of gold and silver, derived some revenue from its colonies from their first establishment, and they therefore attracted the attention of the mother-country from the outset. This was not the case with the other settlements in America; the Portuguese paid little heed to Brazil, for example, which caused Adam Smith caustically to remark that perhaps the Spanish did not thrive the better in consequence of attention, nor the Portuguese the worse in consequence of neglect. He is somewhat inconsistent, however, for a little farther on he candidly says that the Swedish colony might have prospered had it not been neglected by Sweden ; but the former opinion is reasserted when he comes to mention the rapid increase of prosperity of the French colony of St. Domingo during a period when it neither required the protection nor acknowledged the authority of the home government to any substantial extent.

When our colonization had thoroughly settled down we applied to our American and West Indian colonies the principle of *monopoly* of their trade. It was not applied absolutely and entirely, but just so far as, and in such kinds as, *our own interests* dictated. Our method was not so narrow as that of Spain, which limited all trade to two ports in America, Vera Cruz and Carthagena, and two in Spain, Cadiz and Seville; nor did we hand it over to exclusive companies as Denmark, Portugal, and, occasionally, France did. But France later on, and ourselves almost from the beginning, laid down certain conditions under which trade was confined to the mother-country; outside these limits the colonies might sell and buy where they could. The Eastern trade was the monopoly of the East India Company.

We divided their produce into two great classes : (i) ENUMERATED, i.e. scheduled in the act of navigation and some subsequent acts, and (ii) NON-ENUMERATED. The *Enumerated* commodities were either such produce as we needed but could not produce at home, such as molasses, coffee, tobacco, ginger, cotton, furs, dyeing woods; or such as we could produce at home, but not in sufficient quantities, such as naval stores made of timber, pig and bar iron, tar, turpentine, hides and skins. The former we appropriated in order to get them more cheaply by having them direct from the producers; the latter we appropriated in order to avoid buying from our rivals, the foreign nations, as it was a cardinal point of the prevailing policy to preserve a 'balance of trade' by selling as much and purchasing as little as possible in foreign parts.

The *Non-enumerated* commodities might be exported by the colonies to other countries provided it was in British or Colonial ships. They included grain of all sorts, lumber, salt provisions, fish, and (after 1731) sugar and rum.

Perfect freedom was permitted amongst the colonies themselves, both on the continent of America and in the West Indies.

On the other hand, they were limited as to their *buying* from us. They were not allowed to set up such manufactures as would remove the necessity of their resort to the British market, except in very rudimentary stages, e.g. shaping lumber into masts and yards. Sugar might not be refined; no steel might be forged, even for their own consumption; no woollen goods might be sent from one province to another, though persons might weave for immediate neighbours.

Unjust as these regulations appeared to Adam Smith, he is himself scrupulously fair in pointing out that they were not very hurtful to the colonies in their effect :—

(i) The interest of the colonists was so plainly to devote themselves to the *land* and very simple processes of manufacture that the regulations were rather 'impertinent badges of slavery' than actually detrimental to their prosperity.

(ii) *Great Britain gave them considerable advantages* in her own market. She favoured them by imposing lighter duties on some of their produce than were imposed upon foreign goods; colonial sugar, tobacco, and iron were thus helped, and she even gave bounties on their raw silk, hemp and flax, indigo, naval stores, and building timber.

(iii) She gave the same *drawbacks on foreign* goods brought to England and paying duty on landing when taken out for exportation to the colonies as when going to other foreign countries, so that consumers in Massachusetts received such goods without the duty which was paid by consumers in Yorkshire or Scotland.

The net result of the policy up to Adam Smith's time (1776) may be said to be that our *artificial* regulations did not largely alter the *natural* course of industrial development in our colonies. If we confined them in some respects to our market for the disposal of their produce, our market was, after all, the best in the world; and if we compelled them to buy our manufactures and to use our shipping, we were certainly the cheapest of manufacturers, and had the most efficient shipping to offer them. In fact our policy was the expression of the political economy of the time, or rather of mercantile policy before it had acquired scientific principles as its basis, and was chiefly in the hands of merchants aiming at profit and filled with the idea of the balance of trade. But the policy was artificial, and it received two fatal blows just at the same time. In 1776 the situation was altered by the *Declaration of Independence* on the part of the Thirteen Colonies, and in the same year the ideas at the basis of the policy were exploded by the publication of the *Wealth of Nations*. By the one stroke the fabric itself was rudely shattered, by the other foundations were laid for a new fabric, partly built with remaining material, but partly quite new[1].

[1] Adam Smith adds a long argument to show that our *Home industry had really suffered* by the monopoly of colonial trade. He considers that the advantage we gained from it was only a *relative* one, giving us superiority in comparison with other countries; but that, *absolutely*, taking our own country alone, we should have been better off without it. It withdrew capital from our home trade, and from our trade with the continent of Europe; it kept up a high rate of profit, and put us at a disadvantage in other markets: it set up a considerable roundabout trade (e.g. of 96,000 hogsheads of tobacco which we imported we sent out 82,000 again to the continent), and so kept capital inefficiently employed. It narrowed our home industry into working for one great market in place of the more healthy and more secure development where many channels are open. The colonial trade, if left free, would have done us good; the forcing it by the monopoly regulations was hurtful. Professor Nicholson points out in his note that the supporters of the mercantile policy would not on the whole have been moved by this argument, as *relative* superiority, 'balance of power,' was with them the great object as leading to their supreme economic goal, favourable 'balance of trade.'

The history of *Trading Companies* with exclusive privileges furnishes a chapter of considerable interest to the political economist. In these days especially, when aggregation is the prevailing tendency in industrial organization, when conglomerations of companies, firms,

Free Trade.

The movement towards a different trade policy in our remaining colonies and our fresh acquisitions was a part of

and persons are forming themselves into 'Syndicates' to absorb the whole production of some staple of consumption—copper syndicates, salt syndicates, and so on—the working of the great companies in the days of our earlier colonization will be found very instructive. The only difference is that the old companies were privileged by Government, while the syndicates are voluntary associations: but as it was 'smuggling' and 'interloping' that ruined the former system, it is possible that the voluntary associations may prove unable to crush private enterprise.

Adam Smith allows companies for colonization and trade to be necessary for poor countries like Sweden and Denmark, where shareholders must be attracted by privilege and security against competitors; otherwise they will not hazard their small capitals. But rich countries with abundant capital would, he thinks, send out more ships, not less, if trade were not confined, and on the whole he thinks Sweden and Norway ill-advised in attempting on their narrow means to enter on such a trade at all; they would do better to buy East Indian produce from Holland. The Dutch East India Company is convicted of gross dereliction of duty,—if it is regarded as a national institution at all,—in its 'savage policy' of destroying produce when the supply would be too great to enable them to keep up the most profitable price, a procedure known to-day as 'limiting the output;' and the East India Company in regulating the crops of opium and rice according to its own estimate of what they could best make pay. Such proceedings, aiming simply at the profit of the shareholders, entirely unfitted these companies for sovereign power.

Privileged companies were not long required for English colonization and trade; they started the American colonies and then soon disappeared. The East India Company was the only one which had a long history, and it was shorn of its privileges one by one in the course of years. In 1793, at the renewal of its charter, a 'searching enquiry' was made into the effect of the monopoly; at the next renewal in 1813 the Indian trade was thrown open (not the Chinese or other Eastern trade), and in the very next year the private trade just exceeded the Company's—£4,435,000 to £4,208,000. Next year the proportion was even greater. When the next date for renewal arrived the monopoly was discontinued entirely, and not only India but China and the East were thrown open so far as British trade was concerned.

In the desolate regions to the north and west of our settlements in Canada fur trading would not have been carried on at all excepting by the Company plan. Accordingly, the Hudson's Bay Company rethat general movement which, seventy years after the publication of our great classical work in Political Economy, issued in the adoption of FREE TRADE in 1846. Freedom from all Government regulation, control, and direction, liberty to resort to the cheapest market for buying and the dearest for selling, were to be the *natural* bases for our enterprise henceforth.

The change took place by stages. Pitt, a pupil of Adam Smith, took some steps, especially in the consolidation of the Customs; and those very mercantile classes whom Adam Smith had so thoroughly distrusted soon began to see where their interest lay. In the famous petition of the London merchants in 1820, Free Trade principles were explicitly laid down, and all restrictions, except for revenue, were denounced. The Edinburgh Chamber of Commerce petitioned in the same spirit. With political economists and merchants pressing in the same direction, it remained only for the statesmen in front to move. *Mr. Huskisson* was the statesman who directed the progress. The Navigation Act was relaxed in various directions, both as to countries and commodities; heavy protective duties against foreign cotton, woollen, linen, silk, leather, and iron manufactures were substantially lightened by Mr. Huskisson before his death at the opening of the Liverpool and Manchester railway in 1830. In 1842 *Sir Robert Peel* took up the movement, which culminated in the successful opposition to the Corn Laws by Cobden and Bright and the Anti-Corn Law League and their abolition in 1846, and ended in the abolition of the famous old Navigation Act in 1850, which, after two hundred years of service in the building up of England's trade and empire, passed away into the limbo of history.

In the colonies themselves, however, a return to re-

tained its privileges and powers for many years. As lands were taken up for occupation they were removed from the jurisdiction of the Company, e. g. British Columbia in 1858. In 1868 all territorial jurisdiction was taken away, but trading privileges are not yet abolished.

strictive policy has taken place. Two reforms were effected in the same generation—the adoption of Freedom of Trade by England, and the granting of Responsible Government by her to some of her chief daughter-colonies. With what result? That the political freedom acquired by the colonies was used to set up barriers and restrictions in industry and trade! *Freedom was used as a means of returning to Artifice and Interference.* The old restriction by enumerated and non-enumerated commodities was finally abandoned on the part of the mother-country, but the colonies at once set about devising methods of arranging their trafficking so as to secure for themselves the incoming and outgoing of commodities according to their judgment of where their own advantage lay. When Responsible Government was granted it might have been expected that regulation of trade would have been reserved as an Imperial affair. But the granting of the new constitution to Canada and the Australian colonies came at the moment of the flush of the Free Trade victory. In the freshness of that triumph, hopes were strong that the victory won for Free Trade in England was won for the world; only faint-hearted or interested people doubted that the generation before them would see all nations coming into the common fold of natural trade. We might as well have chosen the moment when a Roman consul was descending from the car of his triumphal procession to the Capitol to ask him to acknowledge that the empire was growing too fast, as have asked Free Trade victors between 1846 and 1880 to think of removing the control of trade from the self-government then being granted to the colonies. To have retained trade under our Imperial control would have seemed a cruel slur upon the intelligence of the newly-enfranchised colonies, and therefore no question was raised, and trade was left as a local and internal affair. But our hopes proved to be illusive; no one of the Continental nations has followed our lead, and the United States and our own colonies have most determinedly and decisively taken their stand on the old platform of Government Protection and guidance of industries.

Every Responsible colony but one has a *Tariff* more or less severe; Victoria and Canada very soon pronounced quite definitely for *Protection against all comers*, Great Britain included; New Zealand, South Australia, Queensland, and the Cape *hesitated* at such points as a general 5 per cent. for revenue in New Zealand, 7½ per cent. in Queensland, and so on; but *only* New South Wales took up *freedom*. And since 1880 freedom has continued to lose ground: New Zealand has changed, so has Queensland, the Cape is hesitating. New South Wales is its only stronghold, and even there it is not by a great majority that it is maintained [1]. A New Zealand writer of repute (Gisborne, *Colony of New Zealand*, 1888) shows that the colonists consider it proved that the light duties they levied for revenue had done them good, so far as they had gone, by acting protectively. It might have been thought that Canadians and Victorians would have had more remunerative employment on their *plenty of good land* than in making pianos in competition with our elaborately organized methods of production. As it is, the Canadians 'protect' their piano-makers by imposing a duty of £5 on English and foreign pianos; Victoria a duty of 25 per cent. of the value; the Cape 15 per cent.; whilst Queensland and New Zealand raise revenue by a 5 per cent. duty; only New South Wales admits them free [2]. A walk through the courts at the great *Colonial*

---

[1] In the General Election of 1889 the Free Traders won 71 seats, the Protectionists 60; in Sydney itself only 5 out of the 41 members were Free Traders. This, with the corresponding movement in Victoria towards Inter-Australian Free Trade, largely influenced the acceptance of Australian Union in Trade at the Federal Convention of March, 1891.

[2] Some examples of the duties levied are as follows:—

	Canada.	Victoria.	Cape.	Queensland.	N.S.W.
Agricultural Implements	35 %	20 %	10 %	5 %	Free
Boots	25	(1s. to 2s. a pair)	(3d. to 8d.)	5	Free
Carpets	25	20	15	5	Free
Cottage Pianos	$30 each	25	15	5	Free
Grand Pianos	$50 & 15 %	25	15	5	Free

and Indian Exhibition of 1886 revealed unexpected ambitions; these colonies, with millions and millions of acres yet unoccupied, furnished great stalls with their samples of clothes, hosiery, machinery, and billiard-tables.

Victoria wishes to foster her own manufactures; and her democratic constitution enables her artisans to control her policy. Not only are imported clocks and watches taxed 20 per cent., but even such necessaries as agricultural implements 20 per cent. also; hansom cabs, waggonettes, and buggies, £20 each; medicines, 25 per cent.; silk manufactures, 20 per cent.; articles of apparel, wholly or partly made up, 25 per cent.; coal, 20 per cent. The only touch of liberality in their tariff is the appearance on the exemption list of all works of art; but in view of their own absorption in business this is hardly a self-denying ordinance.

The Representative colonies and the Crown colonies are not free to choose their own course. The retention of imperial control has prevented the adoption of any Protective measures, and customs duties, though largely relied upon for revenue, are confined to that object. The Imperial Parliament had to decide whether to allow India to protect her own cotton goods against Lancashire. The voice of Lancashire prevailed in the name of Free Trade, but there are not wanting those who maintain that it was our duty to India to regard India's needs. However, it is not easy to see how so fundamental a principle as Free Trade can be left optional by us in the government and guidance of our dependencies. It must be noted that in one way the imperial connexion limits the action of the colonies, even of the Responsible ones; they are not as yet competent to negotiate treaties of commerce directly with foreign powers or between themselves. Whatever they do is against the world. But this limitation is being removed. Canada has already a right of treating with foreign countries through our Foreign Office, and in conjunction with our ambassadors, apart from the Colonial Office. Australian Governments are looking for the same liberty, and as a treaty means an exchange of advantages for the two parties it will be very difficult, if not impossible, for such treaties to be made without affecting English interests sooner or later. It is therefore felt in the West Indies to be a grievance that we will not allow them to enter into a separate treaty with the United States, as could be done very readily with great advantage to those islands; nor even with Canada. The Imperial Government cannot, in deference to foreign nations, allow treaties to be made by any parts of our empire, over which it has control, with certain countries to the exclusion of others; nor can it consent to be a party to the exclusion of Great Britain from markets to the advantage of rival manufacturers or producers.

COMMERCIAL UNION?

This situation within the empire is grievously deplored in many quarters. It seems to violate the principles of domesticity which should underlie a really united empire. The day for compulsion is past, but a change might be made by the voluntary formation of the empire into a single COMMERCIAL UNION. The Austro-Hungarian Empire, for example, is more solid than ours: although commercial union was left to the Local Legislatures as a 'national' concern, practically the result was good, as Hungary decided to join the Customs Union of the other states composing the empire, so that that empire is for commercial purposes a unit. Commercial Union might be either complete or partial. In the former case, all tariffs between Britain and her colonies, and amongst the colonies themselves, would be abolished, and a single tariff of duties upon foreign goods would take their place. But it is universally agreed that this is quite chimerical. The practical proposal is that Britain and the colonies should *favour one another* in their tariffs, in comparison with foreign nations. A slight duty on American wheat and none on Indian and Canadian, for instance; an increased duty on French wines, a lower one on Australian; a duty on German sugar, none on West Indian; and other similar discriminations, would be in force. Certainly there is a strong bond in such a connexion as this. Whatever be our opinions as to the strength and efficacy of race-sentiment and political connexion in uniting the parts of an empire, there can be no questioning the reality of a union which diminishes internal dues, taxes, and imposts, and constitutes a single industrial community. Hence we find some imperialists always dwelling upon this idea; nothing else really satisfies them: they like the sentiment, 'love of home,' 'the old country,' and all that. Soudan contingents are quite in the grain of their humour, but in their hearts they believe that *British goods must have an advantage in colonial markets and colonial goods in ours* if the empire is to be placed on a rock.

The general question of a Commercial Union of the empire includes the following considerations at least.

Advantages. (i) The *solid and tangible union* of the empire, amounting, for the colonies chiefly affected, to a re-union, a making real of a constitution which at present is formal and almost intangible, and a strengthening of British influence in the councils of the nations.

(ii) The union might eventually lead to universal *Free Trade.* In one way it would lead *from* it, as Great Britain would have to increase or re-impose duties against foreigners, but on the other it would lead *towards* it, as the colonial series of tariffs against her would be lightened. The area of free intercourse would be enlarged very greatly. Great Britain stands practically alone at present, alone with New South Wales, in abhorring duties, and fundamentally free. No sign of abandonment of the Protection position is palpably evident; we must wait for flow of time or for some catastrophic change. But if Great Britain announced that, failing the adhesion of other nations to the principle, she was obliged to take them at their own word, and to look to her own family of nations for a better reception, we should increase the *freedom of trade* within the most widely extended family of communities in the world. If this proved successful for the development of our empire, it would be a great object-lesson for the cause of 'Freedom of Trade.' And again, the immense importance of the United

Empire as a customer would oblige other nations to consider their present position, and to think seriously about the continuance of a policy which closed British and Colonial markets to their wares.

Difficulties. (i) The formation of such a union could not but give rise to antagonism with other nations. Such a union would be in itself, as a whole, a fortress of defiance. The *whole temper of our foreign relations*, as they have been since 1860, would be so altered that we should have to prepare to pay, in wars and preparations for wars, severer taxes on our industry than all the customs-duties levied from us by foreign nations to-day. At several points, too, special causes of antagonism would threaten. Can we seriously suppose that the United States would sit still and allow Canada to place British goods in privilege in comparison with American? And can there be any serious doubt as to the result if Americans made up their minds that it was detrimental to American progress to suffer it? Can we shut off the West Indies and Guiana from the United States and the South American republics, with which they transact two-thirds of their trade, without causing to arise from all the New World a cry of America for Americans, continent, islands, and all?

(ii) Many Englishmen seem to be committed for life to Freedom of Trade pure and simple. The great contest by which our present system was made possible made a deep impression on the trading-classes and the working-classes of the country. Like the abolition of Slavery, it is regarded as a victory of a moral and social kind which admits of no return to older ways. And many are sanguine that the world will be gradually brought round to this opinion, while others hold it proved that even on purely economic grounds England must stand firm.

(iii) The majority of colonists, on the other hand, are convinced that colonies are in a stage of growth when Protection is a necessity. They base their conviction on scientific principles, and support them by references to definite opinions given by leading political economists even in England. Both

Adam Smith and John Stuart Mill, advocates of freedom of trade as they were, allow that there are circumstances which may make Protection advisable; the colonists claim that these circumstances are found in the colonies. The most recent authorities, Professors Marshall and Sidgwick, give them further support from within what may be called the 'orthodox' school of Political Economy. Especially prominent in colonial minds is the conviction that they have to withstand the insufficiently paid labour of European countries, Great Britain included; and they farther reflect that freedom of trade over the whole British Empire implies competition with the low standard of living of the rice-eating millions of India.

(iv) The *necessity of raising revenue* in the colonies cannot be disregarded, and it is very important in their present tariff-systems. In widely-scattered populations no system so effective for raising revenue has been invented as the imposition of duties on goods as they are landed. The proceeds of the sale of land, the customs-duties, and the receipts of the railways, contribute the chief sources of revenue in our young colonies, out of which they have to defray the expenses of Government, to construct their indispensable public works, and to pay their very considerable interest on debt. The proceeds of land-sales are of the nature of capital, and they should be expended chiefly as capital; the railways yield a commercial return upon money spent; the customs are their chief income for ordinary purposes. The customs upon goods from Britain form so considerable a proportion of the whole that they cannot be substantially lowered until a substitute is found.

Commercial Confederation.

The grouping of colonies *inter se*, as *commercial confederations*, would be an intermediate step. The Dominion of Canada is already confederated in this way; and the movement is on foot in Australia. In South Africa it is already far advanced; in 1890 the Orange Free State joined the Cape Colony in a *customs union*; in the negotiations with the

Transvaal about Swaziland one condition was that the Transvaal should join this union, which it is likely to do; British Bechuanaland will be added by the High Commissioner; Natal will almost certainly follow. In this case we have the noteworthy result that where the attempt to force *political* confederation failed, the exigencies of the situation are leading easily and naturally to *commercial* unity.

Trade and the Flag.

The password most in vogue with those who set great value upon the political bond is the motto, '*Trade follows the Flag.*' It sounds natural enough that it should do so.

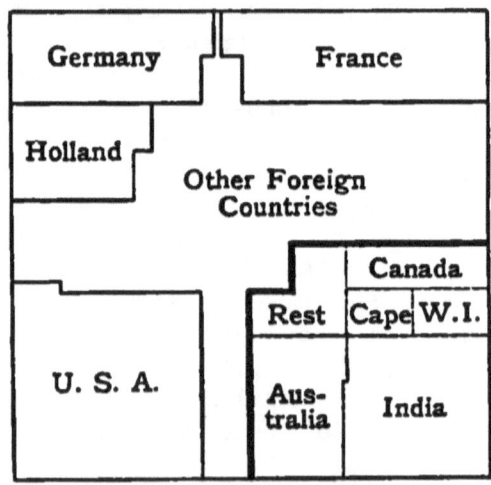

DISTRIBUTION OF THE TRADE OF THE UNITED KINGDOM.

Average of years 1866-1884: Farrer, *Free Trade*. Table vii.

The sentiment of hope suggests it, and statistics of first-rate quality support it. Taking, for example, the year 1884, English trade with the German Empire amounted to 24. shillings per head of the inhabitants of that empire, with France to 35 shillings a head: with the United States to 47 shillings. But there is a great spring upward in the figures when we come to the British North American, South African, and Australasian colonies, with which, as a whole, our trade was at the rate of 168 shillings a head.

How is this to be explained? Are we not yet in a thoroughly mercantile period where the best market is the place where men buy and sell? Or are we to suppose that there is in a Flag some magic which overrides even that tendency of man to get wealth where he can? Of course, much can be put down to community of habits and tastes, leading to community of consumption; they have what we want and we make what they want; they do not read French literature so much as they read English. But this does not really go so far as might be thought. The articles in which national tastes differ are not the most important in the

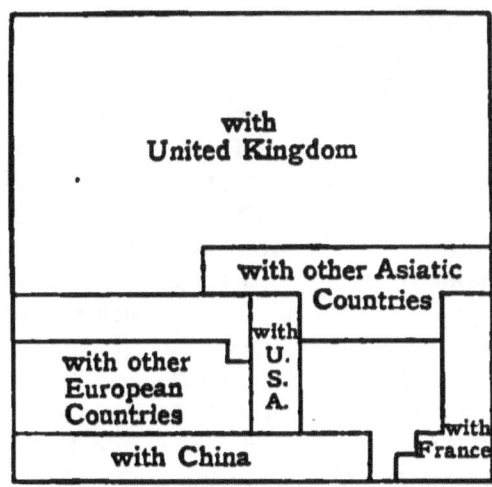

DISTRIBUTION OF THE TRADE OF INDIA.

great commerce; yarns and calico, oil and coal, wool and gold, have an international character about them. And although community of tastes may carry us far in explanation of the 47 shillings of the United States, we have still to account for the spring to 168. Community of law will not do it: and political institutions have not altered the basis of social life or the details of habit in the United States sufficiently to take them out of the same reckoning as the colonies in that respect.

For the efficient cause symbolized by the Flag in relation to trade we must look for a commercial quality after all. The fact is that the Flag represents an element of the first importance for modern commerce, the giving of *confidence*, and thereby the giving of a foundation for *credit*. So long as a community remains a British colony it occupies a special and peculiar position for being trusted with wealth. In the flow of capital, which is vitally important to the prosperity of these young countries, to be in good credit is of primary importance. Under the Flag British capital has flowed out in the belief that the Imperial Legislature could not suffer a colony to become bankrupt: the exact amount of authority possessed by the Colonial Office has not been closely scrutinized, but the fact that these countries are still enrolled as colonies has been taken to imply that we were in some way bound up with them, and would be responsible for them. Labour has not shown any preference for them: but capital has done so. It is not meant that no capital would have gone out, but that less would have gone, and at a higher rate of interest. Further, the imperial sentiment may sufficiently prevail at home to allow of granting of liberty to trustees to invest moneys in colonial securities, which would be a most natural course, and greatly increase the range of their credit.

Since the conduct of the Central and South American Republics some years ago in enticing loans on unjustifiable grounds and the constant difficulties of bondholders of high-rate paying countries of the second or third grade, as Spain, Turkey, and Egypt, taught British investors some severe lessons, the ever-increasing volume of spare British capital has flowed more fully in the wake of the Union Jack. So that now a Colonial Government occupies much the same position in the borrowing market as a British municipality (e.g. January 14, 1891—Weymouth Corporation $3\frac{1}{2}$'s, 98; Southampton, 102; Cape Government, 99; Victoria, 100; Canada, 104). The borrowing of capital determines the flow of trade, for it is not gold and bank-notes that are lent, but purchasing-power, and the colonies are free to purchase where they like ; when the time for payment of interest and repayment of loans comes, they are only too delighted to be able to satisfy us by payments in kind. This keeps us their export trade ; and as trade is set up in one direction there is an advantage gained by using our ships to convey our produce to them instead of going elsewhere to purchase. And the 'exchanges' operate similarly in our favour. The present situation also leads to an Imperial banking system centring in London. Besides the important branch offices which many colonial banks maintain in London, with special London Boards of Directors, some very important banks have their head offices there, e. g. the Bank of Africa, the Bank of Australasia, the Bank of New Zealand, the Bank of British Columbia. There are also many investment corporations which make loans for colonial enterprises easy and secure. Labour is not much affected by the Flag, but recent events have shown that if Trades Unions are to be international it must be by becoming imperial first. The hauling down of the British Flag could not fail to affect considerably the position of the colonies in their finances and their trade. In their infancy it would have been ruinous: even now it would be severely felt for a very long time.

CHAPTER IX.

Supply of Labour.

A CHARACTERISTIC of Europeans at home and abroad is *activity*. Where European civilization is effective Nature is called upon to respond to greater demands upon her; and, as she responds, the demand is only stimulated afresh, and so the wealth of nations goes on growing. In countries where a moderate degree of industrial activity has been found to be already set up Europe has not, as a rule, been able to intervene. In China and Japan industrial pursuits are well established, although there has been found large scope for the wider intelligence of modern European methods. In India, too, the stimulation of industrial activity has not been a pressing need. The expansion of Europe has been mainly into countries occupied by indolent and unprogressive races, or so sparsely occupied as to be practically open lands. Hence the development of civil life has given rise to a fresh demand for labour whenever European energy has placed industry on a new footing.

In *temperate zones* Englishmen are themselves competent to do all kinds of industrial work, but in *tropical regions* they cannot perform heavy physical tasks: they can provide the capital and the managing capacity, but the manual work requires people of tropical birth. In the early days of European colonization the principal movement was into tropical and sub-tropical countries, but later on temperate climates were occupied, and at length the latter movement became the more important of the two.

In supplying labour for the industrial building up of European colonies, *five* expedients have been resorted to at different times in different places.

§ 1. EMPLOYMENT OF THE NATIVE POPULATION.

The employment of the inhabitants found in the new countries was the method adopted by the Spaniards in the New World. As their prime object was gold and silver, they forced the people away from their agriculture and such rudimentary urban pursuits as were followed, into the mines; and ruthlessly driving them they worked them to death. In the group of islands first discovered, the Bahamas, we found only sixteen natives left alive by the Spaniards: in Jamaica not one. On the mainland the populations were too great to make destruction possible, but the natives were subjected to great oppression. English colonists were not placed in this position, so that we cannot tell whether they would have acted with more consideration. We found scarcely any natives in our West Indies, and on the American continent we had to deal with the warrior tribes of the Red Indians, who might be fought and driven off, but could not be drilled into manual labour of a servile kind. Later on we came into contact with others of a similar temper, the Maories, or else with people of very low type like the Australian aborigines. In Africa we are gradually accustoming the Zulus and Kaffirs to be the manual labourers of our colonies, the Hottentots and Bushmen being apparently not of sufficient stamina to bear permanently a part in a higher but more exacting kind of life. In reference to native populations generally, we find a more thorough incorporation of them into industrial life in those regions where the Spanish and Portuguese have been the representatives of Europe than in those which have come to our lot. The mass of the population in Mexico and South America is still of the Indian type, but there is a very large class of people of mixed blood. This admixture has never been an important element in English colonies. The regard for the family which characterizes Teutonic peoples has prevented amalgamation on an extensive scale; we have never Romanized our idea of the family, either in the direction of legitimated concubinage or in the inclusion of 'slaves' in the circle of the household. A Carolina planter's household, of course, included some domestic slaves who were almost part of the family, but the whip-driven gangs of field-labourers living in their cabins were kept outside the pale of household relationships, even when their general treatment was mild and considerate.

§ 2. NEGRO SLAVERY.

The problem of labour-supply in America was early met by a method not in itself indefensible, but utterly unjustifiable and disgraceful as conceived and carried out. The abundant negro populations of West Africa were resorted to for the supply. We may at first ask—And why not? It might have proved a great economic contrivance—a joint working of America's resources by Europe and Africa. But two conditions indispensable to a just plan were entirely absent—(1) the *consent of the negroes*, (2) their transportation in *families and tribes*. As neither of these was possible, so neither of them was thought of, and, instead, there was begun an interference with the common rights of humanity, and a barbarous disregard of compensatory alleviations, which has indelibly blackened the record of Europe in the face of the world. Advantage was taken of the low state of negro society, which made the selling one another into slavery a means of gratifying hatred and of satisfying greed; and agencies for the purchase of negroes from their captors were set up all along the West Coast of Africa. The Portuguese began the system by carrying them from their factories in Africa to their plantations in Brazil; the Spaniards, though never themselves engaging in the trade, took every advantage of it to supply their plantations in Cuba and Porto Rico. Their missionary bishop, Las Casas, unfortunately joined in regarding it with favour, thinking that as negroes could work it was less hard for them to be compelled to do so than for the Indians, who perished when forced to regular toil. England joined both in the trade and in the use of the negroes; and though we must not judge the seventeenth century by the moral standards of the nineteenth, it almost passes marvel to find the nation of Hampden and Milton chaffering with other nations for the *monopoly* of this very traffic, and actually securing it for herself by the Treaty of Utrecht! The lamentable system went on for 250 years, the annual number carried over the Atlantic being some 100,000, at least. So that Africa had to suffer from a double drain—Mohammedans drew negroes from the East for the domestic slavery of Egypt and Arabia and Persia and Turkey; Europe drew them from the West for the plantations of the New World: and of the two ours was the worse infliction, as the domestic servitude of Orientals was less hard than the cattle-like status of negroes in Virginia and Jamaica. In some lately-printed accounts of an old West Indian plantation the entries of purchase and sale of negroes appear mixed up with those of the cattle; combined entries of births of babies, asses, and oxen appear, and in death also they are not divided. In Africa, as a French writer puts it, while Arabs sent raiding parties to the interior from the east, we took advantage of native animosities, and our factories were as 'cupping-glasses' all along the Atlantic coast.

History of Abolition.

A few voices were raised against the trade at intervals, the *Society of Friends* gaining for themselves memorable distinction for their clear perception of its unjustifiable character. In *Pennsylvania* slavery was soon disallowed; and in England Quakers were constantly lamenting over their countrymen's blind greed. Towards the end of last century the suspicion that it was indefensible grew into a conviction that it was absolutely wrong and must be resisted. *Granville Sharp* took steps to obtain a decision that a negro slave brought to England was *ipso facto* freed and could not be taken back to slavery (the *Somerset* case, 1772); the *Master of Magdalene College*, Cambridge, set as a subject for the

University Essay in 1784 the question whether it was lawful to hold men in compulsory service; the Bachelor of Arts, *Thomas Clarkson*, who gained the prize, was won over to the slave's cause, and gave the whole activity of his life to his release. *Cowper* wrote burning verses against it; *Burke* and *Fox* protested against it; *Pitt* was only looking for opportunity to legislate against it, and the popular and influential member for Yorkshire, WILLIAM WILBERFORCE, was so thoroughly convinced of its crying injustice that he joined with Clarkson, and made its abolition the main purpose of his public life. They worked incessantly, and the record of their labour is itself a lesson in arduous and indomitable toil; but it took fifty years to achieve success. The Planting interest was wealthy and compact, and they could buy boroughs and votes, and so prevent the popular voice from being heard; and indeed it was not until the Reform Bill of 1832 cleared away electoral abuses that the thing was done. And it was hindered somewhat by the course which the revolution took in France, which threw suspicion upon all ideas of liberty; many even of those who had held them were affected, and slackened in their zeal. The TRADE was attacked first. In America itself the objection to this was felt even by those who thought the system allowable, and the *Virginia Assembly* went so far as to join in a petition to the Crown against it before Virginia achieved independence. The *House of Commons* passed a Bill for abolishing the trade in 1794, and again in 1796, but the House of Lords threw it out; then a Bill for its suspension (1804) was rejected in the *House of Lords* by 76 to 70; but after the Lower House accepted Fox's resolution in 1806, the next year, 1807, saw victory (though Fox and Pitt were both then dead); the Bill was carried by 283 to 16, and in the House of Lords by a majority of 66. In 1808 the United States abolished the trade. As illicit traffic still went on Brougham induced Parliament to rank the offence as *felony* in 1811, and we kept cruisers on the seas to prevent it. The working of the new ideas of Political Economy was all in favour of abolition; arguments that it was wasteful as well as unnatural and unjust came to the help of the philanthropists; still, in 1823 Buxton's motion was again rejected. In 1825 Wilberforce retired from Parliament, but Buxton carried on the cause there; and at last, in 1833, the Reformed Parliament and the administration of Lord Grey, with Brougham and Stanley amongst his colleagues, *passed the Bill*. The sum of twenty millions sterling was voted as compensation for vested interests; this still remains as the most signal example in history of a nation consenting to tax itself heavily in order to undo a moral wrong. Of course it may be regarded as a means of buying off opposition; but even so, the Abolition party agreed to make the sacrifice, and the nation, as a whole, applauded the decision, and accepted the burden. Wilberforce lived to see the Bill pass its second reading, but died before it came into force. Clarkson lived till 1847. On August 1st, 1834, *the Act came into operation, and 770,280 slaves awoke to freedom*. There was a system of *apprenticeships* attempted, in order to keep the negroes on their plantations, but in 1838 it was given up as it was not working well. In that year the abolition was extended to *our East Indian plantations*. In other countries abolition gradually made its way; in *France* at the Revolution of 1848, *Portugal* in 1851, *Holland* in 1860, and the *United States* by Presidential decree in 1864, during their great Secession War. In the last decade the only relics were in *Brazil* and *Cuba*; but 1886 saw even the remnant of it in Cuba abolished, (1) without compensation, and (2) without visibly affecting production. In Brazil it was arranged that it should end with the century, but any owner setting slaves free beforehand had *pro rata* compensation, according to the time yet to elapse; the effect of this was restlessness on the part of the slaves, and complete abolition was carried in 1887. Thus closes the gloomy chapter.

Significance of the Abolition.

The disappearance of slavery means more than the disappearance of an industrial institution: an *idea* which till this century has been part of the political philosophy of the Aryan peoples has been dissolved. Plato and Aristotle had thought slavery defensible; Sparta and Athens had worked by it. Slavery by conquest, slavery for punishment, slavery to meet debts; not only these, but slavery through birth, by reason of inferiority, and to meet industrial necessity, had been justified. And it was not abolished by political philosophy[1]; the 'rights of man' did not achieve it for France or for the United States. Nor was the idea given up because of express condemnation in the Christian scriptures, but it was dissolved in the Christian consciousness; the simplicity of Quaker belief first, and the Evangelical revival among Churchmen and Dissenters afterwards, brought men to see that it was alien and intrusive in any attempt to realize human life as already within the kingdom of God. The nations of Europe were convinced one by one, and now in tardy recompense they accept with varying degrees of directness the duty of using their influence towards the abolition of slavery within the African continent.

It is often found in human affairs that light springs up out of darkness. Along with the gloomy record of the 250 years of negro slavery we find the history of its abolition; perhaps *the most impressive history* on record of the origin and completion of a *purification of the moral consciousness* of peoples.

§ 3. COOLIE LABOUR.

The place of the imported African is being taken up in many colonies of European nations, and especially of England, by imported Hindus and Chinese; the place of the Slave by the Coolie. The coolie leaves his home *voluntarily*, he works for *wages*, he has full *personal and family rights*, and he can *return home* at the end of the period for which

[1] In 1669 John Locke drew up a Code of Constitutions for Carolina, in which there are inserted definite provisions for 'absolute power and authority over Negro Slaves,' without any apology or explanation even from this advocate of toleration and liberty in England.

he has engaged. By this system thousands of the poorer inhabitants of India are finding regular and well-paid employment in climates similar to their own, and they return home with savings that make them, for the first time in their lives, capitalists. One ship conveyed 320 coolies back to Calcutta with a total of 65,000 dollars belonging to them. They are almost entirely Hindus of the low castes, and they are employed most extensively in our sugar plantations in Mauritius, in Natal, and in our West Indian Islands. Another field has been in the semi-tropical district of Queensland, where natives of the Pacific Islands are employed. In all cases, except the last, Government supervises their original engagement and determines its terms; regulates the voyage and the accommodation provided; receives them on arrival, allots them to the different plantations, and regulates their treatment while in the colonies. Their barracks are built on Government plans, and are inspected from time to time; medical attendance is secured, the food regulated, and the hours of labour and scale of remuneration fixed. At the end of their first period the coolies may re-engage only on certain conditions, and with official sanction, and at the end of two periods may not re-engage at all, as a rule. They may either settle in the colony, or return to India. The Queensland authorities have certainly been remiss, not so much in the regulations which they made, although they were inferior to those enforced in our Representative and Crown colonies, but in the spirit in which they were carried out. Some terrible facts stand on record in the Polynesian traffic; 'blackbirding' was a well-known term, and the class of ships and men employed in it were of the lowest and their proceedings unscrupulous. The Government at length awoke to the duty of looking the evil in the face, but some malefactors condemned by the Queensland Courts under one Administration were released when a fresh Cabinet came into power. The advantage of an Imperial Government in some circumstances is shown in the superior treatment of these people of lower race in colonies where the Imperial hand is still effective. But in all probability the last has been heard of the Polynesian abuses too, although there is peculiar difficulty in Queensland owing to its immense territory and the remoteness of the plantations from the centre of government. The numbers of Coolies in British colonies are approximately: in Guiana 70,000, Trinidad 70,000, Natal 40,000, Jamaica 13,000; in Mauritius there are 250,000, mostly settled there altogether.

A comparison between the slavery and coolie systems shows very clearly how an economic need can be met without infringing on moral rights when nations make up their minds to be just.

The Coolie System.	Slavery.
THE ESSENTIAL DIFFERENCES.	
(1) *Personal Freedom.*	Man a property or chattel.
(2) *Sacredness of Families.*	Family rights allowed only by favour.
CONSEQUENTIAL DIFFERENCES.	
(3) *Homes left voluntarily.*	Prisoners or kidnapped.
(4) *Education and religion open.*	At caprice, usually discouraged, often forbidden.
(5) *Hope securely founded,* either (1) of return home, or (2) of settlement as capitalists.	No future to look forward to.
SECONDARY DIFFERENCES.	
(6) *Government supervision of voyage.*	The horrors of the 'middle passage.'
(7) *Government regulating terms of engagement.*	No proportion between work and reward.
(8) *Government regulating standard of comfort, as to house, food, and medical attendance.*	At discretion of owners.

The above contrast is with Slavery under the English system; under the French *code noir* and the Spanish system there were important differences in the direction of milder treatment.

It is plain that the Coolie system is a good one, if fairly carried out. It may become a *cosmopolitan benefit*. It is, however, the plain duty of Governments to keep a close watch; and in our case, as we control through Parliament both the Indian source of supply and most of the colonies that use the system, the British people can effectively supervise it. Now that we have so much constant communication with India and the colonies we may without difficulty do this. Englishmen travelling abroad should take notice of what they see, and Englishmen at home be ready to give attention to their reports. In this way the planters will feel that proper treatment of coolies is an Imperial question, and that Imperial honour is concerned. On them the brunt of the work of colonization falls, but as they also enjoy the profit, it is no more derogatory for them to accept Imperial help in watching the system than for the schoolmaster of the country to be 'inspected' by national authority. The European mind is made up once and for all on the manner of the employment of inferior races; and though colonists may not all quite cordially agree with us, we cannot forego our responsibilities as we understand them.

The *Chinese coolie* is in a very different position. He goes to many places; often undesired, and in some colonies actually forbidden. But he knows how to take care of himself, and usually becomes a trader, not a field labourer, or he engages in some urban employment. The Chinese question, as a whole, belongs to a different order of topics,—that of immigration of freemen.

§ 4. Convict Labour.

The fourth expedient is still another instance of the activity of the Portuguese in early days, for it was they who first thought of the plan of using *criminals* for profitable employment, in the plantations of Brazil, instead of confining them in indolence or in useless tasks at home. France and England soon joined in using the method. In our case it was first applied to *political* offenders in the troubled times of the seventeenth century. A few Roundheads were shipped off, but Cavaliers were despatched in large numbers to Virginia and Barbados by Cromwell after Dunbar and Worcester and the siege of Limerick. In 1686 there was a similar transportation of prisoners to Barbados after Monmouth's rebellion. Husbandmen, weavers, combers, and 'poor fellows' were sent out after conviction for high treason, to be sold for ten years when landed. Lists are extant of 68, 72, 90, and 100 prisoners thus cleared from the gaols of Dorchester, Exeter, and Wells. When their time was out they were allowed to leave for other islands, and even for Boston, New York, and Virginia, or to return home. Later, *ordinary crimes* were treated in the same way, transportation beyond the seas being the most severe punishment short of death.

Botany Bay.

When we lost our plantation colonies in America we had to look somewhere else for the disposal of our convicts. The West Indies and Canada did not want them; so the results of Captain Cook's voyages were turned to practical effect by Pitt, and it was decided to make a penal settlement on the most remote shore of Australia, at the place named by Cook, from its variety of plants, Botany Bay. Accordingly in 1787 six transport ships and three store-ships, escorted by a man-of-war and a tender, with 757 convicts, of whom nearly 200 were women, arrived there. Some marines accompanied them as a guard, and some live stock and seeds and plants were sent for their support. Shipments afterwards became regular. The convicts were kept in confinement; but after their sentences expired they received land, some stock, and eighteen months' rations. Many wasted this, but a considerable proportion turned it to some account. The supply of convicts was often at the rate of 2000 or 3000 a year, for this was the period when severe penalties were in force: many of them were under life sentences, commuted into transportation, for such offences as forgery and horse-stealing. To return to

England—'home' to them no more—whilst under sentence, was itself a capital offence. Later on, free settlers went out, and amongst them and the *emancipists* the convicts as they arrived were distributed as labourers, instead of being kept in confinement or in Government gangs; as the former classes grew this course was adopted more and more. The state of 'society' was indeed strange: lawlessness was barely kept under control by a military régime; there was a moral chaos, well typified in the unit of their currency, a bottle of rum! Yet a certain element of good nature and cheerfulness in the acceptance of adverse fate on the part of many who were very likely more sinned against than sinning, leavened even this unpromising lump [1]. There were some who candidly accepted the motto enunciated by a convict 'poet,' Barrington, as part of the prologue to a play at the first rough Sydney theatre—the well-known lines—

> True patriots all, for be it understood
> We left our country for our country's good.

Gradually, however, the method became unnecessary for the supply of labour for the original locality: New South Wales expanded; and when the magnificent Downs across the Blue Mountains were opened out by roads a splendid future for agriculture was secured. Free settlers began to come in rapidly, and the reception of more convicts was protested against. The Government were perplexed to know what to do; Victoria threatened to put *her* convicts on a ship for Plymouth; the Cape people successfully objected to a settlement there; Van Diemen's Land repudiated the plan, and with it its own name. Western Australia, at its own request, became a stop-gap, but even there it had soon to be given up. Meanwhile powerful voices were protesting at home in the interests of the wretched people themselves, especially as so many were women. *Howard* had protested against it for

---

[1] *For the Term of His Natural Life*, by Marcus Clarke (London edition, Bentley, 1889), vividly illustrates this phase of life in the early days of the Australian colonies.

some time; the milder criminal law of punishment advocated by *Bentham* and *Mackintosh* and *Romilly* had come into operation. In 1819 there were 1314 persons sentenced to death in England and Wales; of these 108 only were executed, and of these 15 only were for murder. In 1849, when the milder régime was in force, only 66 were sentenced to death; 15 executed—*all* for murder. Archbishop *Whately* insisted strongly that the system was condemned by its failure to *reform*, or to endeavour to reform, moral character; and finally the Home Government acquiesced in these views, and gave up the whole system in 1867.

France still continues it; criminals irreclaimable or relapsed (*récidivistes*) are sent to Cayenne (French Guiana) and New Caledonia; the use of the latter for this purpose is a sore point with the neighbouring Australian colonies.

§ 5. FREE EMIGRATION.

Emigration is now the normal method for supply of labour. By the nature of man's physical capacities it is limited to the colonies of the temperate zone, where it has for some years proved the effective method. For the colonizing country it is doubly important, as it provides for her own surplus population at the same time that it forms new communities: it furnishes not only new customers for her goods, but also employment across the sea for her children. Her merchants are busy, her home factory-chimneys smoke, and at the same time her sons and daughters are finding fresh homes.

Motives for Emigration.

Forces may act by expulsion from within or by attraction from without. New regions may offer new and powerful inducements, or they may be simply openings for a superabundance which is embarrassing the industrial life of an old country. For the capacity of a geographical district to maintain population is a relative matter, and depends upon the industrial organization of the nation occupying it. If this is improved, a territory, already thought full, is proved to have been but inadequately occupied. We do not know whether the single aboriginal per square mile, who once monopolized the whole of what is now our colony of Victoria, thought that the 'Garden of Australia' was already sufficiently populated; but it is certain that people in Elizabeth's day thought that England was getting uncomfortably full with some four million people, and Cobbett called London a 'wen' on the face of nature when as yet many populous suburbs were fields and gardens. But, at any given time, the capability of a country to support population depends upon the stage of organization to which it has attained; and if at any given stage we desire to know how it stands in this regard we may ask at once whether there was any consciousness of being overcrowded on the part of the people themselves. From such a country depletion by emigration is sure to begin if openings are offered.

But a consideration of the early stages of our colonization shows that there were other motives in operation quite as powerful as relief from pressure of population at home. Men went out because they heard of new sources of wealth. The tales of travellers and voyagers fell upon no inattentive ears. Or again, men were driven from home by forces that were extra-economic, political and religious animosities being especially important. There was however for 150 years a considerable stream of voluntary emigration of free labour into our British colonies, strong enough to raise the population of our American colonies to three millions in 1760, when that of England and Wales was about seven.

Cessation.

When we lost America emigration dropped into insignificance for two reasons: (1) Our wealthiest remaining possessions (the West Indies) were tropical; Canada was not easy to open out; Australia was only just known, and was being used for other purposes. But (2) the lull occurred chiefly because at home the pressure outwards had entirely ceased. Population was wanted, our increasing manufactures gave employment to many more hands than they displaced; the barriers of war and the greed of interested legislators compelled us to grow all the corn that could be grown on English soils, however poor; and recruits were wanted for the king's service in both army and navy, where they died by weariness and disease and hard lives, in greater numbers than even the long lists of the killed and wounded in such battles as Trafalgar and Vimeira and Vittoria show. Hence the efforts of statecraft in England for the thirty years before Waterloo were directed towards keeping up population; and emigration ceased.

Movement Renewed.

After Waterloo the whole situation changed. As soon as Napoleon was shut up in St. Helena the Poor Law policy of fostering children, even the children of paupers, was at once changed. Attention was at once turned outwards again, and from 1815 to 1830 an average of 23,000 people a year left the ports of the United Kingdom. Canada and the Cape had some share of attention; the reports from Australia encouraged, as we have seen, free settlers to go there, and the United States received a number which constantly grew. Between 1830 and 1840 the annual average rose to 70,000, from 1840 to 1846 to 100,000. And then came the most memorable single phenomenon in the history of the emigration of labour. In the next few years a movement of the PEASANTRY OF IRELAND began, which must almost be called a national exodus, the displacement of a people. A comparison of the numbers who went out with the population of the island shows *the whole body of the people in agitation*. In no other country of Europe has emigration ever been seen on such a scale. The serious alteration in the Irish industrial system by the displacement of small holdings in favour of larger farms, which was forced upon them by the economic advantages of the latter system under English legislation, operated extensively from the middle of the last century onwards. Then the cultivation of the potato acted in a reverse direction among the peasants, causing increase of population and subdivision of holdings. A large body of people had at any time only a crop of vegetables between themselves and famine, and on the failure of that crop in 1846 and 1847 they turned to emigration as the only remedy. Free Trade mitigated the catastrophe, but emigration was the panacea, and fortunately the Irish did not resist it, but left Ireland. The stream from the British Isles, which was at the height of 100,000 a year in 1840-6, rose to 280,000 a year in the years 1847-50[1], the increase chiefly from Ireland. They went everywhere, but chiefly to the United States, where they carried with them the idea that, rightly or wrongly, they need never have come had their country received considerate, not to say generous, treatment at the hands of Great Britain, not just at that crisis exactly, but during the centuries when it was possible. Since then the stream of Irish emigration has proceeded; her population, which once reached eight millions, has declined from $5\frac{1}{4}$ millions in 1801 to less than 5 now; while England has gone from 9 to 29 millions, and Scotland from $1\frac{1}{2}$ to 4 millions. The number of Irish emigrants from May 1st, 1851, to December 31st, 1889, was 3,346,580.

It is sometimes forgotten in the enthusiasm of Imperialists that the Irish element in every colony, and especially in the United States, is *not* predisposed to the mother-country; and when we speak of the common sentiments of the 'English-speaking peoples' all over the world we must bear in mind that Irish resentment is likely for many years to frustrate hopes of a very cordial attitude to England.

Nationalities in Emigration.

As to nationalities, several marked lines appear. For example, Scotchmen have shown a liking for Canada and

[1] Emigration figures are not easy to obtain satisfactorily, as there is no means of knowing what was *net* emigration, i.e. how many people went out really to settle abroad, and how many must be deducted from the enumerations as travellers only. But still, the figures are useful for comparison, as, at least, we can trace movement by means of a *comparative* examination as between year and year.

also for New Zealand; German vine-dressers from the Rhine have heard of the promising vineyards of Australia. It has been found that a lad from a Cambridgeshire village who had himself done well in London has been the means of bringing a dozen families from his native village to London: in the same way family ties have promoted the mobility of labour nearly all over the world as much as railways or steamboats themselves have done. *French* emigrants proceed only on French lines, to Algeria chiefly, and to places where France has traditional influence, as Egypt. They are not numerous; it is doubtful whether half-a-million people of pure French birth live outside France at this moment, except the French Canadians.

German emigration has been much more important. The Germans have many excellent qualities for settling a country; accordingly they began very early, and their emigration is active still. In Pennsylvania, for example, they always formed a considerable proportion of the people; to the Cape they went under the shield of the Dutch East India Company; and now they go everywhere. To the United States, between the years 1850-70, some 250,000 Frenchmen came to settle; but in that same period 2,267,000 Germans and 2,700,000 Irishmen. In Canada there are over a quarter of million people of German or Dutch origin. If a 'Germany' had come into existence earlier than she did, and a colonizing policy been taken in hand, there can be no doubt that we should to-day have seen important colonies, or even independent States, of German origin. As it is, they are absorbed in the British colonies and the United States, in which they exercise an influence which has hardly yet been sufficiently analysed. *Spanish* and *Portuguese* emigration proceeds chiefly to one or other of the South American states; and *Italians* have shown that the Latin affinity is still strong by choosing the Hispano-American regions of the River Plate and Buenos Ayres as a favourite ground. The *Swiss* have preferred America, but have gone to both North and South. The *Dutch* do not move much now. They were, indeed, once on the point of doing what would have given them a very different place in colonization. Macaulay, in his essay on Temple, says that when Charles II broke up the Triple Alliance and left Holland almost at the mercy of Louis XIV, the Dutch were nearly removing *en masse* either to America or to their Eastern colonies. But they had their place preserved for them in their narrow home, and their numbers have never given them the power of supplying many emigrants; about 4000 a year went to the United States in 1882-89.

Scotland made one or two separate attempts at colonization: one to Nova Scotia in 1621, to be under the 'Crown of Scotland,' and governed by Scottish law; the other, the disastrous attempt at Darien. But their separate endeavours were not prolonged, and Scotchmen soon threw in their lot with Englishmen.

Mr. Payne, in his able review of the whole subject of European emigration (*European Colonies*, pp. 383-386), states his opinion that the most successful element in it is contributed by the Scotch, that the English come second, and the Germans next.

The State and Emigration.

It is difficult to remain satisfied with Government inaction in so important a movement. Without going so far as to desire to see a Government collecting information about the condition of its people, or about the openings abroad for labour, for the purpose of *compelling* people to move in accordance with the situation disclosed, we may still think that much might be done. As a matter of fact, a good deal has been done in France, for example, to stimulate colonies, and in Germany to keep her people at home. In England there was a beginning of Government attention in the reign of Queen Anne, when free passages to our American colonies were offered to labourers and their families who were out of occupation. In this century the House of Commons first considered the subject about ten years after the Great Peace had begun, and in 1871 a Royal Commission examined it. The Government accordingly adopted the plan, very much like that of Wakefield, of using the proceeds of colonial land-sales in premiums to emigrant labourers; and bounties of £30 for a man and £20 for a woman going to a colony were given. Afterwards the Governments of the Responsible colonies had to take their own measures for attracting labour; but before they had time to effect much, the gold-discoveries in Victoria gave an independent impetus, although they caused a diversion of the stream. But nearly all the colonies offered either free or assisted passages to labourers, and on arrival granted land on easy terms, as it was not wage-labourers they were likely to get, so much as men who were tired of wage-paid labour in England and yearned to have a bit of land of their own. This might very well have gone on for a long time, as there were immense territories to be occupied, but soon the influence of democracy was seen in the colonial governments; the men already in the colony began to regard with jealousy the arrival of further 'supply'; the votes for assisting immigration were reduced, and in most cases withdrawn altogether.

Opposition from Colonial Governments.

But the course of development has led to a still stranger position: here again the granting of liberty has been turned against ourselves. Our young colonies took early opportunity of independence in Government to set up hostile tariffs against the *produce* of Lancashire and Dundee and Belfast. They are now tending towards a *hostile attitude towards the migration of British labourers* into their vast regions. They say that they will have them when of the right sort, and will welcome such. For this no thanks are due; as we have seen, each such person has cost Britain £175, and he is lost just as he begins to be a builder up of our national wealth. But her nondescripts they have ceased to invite, and ominous threatenings are heard that her failures they will not have. Even the strong, able-bodied man is told that he ought to have a little capital, say some twenty shillings an acre; so that *the British labourer pure and simple sees the gate practically closed*. In the United States the notions of liberty and equality are ceasing to be applied outside their own boundaries; a Congress-man and well-known writer, *Mr. H. Cabot Lodge*[1], has expressed the opinion that the time is coming when America must begin to consider whether the tide of immigration of people of inferior 'morale' is to be allowed to continue. The old boastings about the vast continent and its arms open to the oppressed European are giving place to scowls at these victims of decayed civilizations, as competitors for the American's high wages.

IS AUSTRALIA TO BE APPROPRIATED BY PRESENT COLONISTS?

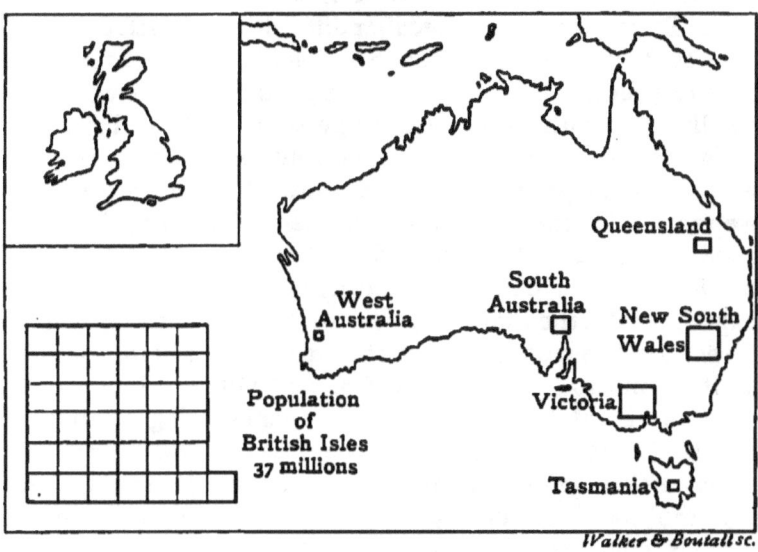

A somewhat troubled sky is over the prospect; certainly if the colonies are not ready to take British people, rough and smooth together, as in the past, they will cease to concern us in reference to our labouring classes and the question of how to do the best for our ever-growing population. A war to force immigration or to compel a re-allotment of some territories

[1] *North American Review*, January, 1891.

P

which colonists cannot fill themselves would be an incongruous conclusion to our colonial story. Other means must be hoped for; perhaps imperialism in labour, or even cosmopolitanism, will take the place of nationalism, and labourers themselves will insist on the world being open. Meanwhile the question, though not urgent, is unmistakeably becoming so.

The English Government and Emigration.

In England the opinion of those who know much about the subject has led to a discountenancing of State aid of a pecuniary kind being given to emigration, on the ground that the State is not likely to do it best, and that the intervention of the State gives rise to peculiar difficulties best left dormant. It would be quite easy for the Colonial Office to raise a loan of a few millions at 3 per cent., and by advancing this in small sums, with great care, to persons ready and fitted to emigrate, to set a considerable current in motion. But are we willing to promote the departure of such people? Do we really wish to see men and women of fine physique and good moral character deported? If they want to go we will not hinder them, but we can hardly speed them at the public expense. But the State may very well be asked to place at the disposal of the nation at large the ample stores of *information* at its command through the Colonial Office. The request for this has at last resulted in an agency being established by the Colonial Office, under the title of the *Emigrants' Information Office*[1]. A quarterly statement is issued, showing the condition of the labour market generally in the various colonies, and as modified from time to time. The peculiar facilities for distributing information which Government possesses are utilized by the exhibition of this quarterly circular at every post-office in the kingdom. But this provision hardly seems adequate for the supply of information to so large a number of the population as is

---

[1] The effort is very slight: the whole 'department' costs only £650 a year.

concerned. The conditions of industry are very varied, and the legal regulations are very complicated and perplexing, there being some 550 statutes, British, colonial, and foreign, bearing on the conditions and status of persons changing their country of residence. But the institution of this central office is a boon, and farther development may be pressed for in time. In Ireland more is done: there is in Dublin an Emigration Department of the Board of Trade, with a chief inspector, nine assistants, and seven medical inspectors.

Another branch of the work is taken in hand by the favourite English method of *societies*, private and irresponsible. Amongst these are the Self-Help Emigration Society, for Great Britain (not Ireland) at one end of the line, and Canada at the other. This society has correspondents in Canada, who are men of some standing, to whom emigrants take out letters of introduction, and who look out for work for them. Aid is given when necessary; and the society placed out 816 persons in 1889 at a cost of £2 10s. a head, besides their own contributions. Employment, it is reported, was found for all who were really willing to work. There is also a Church Emigration Society, which aims especially at utilizing the advantages possessed by the English clergy in their knowledge of the labouring classes, and in their ability to give them introductions to the clergy in the colonies. Many orphan societies and institutions adopt this method of placing out some of their charges. Still, all is on a small scale; the number assisted by societies in the year when last an enumeration was made was only 3000. The Emigrant and Colonists' Aid Association is another society; it has formed a complete settlement in New Zealand of 4000 people, advancing capital to people of the wage-earning class until now they possess holdings assessed at £200,000, and its transactions yield a remunerative return. Individual enterprise is not lacking: one lady supported with £100,000 a scheme for a settlement in the eastern part of Cape Colony.

System in Emigration.

Emigration has hitherto proceeded very much at random as regards the industrial aptitudes of the emigrants. Sometimes their aptitudes have been much alike, whereas a *composite* colony would have many advantages; a well-assorted group of capitalists, foremen, and farm labourers, of blacksmiths, joiners, and other handicraftsmen, would at once form a settlement in which variety of work would be for mutual good; and if we go on to add as a necessity the schoolmaster, the doctor, and the minister of religion, we have a mixture of urban and rural 'industry' such has grown up in old countries. It would therefore be only the conscious imitation by policy of the procedure of Nature herself.

The emigration parties of our early period were, in a rough way, composed of such various elements as these. John Smith, for example, besides asking for young married people who wanted better employment, and 'fatherlesse children of thirteene or fourteene yeeres of age,'-promises sport to the gentry, pleasure and profit to planters, and to all fishing whereby they may take more in a day than they can eat in a week, and the delight of 'crossing the sweet aire from Ile to Ile over the silent streames of a calm Sea.' And of late years much thought and a good deal of enterprise has been directed to *systematic colonization*. The name of Edward Gibbon Wakefield stands foremost, perhaps, among those who have urged it upon public attention. He is a figure of considerable interest in the colonial history of the nineteenth century: one of those who combined practical enterprise with some originality and force in the region of ideas. He wrote *The Art of Colonization*, and is regarded on the best authority as the 'eminent founder of South Australia and New Zealand,' and he proposed the resolution in the New Zealand Legislature which led to responsible government, as in Canada, being granted to the Southern colonies even in their infancy. As stated in Chapter vi, his aim was that both capital and labour should be applied together, and that this should be done by the colonial lands being sold only for considerable prices, the proceeds to be expended in importing labour. Although his efforts were not permanently successful, it was under their impulse that South Australia was cut off from New South Wales, and that New Zealand was first settled. The South Australian Company was formed to carry out these ideas; a New Zealand Company was formed, with an influential directorate, which founded Wellington and Auckland; later, a company of Churchmen established Canterbury, and one of Presbyterians, Otago. But the policy did not long continue even in those colonies. At home it was attacked by an influential exponent of the 'natural' school of Political Economy, M'Culloch; the gold-rush to Victoria in 1851 upset all *systems*; and when the colonists had matters in their own hands they abandoned the method and left colonization to flow along the easier ways of natural inclination. Sir Frederick Young, a great living authority on colonial subjects, writes of the system thus: 'I confess that many years of study, reflection, and experience have led me more than ever to the conclusion that the main features of Wakefield's system were sound, and in my opinion it has been an unfortunate thing that they were ever repudiated and abandoned, as well for the colonies as for the mother-country.' (*Roy. Col. Inst. Transactions*, xvii[1].)

Another method proposed has been to mark out the land into townships in an orderly fashion, providing at the outset sites for churches, schools, institutes, and hospitals, in central positions.

But, on the whole, we are thrown back on what Adam Smith said a hundred years ago. 'According to the *natural* order of things, the greater part of the capital'—he does not exclude labour though he is not concerned here to mention it; it follows capital so far as his argument is concerned—'of every growing society is first directed to *agriculture*, afterwards

---

[1] For farther commendation of Wakefield's principles see J. S. Mill, *Political Economy*, Book V, Chapter xi, § 12; and again, § 14. For a contrary opinion see E. J. Payne, *European Colonies*, p. 173.

to *manufactures*, and last of all to *foreign commerce*. This order of things is so very natural that in every society that had any territory it has always, I believe, been in some degree observed.' And in accordance with his fundamental views he goes on to stigmatize the inversion of these by modern States as 'an unnatural and retrograde order.' But our own recent colonial history, in Australia especially, has shown that in the early stages this inversion could not be imposed, but that as soon as the colonies acquired some substantiality they have themselves inverted this 'natural order,' and given us such a colony as Victoria, where urban and rural industry already proceed side by side as in countries hoary with centuries of natural life.

Lord Granville once expressed the opinion that it has been for the advantage of recent colonization that it has proceeded at a time when the prevalent doctrine was *laissez faire*; that it has been fortunate that so many new colonies have had an infancy and a youth not hindered by futile attempts on the part of the State to direct them. But the truth of this must depend upon one or other of two assertions, either (1) that during this period activity and energy were so intimately bound up with individuality that if Government restraint had been imposed, the springs of individual energy would have been dried up, or at least parched, and we should not have had the copious outflow we have witnessed either of capital or of labour or of employing enterprise; or else (2) that the Government of the time was not of a character to fit it for such a task. One or other of these may have been true; if so, Lord Granville was right. On the other hand, John Stuart Mill, as ardent a lover of liberty as modern English politics have produced, gave his strong adhesion to the opposite view, that we ought to have had *more* Government guidance in colonization than we have had. In the last Book of his *Political Economy* he takes colonization to be one of the spheres of activity for which there are plain grounds for the action of the State. 'If it be desirable, as no one will deny it to be, that the planting of colonies should be conducted, not with an exclusive view to the private interests of the first founders, but with a deliberate regard to the permanent welfare of the nations afterwards to arise from these small beginnings ; such regard can only be secured by placing the enterprise, from its commencement, under regulations constructed with the foresight and enlarged views of philosophical legislation ; and the Government alone has power either to frame such regulations, or to enforce their observance.' Of course, if no 'philosophical' legislation was attainable, this opinion is out of court, and we must be satisfied with what has been achieved without it.

CHAPTER X.

Native Races.

EUROPEAN colonization is the latest phase of the Aryan movement, and must be the last, as there is now no fresh field to occupy. At least, it already concerns all those regions where the Aryan can live and continue to possess the characters by which we know him, and it must therefore be the beginning of the last movement of Aryans; its volume may be increased, but all the probable lines of direction seem to be already laid down. There would be no gain from an attempt to analyse and summarize within our brief limits what this movement has meant for all the races of the world, but our subject requires some consideration of the way in which it has affected such non-Aryan branches of the human family as have been brought within the British Empire.

Classification of the Races of Mankind.

The power of variation has been given to man to a degree which certainly prevents any feeling of monotony from arising when we survey the world. Colours and shades, statures, shapes of skull, angles of face, relative development of organs, and other physical differences, have been abundantly distributed; while as to languages and dialects, mental capacities, sentiments, dispositions and tempers, moral ideas and religious hopes and fears, of these we can but say that, like Cleopatra's charms, 'Age cannot stale nor custom wither their infinite variety.'

The efforts of ethnologists to attain a satisfactory grouping of races have given rise to much interesting research and argument, and some lines of demarcation not difficult to follow have been attained, provided we bear in mind that the lines are not sharp-cut all over the field, although definite enough when extremes are brought into contiguity. One leading ethnologist has not been able to reduce the fundamental division to less than eleven; another requires fifteen; another, sixteen. *Blumenbach* gave the arrangement which has been in popular use for a considerable time—CAUCASIAN, MONGOL, MALAY, RED INDIAN, and NEGRO. *Professor Huxley* in 1870 gave a fivefold division—XANTHOCHROIC (fair whites) and MELANOCHROIC (dark whites), closely allied; MONGOLOID; NEGROID; and AUSTRALOID. But these denominations are hardly suitable for ordinary use, and, on the whole, we may replace them by more familiar terms with much the same effect as to classification. Thus:—

ARYANS : (*a*) Fair-skinned and fair-haired, as Scandinavians.

(*b*) Darker-skinned and dark-haired, as high-caste Hindus.

These have their present abode from Ireland to the Ganges, the southern boundary being the Sahara Desert and the Indian Ocean.

MONGOLS : From Lapland to Siam, with a considerable variation in the Malay Peninsula and adjacent archipelago, and further variations in the Pacific Islands, and other variations in America.

NEGROES: Central and Southern Africa; and with variations extending to some islands in the Eastern Archipelago.

Some BROWN peoples : The earlier inhabitants of India; Australian aborigines, and possibly, though doubtfully, Egypt and Nubia.

The use of colour as a mark is often convenient for memory, and corresponds fairly well with the above : *White* for Aryan; *Yellow* for Mongol; *Black* for Negro; and *Brown*. But, closely pressed, it would remove the Hindus from their proper place, which is nearer to Europeans than to other brown races, and it is rather straining words to speak of them as 'white.'

This classification leads to much the same broad result as

is arrived at by comparison of the fundamental structure of languages—the *Flexional*, the *Monosyllabic*, and the *Agglutinative*.

Unity of the Race.

That community of race runs through all these varieties is beyond doubt. Ethnologists again incline to assign to man a single origin. The other view, that man had arisen in different centres, was gaining ground for a time, until (1) the advance of geology placed longer periods at disposal for the working out of variations, and (2) the evolution of species became the predominant general position in all Natural History. So that Darwin came to maintain the single-origin view of the older ethnologists, Blumenbach and Prichard; the eminent French ethnologist, M. Quatrefages, is strongly in favour of it; and Dr. Tylor regards it as now the prevailing opinion. The existence of non-Adamite man is still an open question; indeed M. Quatrefages thinks that there were men both in the tertiary and the quaternary geological periods, but human beings as now known 'seem to have originated in one place, and multiplied and multiplied until the population overflowed, as from a bowl, and spread themselves in human waves in every direction[1].' In spite of all the difficulties placed in the way of such movement by the seas and oceans, its feasibility was maintained by Lyell in the following strong terms: 'Supposing the human genus were to disappear entirely, with the exception of a single family, placed either upon the Ocean of the New Continent, in Australia, or upon some coral island of the Pacific Ocean, we may be sure that its descendants would, in the course of ages, succeed in invading the whole earth, although they might not have attained a higher degree of civilization than the Esquimaux or the South Sea Islanders.' That this centre of origin was somewhere in Asia is the common opinion. Granting that man appeared before the present geological and geographical conditions of

---

[1] *Human Species*, chap. xv.

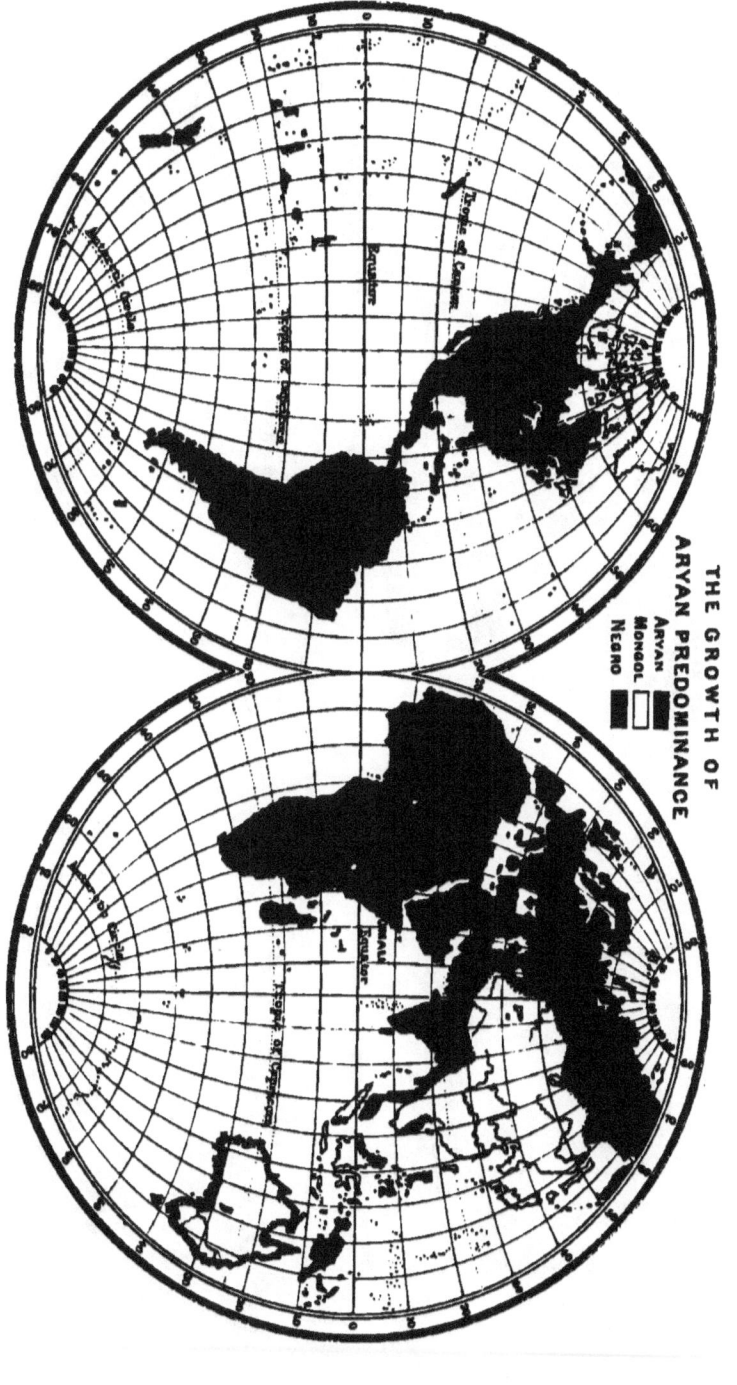

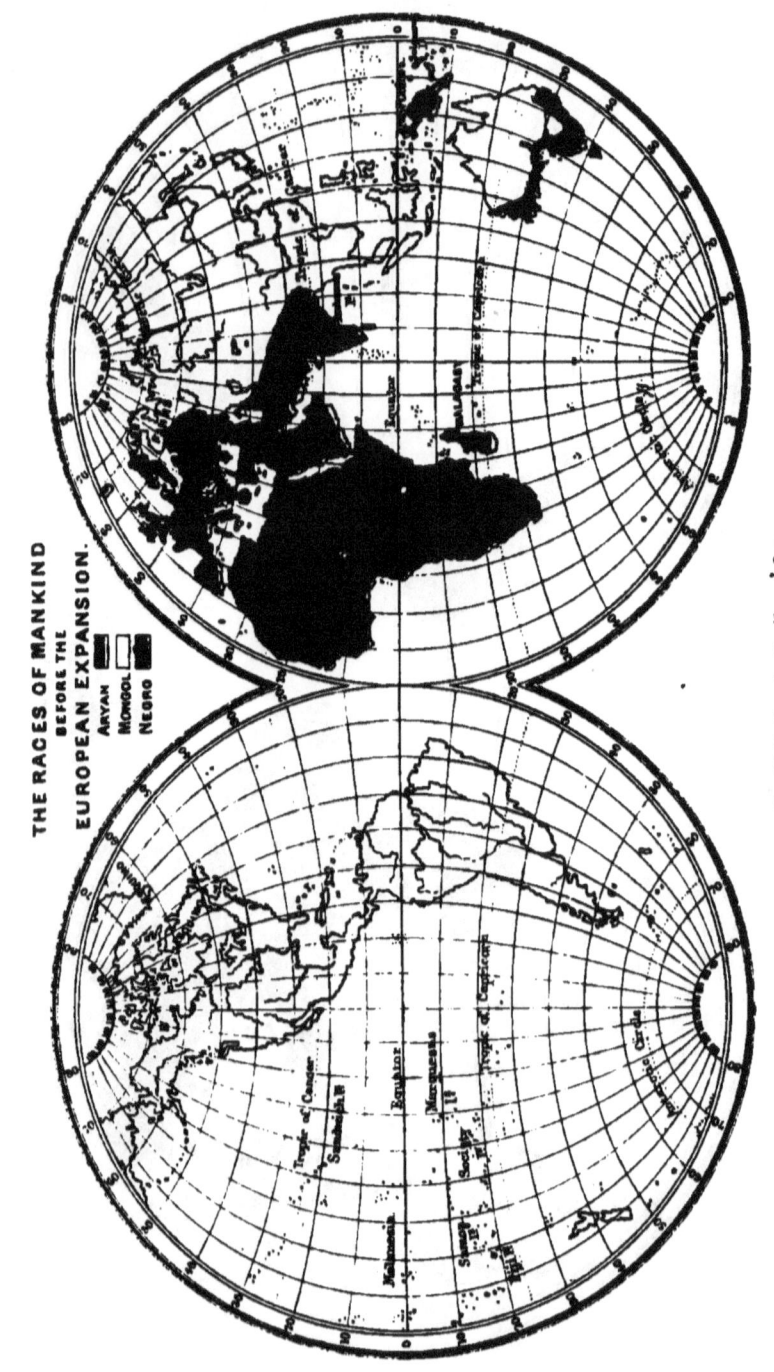

the earth, the facts point to the far north, if a higher temperature was prevalent there in earlier epochs; or to the *central plateau between the Himalayas and the Altai mountains*, if the conditions were then as now. Towards this plateau we find the *four fundamental races converging*, and nowhere else; around it the *three fundamental types* of *language* are grouped; and the *domestic animals* in their early forms are derived from it as from a central habitat.

If the inhabitants of the earth to-day can be taken at some 1300 millions—which is rather below than above the recent estimates—we must assign about 600 millions each to the Aryans and the Mongols, perhaps 80 millions to the Negro, and 10 millions to the relics of the Brown races. In addition, there are some 20 millions of a mixture of races so recent as to fall within modern times, such as the half-breeds of North and South America and the Mulattoes.

RACES MET WITH IN OUR EXPANSION.

The extension of the Aryans since 1492 over North and South America and into Australia, and their assumption of the government of other regions where other races are still the main body of the inhabitants and likely to remain so, has brought Europeans into contact with men of every race.

This has resulted either in *Extirpation* or *Subjugation* or *Admixture*.

Expansion of other Nations.

The *Spanish* movement involved extirpation at the outset, as already described, in their West Indian Islands. It seems almost beyond belief, but it is said that the native population of Hispaniola (Hayti), estimated at something between one and three millions at the time of the Discovery, had in fifteen years fallen to 60,000. But in relation to the Mongoloid inhabitants of Central and South America, the Spanish and the Portuguese have effected a complete subjugation and a very considerable admixture. M. Quatrefages reckons the mixed European and native population of Mexico and South

America as one-fifth of the whole. The Portuguese have mixed very considerably with natives of Africa and of India.

French movement has not been on a scale sufficient to exercise any important influence; their acquisition of Algeria, Tahiti, and Madagascar is of too recent date for any marked result to be seen. What influence there is resembles that of the Spanish, the Latin nations lending themselves easily to the formation of mixed races.

The *Dutch* have exhibited the Teutonic objection to mixing with other races. At the Cape they came into contact with isolated offshoots of peoples who are either yellow or brown, in admixture with black, the Bushmen and Hottentots, stunted in body and degenerate in character, and the record is one of harshness and extirpation. The Dutch, indeed, are reported to hold views which place such races out of the pale of Christendom as the Canaanite and Hittite were outside the pale of Israel; and their conduct has been regulated by this belief; 'no slaves or dogs admitted' was the inscription on one of their two churches in Guiana in 1803. But in Java they have had other ends in view than settling in a promised land: their business there was so plainly to direct the labour of the natives that they have organized a *modus vivendi* in an industrial system with very considerable success, and with benefit to the Javanese themselves. This was not attained for a long time; the early years of the Dutch East India Company's management gave a result so bad that Dutchmen in our day join in repudiating the system of oppression which was set up. But they have now in operation a policy which is a remarkable combination of liberal and aristocratic principles. On the one hand they frankly recognise native local government by allotting local functions to the native chiefs— for example, the enforcement of sanitary laws in the towns and villages. But, on the other hand, there is no pretence at equality as part of public policy. Marriage between a native regent-chief and a European domestic servant was not only forbidden, but the chief was severely reprimanded for asking for permission. No European may on any account be a domestic servant to a native chief, and any European sailor or soldier found intoxicated in public would be promptly shut up in ship or barracks[1]. Thus we have here a thoroughgoing aristocracy set up by a democratic people—a frank adoption of Oriental method. At the same time, the Dutch do not recognise educational or religious responsibilities: they consider our present policy in India suicidal; but that is, of course, because they do not hold by 'Java for the Javanese.'

BRITISH EXPANSION.

British colonizing energy has borne us into the front place in the contact of Europeans with men of other races, and especially with the 'Nature-peoples' of the world, to borrow a German expression. Leaving out of account our contact by commerce with China and Japan, and the various Persian and Arab populations between India and Morocco, we have brought under our flag peoples belonging to all the chief divisions of the race.

In *India* we have assumed the direction both of the Aryans and of the mixed races throughout the peninsula and the island of Ceylon; and this is, of course, our chief achievement and our most splendid opportunity (see Chapter v). It is to the beneficent results of our contact with the native races of India that we must turn from the sinister records of our influence elsewhere if we would recover our national respect.

The Negro Race in West Africa.

The NEGRO has known us in two ways, as we have dealt with him in the West of Africa and in the South.

The *negro of West Africa* is the purest type of the black race. When we see the familiar pictures of the woolly hair, the thick lips, the bridgeless nose, we are contemplating, as a rule, the typical native of the Guinea coast, where first we came into contact with the race. Our contact has been to him a series of rude and heavy blows: the trading factory of

---

[1] *Java, or How to manage a Colony.* J. W. B. Money, 1861.

the white man became the market where he was sold into hopeless slavery, the place where tribal feud and chieftain's greed found themselves rewarded by the sale of the hapless victims of war or of plundering raids. This went on for 250 years. In 1806 came the change, and Great Britain sent the cruisers of her navy in chase of slave-ships, and founded Sierra Leone as an abode for the homeless rescued slaves. And during this century the 'factory' element has again been fostered, so that we have in Free Town and Cape Coast Castle and Lagos the chief outlets of Guinea trade, and shall soon have another still more important where our Niger territory touches the coast. Many points of interest are raised by the history of our relations with the Negro race.

(i) Travellers make very serious charges against our action on that coast in carrying on a *liquor traffic*; the results are so pernicious that it is alleged that this wrong is not less than that of the slave trade itself. Charges stronger than anyone who is not speaking from personal observation ought to bring have been publicly made, and have met with no authoritative refutation.

Our only consolation is in learning that the worst offenders are not English but Portuguese, Dutch, and German firms, who have entirely ignored the claims of common humanity in the fierce race for business profits.

(ii) Our attempt to civilize the negro in our settlement at Sierra Leone is generally considered to be far from a distinct success. To put it briefly, what we have done is to give an opportunity for the *imitation of Europeanism* by people who cannot possibly really live in our way yet. Exceptions there may be and are, but they stand out above their countrymen too distinctly to enable us to found general conclusions on their individual worth. An imitative civilization, like an imitative morality, is as a hollow reed, which in time of stress will pierce the hand that leans upon it. The Church Missionary Society has found it necessary to take steps for the purification of the native church of Sierra Leone; and Lord Wolseley has declared his conviction that if white men left the colony free there would be a relapse into savagery on the part of the majority, and that human sacrifices would again be offered in every market-place, on the West Coast. The American free colony of *Liberia* is, perhaps, more successful. Time must show what else we can do. Relapse is possible; but it is yet quite open to a hopeful mind to believe that some good has been done, even if not exactly in kind or degree what we have aimed at.

(iii) The influence upon the race of whatever has been achieved for and by the *Negro* populations in their new homes in *America* and the *West Indies* must not be left out of account. Opinions differ on that, too; but no ingenuous and disinterested observer can doubt that their condition is almost immeasurably higher than that of their original tribes. We must not judge them by an Aryan standard because they live within our society; we ought not to expect more progress than the time elapsed makes likely, especially when we remember the abject and depressing condition in which the time of their enslavement was passed by very many. 'Chattels' do not at once become thrifty, self-reliant, upward-moving, responsible beings because an Act of Parliament alters their status in a day. The impressions of visitors to Martinique and Guadeloupe, and of Mr. Froude in the British West Indian islands, where he found what seemed to him the happiest peasantry in the world, can be set against Sir Spencer St. John's gloomy account of the Negro Republic of Hayti. And even in Hayti it comes out that it is (1) only in remote places that superstitious cruelties are practised, and (2) in the imitations of political life that the imitative element leads to absurdity. In all this imitation there is much of grotesqueness, no doubt; but some minds are even more impressed with the pathos of the endeavours after better things. Let us wait until another Toussaint l'Ouverture arises; if the race had such a man once, it may have others.

In the *Southern States of America* white men say that the negro question is still unsolved. But do the negroes say so themselves? It is so much easier for one side to make itself heard by us, and 'bias' is so palpable, that it is doubtful whether what material we have before us is of any value. Negroes appear unable to enter into those combinations and organizations which are so effective in America; certainly unless they improve in this respect they must remain in a subordinate position indefinitely.

Those who advocated the abolition of the slave trade always hoped that some good would come out of that evil. But abolition is too recent in the United States for us to be able to say whether or not their hope was without foundation.

The Negro Race in South Africa.

The natives of the East and South-East of Africa are not so purely of the Negro race as the West Africans: they have a strong dash of the Arab in their blood, and with it a considerable increase of stamina, both physical and moral. Europeans of the last generation had no lack of reason for recognising the metal of which the various Kaffir tribes in and around our growing Cape Colony were made. Their resistance to our encroachments was vigorous, and cost us many anxious campaigns and some disasters. In our own generation the Zulus have impressed themselves very forcibly on popular imagination as 'neighbours' of stubborn stuff.

There is a fair hope that in South Africa we have reached the end of military hostility with the Kaffirs and Zulus. It is believed that the industrial era has dawned for them; that as labourers and perhaps as small cultivators they will find comfort and contentment. Here again, however, distrustful voices are heard: from Natal there is a cry that the inrush of Zulus has ruined the colony, and that we shall have to let them take possession of it, not perhaps in their former savagery, but in such stage of civilization as they have so far reached. And in the provinces of the Cape Colony there is the Dutch majority who doubt strongly whether there is progress in store for these races at all, and many English colonists agree with them. But on the other side there is the demonstrated fact that the negro is not suppressed when he comes into contact with the white man; he can live by his side and work with him. And, what is more, he can do it cheerfully. This is the sign that contact is *congenial with his health* on the whole, and, if so, the natural wholesomeness will tell as the great factor in the final solution of the case. And when the new regions are opened out, and Bechuanaland and Mashonaland and the Transvaal and the Orange State are all connected by railways, and so with the Ocean and Europe, we may expect to see a supply of capital and employing talent going out which will make a moderate amount of labour so palpably to the advantage of the strong natives that they will fall into place as readily as their less promising fellows have done in Barbados and Martinique.

The Bushmen and Hottentots, however, are almost certain to be exterminated. It is not that we are purposely injuring them, but they do not seem to be able to live under the conditions of our life. They are being pushed farther and farther inland, and in their displacement they become depressed, and their numbers are diminishing.

For the majority of our South African negro fellow-subjects, however, we may fairly hope that our advent has meant a change of life for the better. When it is remembered that their past history—if such a term can be applied to events so disconnected—has been one of ceaseless tribal wanderings, changes of abode, periods of conquest and periods of subjugation, there is reason for trusting that European civilization will prove eventually to be their salvation, not their destruction.

North American Indians.

The natives of North America have won for themselves a place in the European imagination far above that to which their importance in the human family would have entitled them. Besides the Red Man there are also in America peoples who went over Westward from Scandinavia as well as Eastward from Asia; such people of 'white' character have been found in isolated groups far South as well as in the North. But the Red Indian, a comparatively late arrival himself, has been the native who has concerned us. The *Red Indian*, as he is incongruously yet unalterably called, is of predominantly Mongol type. It is not certain that he has been in America very long, but when we arrived we found tribes of varying strength wherever we went between the St. Lawrence and the Mississippi. Opinions vary as to what was their industrial condition; it has been usual to regard them as simply in the *hunting* stage: certainly they were not *pastoral*. The wild buffalo occupied much of their attention, but they had some rudimentary agriculture, growing maize—'Indian corn,' as we used to call it—and tobacco; they made pottery: and some tribes had villages or encampments of some fixity. Still even these were composed of moveable wigwams: they cleared no ground. The women merely sowed maize in the glades as a subsidiary employment, while the men were out in the hunting-field or on the war-path.

Our usual procedure with them was, first, peaceful reception, purchases and contracts; then, contracts broken by individual whites who desired new ground, or by tribes who either did not understand what they had agreed to surrender or could not consent to abide by it when they came to understand it; reprisals, attacks on settlers' houses, massacres, struggles, and—as a result—a gradual displacement. They gave ground slowly, and for a century and a half the contest was very bitter. So late as 1756 New England Governments paid money for Indians' heads. When the colonies went to war with Britain, the Indians were for the Royal troops, or rather, against the colonists; to this day a tradition lingers that 'Britishers,' 'King George's men,' were their friends.

After the division of North America between Great Britain and the United States, the lot of the various tribes of Indians ceased to be uniform.

In Canada.

In Canada the milder attitude of the French to the Indians left us a legacy of friendliness to the white man which it is pleasant to think was not dissipated by us.

We have now in Canada about 100,000 (more than a fourth of the whole race), some of them following agriculture on reserved lands in the settled provinces with subsidies at so much per head from the Government; others engaged in hunting for furs in the territories still worked commercially by the Hudson's Bay Company. They appear contented: a revolt in 1885 of half-breeds (French and Indian) under Riel was not sympathized with by the Indians themselves. Lord Dufferin was able to say to the chiefs of the Six Nations at Tuscarora in 1874 that 'he found from ocean to ocean, amidst every tribe of Indians, the name of Canada to be synonymous with *good faith, humanity*, and *benevolent treatment*,' and he specially commends as one of the methods —taken from the French, no doubt—' a careful recognition of the position of the chiefs, and an encouragement of the continuance of their own tribal organization.'

In the States.

But in the States the conditions of peaceful settling seem somehow to have been wanting. The Government took measures for dealing with the Indians—reserves were allotted to them—but the pressure of the white population prevented the Government from being able to secure the reserves. They were invaded and appropriated where the writs of the Federal Government could not be effectively executed. In some cases deportations of Indians were made. It was a case of the people being too strong in their individual capacity for the Government which they set up. Up to 1872 some 400 treaties with tribes of Indians had been signed: but an American[1] confesses that 'it is hardly too much to say that every one of these solemn conventions has been broken by the United States, and many of them were violated almost before the ink was dry on the parchment.' The fact is, the Government has been powerless: the treaties could have been enforced only by a strong military arm, and this a democracy was in no way likely to furnish against itself.

[1] Mr. L. A. Lathrop, *New Review*, Dec. 1890.

And so the settlers spread out: hills and plains became 'territories,' then 'states'; the Indian was thrust aside, and his buffalo disappeared.

Could nothing have been done? Even in the little Dutch settlement of New Amsterdam in the seventeenth century two parties arose, one counselling patience and kindness, in confidence that the Indians would thereby be won over; the other restless, passionate, clamouring for extermination as the only means of safety. And the noble principles on which Pennsylvania policy was based led to results of themselves sufficient to prove that it is not the inevitable that has taken place. The condition of some tribes now existing points to a decisive answer in favour of the Indian. The *Cherokees* are agricultural and rear cattle; they maintain schools at a cost of 70,000 dollars a year; they have a newspaper; they own private property; they increase in population in a fair ratio; and they are not despised by their white neighbours.

The *Oneidas*, the last remnant of the famous Iroquois confederacy, still persist in the State of New York, having adopted the white man's habits and customs. Mr. Lathrop states that 'they are strictly temperate, industrious, and Christian.'

The number of Red Indians in the United States is now about a quarter of a million, mostly scattered over nearly a hundred reservations, and some fifteen thousand living among the whites.

That the Red Indian will disappear is beyond doubt; but as (1) it will be long before all the reservations are wanted, and (2) the Government is stronger now, and as (3) in Canada the fur-hunting grounds at least will long be open to him, a farther lease of life is before him. A graphic picture of a Red Indian chief's view of the disadvantages of their life in comparison with that of the white man is quoted by Lotze[1]. He speaks of the white man's corn soon raised in comparison with his own *meat* requiring thirty moons to grow, of the animals with four legs to escape, and themselves only two to follow, of the security of the grains of corn remaining where they were placed, and of the hundredfold return. 'That,' said the chief,

[1] *Microcosmus*, vol. ii, p. 239.

'is why they have so many children and live longer than we: the race of the corn-sowers must supplant the race of the meat-eaters unless the hunters make up their minds to sow too.' If this economic change is as fundamental as the wigwam philosopher thought—and who shall say that it is not?—there is room for expectation that his race may endure. He will, however, gradually cease to be the Red Indian, except in blood: different occupations and other hopes will have become his before he passes away; or, as he comes nearer to the white man, perhaps he will be absorbed as an 'element' in a compound race.

The Maori.

The Red Indian suggests at once another Native Race of warlike character and fine physique—the Maori of New Zealand. Though he is black in colour, he is not negro, but Polynesian—that is, a mixture of yellow, black, and very probably brown, blood runs in his veins. He has proved a valiant defender of his soil, and has secured for himself an honourable peace. Our proceedings in New Zealand have been straightforward, on the whole. Captain Hobson, the first Governor, recognised the Maories' right of possession, and proceeded by treaty in his dealings with them, and regarded them as in direct communication with the Queen of England. *The Treaty of Waitangi* in 1841 was the Magna Charta of their position. But the solution was not to be without blood. The tribes did not altogether realize what they were giving up in the treaty, and did not recognise the right of the chiefs to sign away the land for ever, and thus we had the Maori wars. The result was inevitable. They were not using the islands as Scotch and English settlers could use them, and they were bound to give way. They now live in the North Island to the number of about 40,000. Fairly settled in their habits, they yet are on the decline in numbers. This seems not to be the result of our action, but to be the continuation of a decay recognised by themselves. They migrated probably not more than four hundred years ago, and have been successfully acclimatized. But our coming has no doubt affected them : their grass is conquered by ours, their rat by ours, and so, as they say, they themselves must expect to disappear. Whether presently, if they pluck up fresh heart, their new civilization can help them remains to be seen. Sanitation can do much; but they may be unable to conquer despondency and gather courage for a fresh career.

The South Seas.

In *Fiji* our contact was at first through individuals; the civilizing was done by missionaries, and done well. The natives have placed themselves under our protection as against any other foreign countries, and we govern them as a Crown colony.

In *New Guinea* our protectorate has only just begun. The Government has determined to protect the natives thoroughly against irregular settlements of white men; and for the present, at least, is more concerned to attend to the natives themselves than to invite immigrants. It is at least likely that what white men do in our part of New Guinea will be done in an orderly and considerate way.

The Australian Races.

Two races remain for consideration, but these open out pages which it is England's disgrace to find written against her in the book of human history. The aborigines of the Australian continent were not an attractive people, no doubt; nor did they offer promising material for development into permanent elements of Australian life. But their fate has been to be traduced before the world as hardly human, and to receive a treatment which, as the common saying is, no one would visit upon dogs. The story of the Red Indian is repeated, only without any gleam of romantic incident on either side. The Australian aboriginal belongs to the Brown race; he is different from either the Papuan of New Guinea just to the north of him, or the Tasmanian just to the south; hence Professor Huxley made an Australoid class, with him as type. There are, however, different tribes on different sides of the continent; some almost African, some on the east almost Polynesian, and some Malayoid on the north. There is good reason for placing all of them very low in the scale of humanity, perhaps at the bottom; at any rate, close by the Bushman and Hottentot: but the denial to them of any human qualities was due to indifference or to malobservation through bias. An outsider has judged differently. 'I approach this subject of the Australians very unwillingly,' writes M. Quatrefages (*Human Species*, p. 453); 'in no part of the globe has the white shown himself so merciless towards inferior races as in Australia; nowhere has he so audaciously calumniated those whom he has plundered and exterminated. In his opinion the Australians are not even *men*. They are beings "in whom are combined all the worst characters which mankind could present, at any of which monkeys, their congeners, would blush" (Butler Earp). Noble minds have doubtless protested against these terrible words, addressed to convicts who were about to seek their fortunes in Australia; but what could be expected of them when every evil passion was called forth and supported by similar arguments, which, again, rested upon assertions supposed to be scientific? The result of those experiences in Australia and Tasmania is well known; and those who wish for information have only to consult travellers of every country—Darwin as well as Petit-Thouars.'

In refutation of the falsehood of the statements that were commonly circulated as to the absence of human faculties in the Australian, such facts are now made indisputable as that they organized the family and divided their tribes into true clans, and even now remember the reasons for the division. They marked out land (mentally) and respected boundaries, they hollowed out canoes, and made nets strong enough to resist the not trivial strength of the kangaroos. Sir John Lubbock, relying upon one set of authorities, has denied them any religious beliefs or habits. M. Quatrefages, who has read Sir John and his authorities, produces others who show the Australian as conceiving of the world as created, as offering prayers and oblations, as recognising evil and good, and as having a belief in another life. Mr. Bonwick, an Australian colonist, told the Royal Colonial Institute in December, 1890, that the Australians, before their decay set in as we see it, had considerable intelligence; they were admirable mesmerists and thought-readers.

Now, if one set of authorities has not found these signs of intelligence, it does not therefore follow that other investigators have not found them either. The inability to see what others see does not prove absence, and although Eyre, Collins, and MacGillivray are on the negative side, we cannot possibly count as nothing the evidence of Cunningham, Dawson, Wilkes, Salvado, Stanbridge, and Lumholtz.

The attempts to civilize the Australians have not been largely successful, yet Dawson made some of them into rudimentary farmers; Salvado had some useful workmen around him; Blosseville found them of some service when the gold-fever drew away all his white work-people; and Buckley, a deserter, made considerable advance in the direction of civilizing some tribes. The effects of the missions will be dealt with in the next chapter.

The deteriorating effects of rum are, however, beyond doubt. The Anglo-Saxon can drink rum without necessarily being ruined; the native cannot. From this and other causes their number in the settled districts, even with all the care that is taken, is not maintained, and their disappearance is only a question of a few generations; perhaps there are not 10,000 now in the more settled parts of the colonies.

The colonial governments, stronger now than of yore, and expressing the voice of orderly communities, have organized protection for the aborigines, so far as they will accept it. From West Australia and North Queensland some dismal stories continue to be heard[1], but, on the whole, there can be no doubt that the mass of the inhabitants of Australia are anxious to do their duty to the fast disappearing remnants of their precursors in the possession of that continent.

[1] See Lumholtz, *Among Cannibals*, Murray, 1889.

The Tasmanian.

The Tasmanian has formed the subject of a dismal episode in the drama of human history. It is an episode complete in itself; the story of his contact with the white man has begun, has run its course, and has ended. *The Tasmanian is no more.* It is a sombre story—of rude, rough men landed on an island, finding weaker men in their way; the newcomers, impatient and ruthless, were resisted, and were roused to passion. Gerland, a German writer, thus characterizes the disappearance: 'The Tasmanian population has not vanished before the civilization—as the modern theory represents it—but before the barbarity of the white men. They were shot down like wild beasts; regular hunts were undertaken against them through the island.' Until 1810 the killing of a native was not murder in the colonial law: in 1826 the war of extermination began; £5 was offered for the capture of an adult, £2 for that of a child. They were pressed into a corner of the island and practically exterminated; the story was closed in 1876 by the death of a woman who was absolutely the last of the race. The condemnation of the whites is absolute. The present Agent-General for Tasmania expresses a belief that they would have 'succumbed to kindness, which endeavoured to preserve them, as well as to the enmity that would have slain them.' Probably this is so, judging from what is taking place in Australia; but they need not have been hustled out of existence, hunted down, as no less an authority than Darwin said, as at some of the great animal-hunts in India.

The South Sea Islanders.

In the South Seas wrong has not been done since any islands, such as Fiji, came under our empire; but the intercourse of white traders had inflicted much deadly wrong upon the native populations. The materials for judgment are abundant, and gloomy indeed is the reading of them. But the chapter has closed, and the occupation by European Governments of most of the important groups, and of many scattered islets too, has interposed the public opinion of Europe between them and the passions and the greed of individual Europeans.

Perhaps now it is sufficiently evident why Englishmen—leaving others to bear their own burdens—dwell with so much thankfulness on our present philanthropic mission in India. There we may redeem the past. And the scale of our influence upon the Hindu peoples renders the aggregate of the transactions with all other inferior races slight in comparison. The Tasmanian's wrong is not atoned to him by the welfare of the Bengalee; the crushing of the Red Indians is not compensated for by the careful tending of Fijians, any more than the contentment of the negro of Jamaica compensates for the wretchedness of his slave-ancestors. But it is all the compensation possible. We must hope that the sins of our fathers have wrought havoc for but a few generations, whilst for a thousand generations of the future the peoples endowed with culture will redeem the time by kindness and helpfulness to the Nature-peoples of the world. To have the leading share in this redeeming influence is part of the Imperial charge laid upon the people of Britain, America, and Australia.

The Past Unjustifiable.

Looking back over this whole history it does not appear satisfactory to our ideas of morality and humanity, to say nothing of Christian charity, for us to seek palliation or justification for our treatment of these Nature-peoples, especially in America and Australia, by referring to the necessity for the survival of the fittest in the struggle for life. Man, as a spiritual being, cannot be judged by reference to the laws of the non-spiritual sphere of being. And that the spiritual principles of justice, kindness, and human brotherliness would have yielded different results is (1) certain on abstract principles and (2) confirmed by many isolated instances, notably the brightest spot in all the history, the method of Penn and the colonists of Pennsylvania, and (3) ratified by the comparative success in this century since higher principles have been both invoked and made effective. Where justice and charity have been combined, where courtesy and trust have been our weapons, even with high-spirited peoples, response has not been lacking on their part.

The past is irrevocable, and in the future men must move on. Some of these peoples are plainly passing away: they are unable to live when called upon to make a sudden and almost a spasmodic effort to live in a higher stage of culture. But even for these it is not difficult to determine what should be our attitude. What is our conduct to the sick and dying among ourselves? All the alleviations and comforts we can think of are placed cheerfully at their disposal. Let it be so for these sick and dying tribes. Let us walk gently *as in the sick-chamber*, and be ministers to their closing years in comfort, patience, and tenderness.

It is two hundred years ago since the following words were written down by a man of an eminently kind heart and acute observation; we may transcribe them, for the two centuries of our own history since have given further evidence of their truth. .' 'Tis hard,' wrote Sir Thomas Browne, 'to find a whole age to imitate, or what country to propose for example. History sets down not only things laudable but abominable; things which should never have been, or never have been known; so that noble patterns must be fetched here and there from single persons, rather than whole nations, and from all nations, rather than any one.' In a spirit chastened by such reflections as these Englishmen must read the history of their relation to the Nature-peoples.

CHAPTER XI.

EDUCATION AND RELIGION.

I. EDUCATION.

IN the minds of the founders of British Colonies care for the Education of Youth held a very prominent place. The educational institutions of England, with their traditions and endowments, were left behind; but in almost every colony attention was given to the schools and colleges for both religious and general education. In colonies founded by companies, as Virginia, the settlers had the advantage of the help of leading members of the companies at home; in those which were places of refuge, like Massachusetts, the settlers themselves took good care not to let their children suffer from an expatriation which was due chiefly to intellectual and religious causes. The history of Education in America up to the time of the independence of the thirteen colonies shows some noteworthy features.

(i) *Provision for Education was made from the outset.* The second Virginian Company (1610) had amongst its most active members Henry, Earl of Southampton, the patron of Shakspeare; Sir Francis Bacon; Bishop (afterwards Archbishop) Abbott; Richard Hakluyt; Nicholas Ferrar; Sir Thomas Smith; and Sir Edwin Sandys, a favourite pupil of Hooker. It is not surprising therefore to learn that the Company obtained from James I a Royal Letter authorizing an appeal to the nation for funds for a college at Henrico, in Virginia. The appeal was made, and the Bishop of London paid in £1000 from his diocese alone. The Company raised £1500, and set apart 10,000 acres of land for the same purpose. The colony of Massachusetts was only ten years old, and consisted of but five thousand families, when it applied itself to providing for education. So important did they regard it that they voted £400 for a college, a sum equal to a year's general revenue. This public-spirited policy promptly called out private beneficence: two years afterwards (1638) John Harvard, a refugee clergyman, bequeathed half his property and his whole library to this college, destined to become the most distinguished educational centre in the New World. But a still more remarkable evidence of the thorough determination of the Massachusetts settlers not to allow their children to lose the inheritance of the past is found in two laws passed by their Assembly:—

(*a*) In 1642 it was ordered that—

'None of the brethren shall suffer so much barbarism in their families as not to teach their children and apprentices so much learning as may enable them perfectly to read the English tongue.'

(*b*) In 1647 it was further ordered—

' To the intent that learning may not be buried in the graves of our forefathers, every township, after the Lord hath increased them to the number of fifty householders, shall appoint one to teach all children to write and read ; and when any town shall increase to the number of one hundred families, they shall set up a grammar school ; the masters thereof being able to instruct youth so far as they may be fitted for the University.'

A comparison of the spirit animating these 'orders' with the spirit which guided public opinion in England for a considerable part of this century shows how far we are from the truth in supposing that modern ideas have proceeded uniformly in the direction of progress.

(ii) *Education in the colonies was at first liberally supported in England.* The national appeal for Henrico College was only the forerunner of frequent applications of a like kind. This particular college was a failure; but in the reign of William and Mary a clergyman named Blair took up the matter again, and raised £2500 from merchants of the city of London for the 'William and Mary College' which was instituted in 1692; and William III assigned to it

£2000 due to the Crown at that time from certain quit-rents in Virginia. But it must be confessed that a different spirit began to manifest itself at this very time; the Attorney-General of the day (Seymour), reluctantly engaged in drawing up the charter for William and Mary College, vented his wrath in the notorious reply to Blair's representation that the people of Virginia had souls as well as the people of England: 'Souls? damn your souls! make tobacco!' And not much more creditable to the state of public feeling rapidly becoming prevalent was the unsympathetic and disheartening treatment by Sir Robert Walpole of Bishop Berkeley's strenuous endeavours to establish a college in Bermuda: endeavours which Berkeley had finally to abandon after years of procrastinating promises on the part of the Prime Minister. But public help was not altogether withdrawn; George II gave £400 to help a college in New York, and £200 to help another at Philadelphia. It was, however, to private persons, to the Society for the Promotion of Christian Knowledge (founded 1698) and to the Church of England, that the promoters of these colleges appealed, not to Parliament. The Archbishop authorized a collection throughout the kingdom for them, and a sum of nearly £10,000 was received (1755).

(iii) *Education was extended to the children of the poor.* For instance, the Massachusetts laws already quoted make no distinctions: the townships were to provide schools open to all. There was a free school in the island of Bermuda as early as 1662, amongst its benefactors being Nicholas Ferrar, who gave it 'two shares of land in Pembroke tribe'; in South Carolina large legacies were left in 1721 and 1731 for the education of the poor of the Parish of St. Thomas. The Society for the Propagation of the Gospel in 1702, after drawing up a code of instructions for its missionaries, proceeded to draw up a similar code for the parochial schoolmasters whom it was to send out to the colonies and plantations.

(iv) *Education was closely associated with Religion.* The idea of 'secular' education was hardly conceived: in public education the religion of the colony was taught; or, if there were no established religion, then colleges and schools were denominational. Yale College, in Connecticut, was founded by Congregationalists; Princeton College, in New Jersey, by Presbyterians; Columbia College, in New York, and Philadelphia College, by members of the Church of England. The exclusiveness in some of them was uncompromising: at Yale the professors had to sign a Confession of Faith, and attendance by the students at public worship of the Church of England was punishable by fine, except for communicants on Christmas and Sacrament Days. At Harvard the charter was entirely free from any exclusive provisions; but, as a matter of fact, the curriculum in divinity avoided the works of Hooker, Usher, Jeremy Taylor, Chillingworth, and the other Anglican divines who contributed to 'the golden age of English theology.' The schools were usually attached to the churches, and the children passed naturally from them to membership of the various denominations. When Great Britain acquired Canada it was found that it was the activity of the Jesuits which had been effective for education: they had organized, side by side, their churches, their hospitals, and their schools.

(v) *Education was not very highly valued in the Plantation Colonies.* In Virginia the two attempts to establish a college ended in failure. The Henrico scheme fell through, and the William and Mary College never flourished. In spite of liberal endowments and the encouragement of leading men at home—Archbishop Wake was its Chancellor, for example—it was not supported by the gentry of Virginia. In 1724 it was—

'A college without a chapel, without a scholarship, without a statute; having a library without books, a President without a fixed salary, a Burgess without certainty of electors.'

In the West Indies the Propagation Society was unable to organize a college until 1830, although two fine estates in Barbados were bequeathed to it for this purpose by General Codrington so early as 1710: a school was all that the West Indian colonies were during that period capable of supporting.

Apathy.

The later years of the eighteenth century and the early years of the nineteenth were a period of general apathy as to Education, in England and with English people generally. The Universities had gradually declined in zeal and efficiency: although from time to time a scholar or a mathematician appeared, the range of studies was very narrow, and the tone of intellectual and moral life very unworthy of the traditions of the century before. In the college of Fisher and Ascham, of Falkland and Strafford, Wilberforce was told that as a young man of wealth and great prospects he need not trouble himself to study; and Wordsworth had to declare that he himself 'was not for that hour, nor for that place.' The Grammar Schools were given over to a pedantic routine; and, although the Christian Knowledge Society supported about 500 schools, the Bishop of Norwich asserted in 1810 that 'nearly two-thirds of the children of the poor had little or no education.' A change was imminent, however, which was definitely, but slowly, to take Englishmen back to their former high position.

In 1807 the British and Foreign School Society for undenominational Schools was established; and the Church of England founded the National Society in 1811, which aimed at planting a good school in every parish in the kingdom. Still, progress was slow; by 1833 the former Society had only 160 schools, and the latter only 690, in the 11,000 parishes of England and Wales. In that year the Government made its first timid grant; in 1839 the Committee of Privy Council on Education was formed, and by 1870 there were nearly 2,000,000 children in the National Society's Schools. In 1870 elementary education was made compulsory, and the efforts of voluntary societies were supplemented by State action.

Present Condition.

In the colonies the apathy of this period had but little effect, in consequence of our empire at that time consisting chiefly of the plantation-colonies of the West Indies, and settlements like Canada and the Cape, which were in a very rudimentary stage of growth. When the English-speaking colonies attained greater advancement the apathy was past; and they have one and all most thoroughly participated in the progress indicated. Indeed it may be said that they have anticipated it; for several of the colonies were beforehand with the mother-country in recognising the right of all children to have some education, and the great advantage to society in there being opportunity for some children to have the best education that can be given.

In every English-speaking colony there is now a complete apparatus for education, at least in outline. Universities and High Schools for both boys and girls are supported by endowments or Government subsidies, or by both of these. Elementary education is universally provided for: even the sparsely inhabited districts of New South Wales are not allowed to be outside its range, as teachers are appointed to travel from place to place when necessary. In most of the colonies the Elementary system is based on four principles: it is (1) compulsory, (2) secular, (3) free, (4) directed by the central authority. In some of the colonies provision is being made for technical education at the public charge. In the larger colonies there are schools of medicine and law attached to the Universities, so that the whole range of education is covered, and resort to Europe rendered a luxury, not a necessity, even for professional men. The Universities are upon the Scottish model, not upon the English: the students are not resident under discipline, unless they choose to enter the Halls established in the University towns by several of the Churches. When school and college days are over, the pursuit of learning and science is encouraged by societies after the model of those in Great Britain. New South Wales, for example, has a Royal Society, a Medical, a Linnaean, and an Art Society. Several of the colonies which are too small to support a University give liberal exhibitions to enable sons of residents to proceed to British Universities.

Educational Federation.

There is still a double tie between the colonies and home in educational machinery. Not a few of the higher posts in their Universities are filled by men invited from Great Britain to the colonies for that purpose; and not a few of their students resort, sometimes after passing through their own Universities, to Oxford and Cambridge. Both of these Universities have power by their new statutes to affiliate Colonial and Indian Universities or Colleges, under which residence at the latter counts for part of the required residence in the former. Four Universities are already formally affiliated with the University of Oxford. There is at Cambridge a Canadian Club and an Australasian Club; and there are nearly always men from the Cape and the West Indies in residence. The famous Medical School of Edinburgh is, however, perhaps the chief resort of colonial youth, as advanced medical studies require more apparatus than the colonies can well supply, and medicine and surgery have only lately become an effective part of the education offered at the English Universities. Many go to the London hospital medical schools, and many law students resort to the Inns of Court. The Royal College of Physicians and the Royal College of Surgeons of England have gone so far as to accept the diplomas of the Australian Colleges as qualifications for practice in England. There is not, however, reciprocity between the Bar of England and of Australia, nor even between the Bars of the different colonies.

In the wider sense of 'education' as covering the whole of life it is sufficient to say that two great instruments of culture are very effective throughout the empire.

The *Press* is a far-reaching and complicated mechanism for the diffusion of knowledge. Most leading colonial clubs take in some English daily papers,—delivered in batches, of course,—while all the weekly and monthly and quarterly journals of reputation are taken in the centres of colonial life. On the other hand, colonists have themselves organized an extensive press; daily papers in the towns, and weekly or bi-weekly papers everywhere. At the Colonial Institute in London 170 journals are taken in regularly from all parts of the empire. The colonial newspaper is edited with a definite belief that colonists have their wits about them, and use them, and a smartness closely akin to that of the American press is an almost universal characteristic—in attempt at least.

Travel, becoming easier, less irksome, and less expensive every year, gives all colonists who have inherited or earned a few hundreds an opportunity of seeing the rock from which they were hewn, and they are not slow to take advantage of it; while Englishmen in increasing numbers go out to study these new communities for themselves. Lord Rosebery set a good example to young men with ambitions of public usefulness; and soon it will be difficult for purely insular persons to look beyond aldermanic chairs in town or county councils. Members of either House who desire to be heard with authority on questions ranging above cattle-disease or incidence of highway rates must have looked farther afield than their own counties; and certainly the direct control of colonial affairs at the Colonial Office can hardly be again, as a thing of course, entrusted to a man who has not had some experience of the lands and the peoples with which he is concerned.

Of the *material* of education, so to speak, little need be said. That grand common possession, our language, places at the disposal of colonists, as at our own, the treasures of our literature and the discoveries of science. Colonial genius will no doubt be overshadowed by the mass of home *literature* for long; not only by the great classical writings of which they as well as we are the inheritors, but by the current literature and the higher literature of the passing generation. In *science* they at present contribute new material chiefly: but in this field the levelling of intellect will tell, and they have special opportunities in some fields of research. In *art* they are at the greatest disadvantage. The picture-galleries and the sculpture-galleries of Europe must ever remind them that they are offspring, or rather, later stages, of an older civilization than their own. Science gives her riches in accumulation to the succeeding generations. But Art is more reserved, in that to some generations she gives little or none; more free, in that upon some she confers gifts which she never after exceeds. Choice engravings, accurate photographs of rare old buildings, and careful casts of famous statues, must be gratefully accepted as their temporary resource by the colonies till their own full development comes, or until by their wealth they can persuade Europe to part with some of the treasures of her art-galleries. Perhaps the decreased value of English land, the owners of which possess so great a stock of treasures, will in time tell for the advantage of colonial governments and municipalities in this way. At present, when it is said that the level of education and of intelligence is higher in a colony than at home, we must acknowledge this, and yet allow for a certain lack on their part of many 'educational advantages' not scheduled by any Government department, which our old-world people enjoy, or may enjoy. It is the lack of this touch which gives a certain hardness to the colonial character; even when a colonist visiting Europe is evidently endeavouring to appreciate a picture-gallery there is frequently something which strikes harshly on his English friends of the same standing. Intellect without experience cannot give judgment, in its special sense as a kind of 'taste.'

Education for Natives.

The education of people of Native Race was at the outset associated so closely with their religious conversion that a separate treatment is impossible in the early period of the history. A few instances of the actual connexion of the instruction of the natives with the instruction of the children of the colonists will suffice to make it clear how far removed the early colonists were from despising the coloured peoples as not capable of instruction as distinguished from conversion.

The Royal Letter of James I recommending the proposed Henrico College, speaks of 'propagating the Gospell amongst Infidells, by the erecting of some Churches and Schooles for the education of the children of those Barbarians.' Sir Edwin Sandys, Treasurer of the Virginia Company, received an anonymous donation for 'the training of Indian children from seven to twelve years of age in the knowledge of the Christian faith,' and then 'until they were twenty-one in the knowledge and practice of some trade, when they were to be admitted to an equality of liberty and privileges with the native English of Virginia.'

Governor Yeardley made a special treaty with the successor of Powhatan for the introduction of Indian children into Henrico College. At Harvard also provision for them was to be made; and the first building actually erected on the college ground was 'the Indian college.' It was at Harvard that the missionary, John Eliot, had his Bible and tracts in the Indian language printed for use in his work.

Again, sixty years later, when William and Mary College was instituted, Robert Boyle endowed an extra professorship at the college for the conversion and instruction of the Indians.

The education of the Negro slaves was, as a general rule, forbidden, or at least not promoted or encouraged, in the English colonies. The plantations were scattered at considerable distances; the children were set to tasks of some simple sort, such as picking up stones, or weeding, at a very early age; and on Sundays and such Saturday holidays as the negroes had, there were the plots on which they grew their own food to be cultivated. A Catechist of the Propagation Society opened a school in New York for negroes in 1704, and the Society had schools on the Codrington estates in Barbados. But of education apart from worship there was practically none in the plantation colonies. 'If you attempt to teach the negroes to read and write,' said the British Governor of Guiana to a chaplain in 1817, 'I will banish you.'

In India the apathy as to education at home prevented our seriously entering upon any education policy until the middle of this century. Until 1813 the Company hindered any attempt to 'Europeanize' the natives of India: in 1833 came Macaulay's method of educating some of the upper classes; and then followed the complete change which has issued in the system which is fast spreading over the whole peninsula. There are about three and a half million scholars and students; this is only a fraction of the children of India, but it is twice as large a number as that of ten years ago. Scarcely a tenth of these are girls, however, India not being yet ready for female education on an extensive scale. In almost every district there is a higher-class school, where English, and Sanskrit or Arabic, occupy the position of Latin and Greek in European schools. There are six Universities, several Government colleges, and many excellent colleges aided by Government grants, but mainly supported and manned by the Missionary Societies. For many years the Missionary Societies held the field in education, Carey's College at Serampore and the Presbyterian Colleges at Madras having earned special honour in Indian history.

In our Crown colonies education has become one of the chief objects of Government care since the increased attention to it at home. In Jamaica, for example, there were 19,000 scholars on the books in 1866; there were 75,000 in 1888: there is now a Government School under inspection, and taught partly by trained teachers, to every 800 of the 600,000 people in the colony.

II. Religion.

Among Colonists.

The general impression formed by a survey of the religious condition of the European people in the Spanish and Portuguese colonies is, that religion has suffered in quality from removal from the centre of Christendom, and from a lowering of moral tone due to the enervating influence of climate and the intermixture with heathen people. The history of Portuguese Christianity is undoubtedly that of a decline, and the accounts given by the South American republics agree in showing a condition below that of the Roman Catholic countries of Europe. In the French colonies, the decay of the influence of the Roman Church is only a reflection of its decay in France, but it goes even farther, for the reasons just indicated.

The religious element in British colonization has on the whole been continuously present, but in varying degrees. There never was a time when colonization totally lacked it: and as a rule it was incorporated with it in about the same degree as it was vitally operative at home. The Hakluyt records show it always present in the early stages, and men eminent for piety at home were amongst the chief fosterers of early colonies. A Royal Ordinance was attached to the Virginian Charter to the following effect :

'That the said presidents, councils, and the ministers, should provide that the Word and Service of God be preached, planted, and used, not only in the said colonies, but also, as much as might be, among the savages bordering among them, according to the rites and doctrines of the Church of England.'

The expedition contained a chaplain, Robert Hunt, who received official authority from the Archbishop of Canterbury by the special recommendation of Hakluyt. How amid the log-cabins of James Town worship was performed with a sail for a roof and a bar of wood nailed to two trees for a pulpit, until presently 'a homely thing like a barne' was constructed, we read in John Smith's narratives. In these rude tabernacles, however, 'we had,' he says, 'our Prayers daily, with our Homily on Sundaies.' When the colony was settled the Assembly assigned tithes to the clergy, imposed penalties on absence from public worship, and on breaches of the law of rest for the Sabbath, and otherwise clearly and definitely assumed that Virginia was to be like home.

In the New England States the refugees organized their churches according to their own ideas, but the local Governments had control, while in the Middle States religion was organized for the most part without the direction of the political Governments. Help from home was never quite lacking. A company to promote religion in New England was formed by Act of the Long Parliament in 1649, and a general collection on its behalf ordered by Cromwell ; and this same company afterwards enjoyed the support and counsel of Robert Boyle. In Queen Anne's reign Dr. Bray was the chief instrument in founding the oldest existing societies for this purpose —the Society for Promoting Christian Knowledge, and the Society for the Propagation of the Gospel. Of the five persons present at the first recorded meeting of the former, a peer, two lawyers, and a soldier, met to deliberate with Dr. Bray; the scholar and soldier who founded All Souls' Library at Oxford founded also a college in the West Indies of a clearly religious type and for mainly religious purposes. Bishop Berkeley tried for years to obtain a college for the North American colonies, but ineffectually, owing to the indifference of Walpole. The two most eminent Bishops of the eighteenth century, Butler and Wilson, were ardent supporters of religious enterprise for both colonists and native peoples. Even in the moral chaos of the convict settlement at Botany Bay in early days the religious element was there, and of a high quality. Mr. Payne, a very reserved writer, says (p. 168), 'The only civilizing element in the place was the presence of a devoted clergyman named Johnson, who had voluntarily accompanied the first batch of convicts.' Johnson laboured unceasingly among the convicts: he built a church for them at his own expense, although he is obliged to add that 'they soon burnt it down.' And so it has continued. Every branch of the Christian Society which has flourished in England has been able to reproduce itself abroad; and on the whole we may say that, as a reproduction of British Christianity in its varieties, and to a very considerable degree in its range of influence, the work has been done. In most of the chief colonies all the great branches have a representation, and usually in proportion to the numbers of those of their members, not who remain at home, but who have taken part in emigration. Of course there is some change in relative strength, some shaking loose from old associations, and forming of new ones; and it would seem, if we take the English people in America into account as well, that Methodism has been most successful in gathering those who have made a change. The *State* Church has of course lost many adherents in colonies where there is no religion 'as by law established,' but not so many as might have been expected in our present colonies, where the 'Church of England,' as they insist on calling it still, has on the whole more adherents than any of the divisions ranked as 'Nonconformists' at home.

In the British colonies religion is affected by the scattered character of the occupation and the comparative isolation of many of the colonists; but even more by the general absorption in industrial life, and a considerable materialization of thought and life. Hence we do not find either (1) that striking spiritual power has been developed among them as a whole, or (2) that there is so large a residuum estranged from religion by the absence of opportunities to discharge the elementary duties of orderliness, thrift, temperance, and mutual help. There is a greater general satisfaction with everyday life, on the one hand, and less call for militant evangelization on the other. That the Christian virtues flourish in personal character and family life is not, however, to be denied because the zeal which works out of doors is less needed. As the towns grow larger, and the residuary class at one end and the idle class at the other grow larger, the experience of Europe may be repeated, and an aggressive character be called out in men and women whose ardour is latent as yet.

But on the *intellectual* side a competent observer, Bishop Moorhouse, has publicly expressed his opinion that religious interests are on the whole more active in the colonies than among the industrial classes at home. The problems raised by religion, and their treatment by the intelligence of men, find interested readers and thinkers in many a remote township or solitary agricultural station. Such are some of the men who pass lonely evenings over their log-fires with books and newspapers of whom the Bishop said, 'It is a bracing exercise, and a keen delight, I can assure you, to pour out the deepest thoughts of one's heart to such an audience of thoughtful men, so still, so eager and appreciative. Thought is alive, feeling is intense with them.'

Religious Federation.

Religion contributes a powerful element in the union of home and the colonies. The Federations of the Churches form an important mechanism of sympathy and common interest. The gathering of nearly 150 Bishops of the Church of England and her daughter-churches in a Pan-Anglican Conference every ten years under the Archbishop of Canterbury is a federative event of great effect—the political barrier between us and the United States being in this rendered inoperative by union for the high purposes of religion. And the majority of the colonial Bishops at present are English clergy, the important dioceses especially desiring to place themselves under the direction of clergy of standing and experience gained in work at home. The Presbyterian churches have had conferences; the Methodists are accustomed to send delegates from home to colonial conferences and to receive colonial delegates here. Even the essentially detached character of the Congregationalist system proves to be not incompatible with mutual aid and counsel by utilizing the travel of eminent preachers from time to time in the colonies, and even occasionally by arranging expressly for visitations of this kind. The Roman Church is, of course, federative in influence, but it looks to a centre outside the empire.

Religion and the Native Races.

The records of the missionary enterprise of the Christian Church since the opening out of the way to the East and the discovery of the New World form a chapter of history of special interest, variety, and depth of meaning. It must necessarily awaken very different feelings in different minds, and a summary of a kind likely to be satisfying to all is out of the question. Elements vital to some are dubious to others; but though the relative importance of both efforts and results cannot be estimated in the absence of agreement as to a common measure, there are some aspects which can be dealt with by history as an investigation of events purely secular. The *ultimate issues* of these enterprises may be in another world, but they have had *immediate issues* within the realm of things strictly belonging to the life that now is. If holiness and righteousness are the ways to God and the results of conversion to the faith of Christ, it can be seen whether men have walked in these ways and shown fruits of such a faith while still on their road towards the portals beyond which history cannot penetrate. The moral and social lives of the peoples influenced by missionary enterprise form, therefore, an objective study which history can estimate, and without a consideration of them no history is either candid or complete.

In this way some objective results may be given: there may be others; the following are offered as indications and outlines of the influences which have been exerted.

(i) THE EXHIBITION OF CHARACTER.

There is good reason for placing this as the foremost influence of all: for the preachers of Christ have themselves placed His character in the front of their teaching, and their own influence has to a great extent followed from the exhibition to the Nature-peoples of their own character as influenced by His.

The range of choice for examples is marvellously abundant: before every mind there arise at once memories of some devoted men and women; before each, perhaps, some chosen heroes or heroines set firm in regard and love. There are limitations in our capacity for admiration, and these limitations are reached, to some of us, again and again when we think over the romance of missionary history. St. Francis Xavier and Henry Martyn; John Eliot and William Carey; Adoniram Judson and Alexander Duff; and many a noble wife with name indelibly associated with her husband's,—do we need to wish men and women to be better than these? There have gone to every part of our empire where Nature-peoples have been touched, men of the finest moral qualities—some rough in manners, others of the highest refinement, but in the force of moral and spiritual energy alike. Every Native Church is built on some one or more of these as foundation stones; some of them laid in short lives and heroic deaths, others in labours continued from youth to advanced old age.

If these characters had been only grand their objective influence would have been less. But they were *grand on simple lines*, and Selwyn and Patteson, the flower of Eton and Oxford and Cambridge, washing and nursing their Polynesian boys, are only like the rougher-bred shoemakers and factory-hands, such as Carey and Livingstone, in their inability to regard kindness between one human being and another as anything else than both the law of nature and the law of Christ. Let us sum up their virtues and analyse their ethics, if we can: their characters have lived before these peoples, and the Aryan at his highest has moved among the Mongols and the Negroes, and that directly in the name of the supreme object of his worship.

(ii) The Native races owe to the religious preachers and their mere presence among them the IDEA *of the* UNITY *of the whole race*. From their contact with the white man apart from missionaries they could never have drawn this inference. Of course, some races offer no particular welcome to this idea: the Brahmans probably despise us in their hearts as outside caste, and refuse to admit us within their sacred pale. But taking a broad view of the race, the lifting up of all peoples to the level of the foremost has no more potent instrument than this *idea* that they *can* be lifted up. In classic antiquity men thought that Nature might and did produce many human 'races.' Christian civilization has been the first to insist on *humanity* as implying a reality which has no counterpart in the cognate conception 'animality.' A unity is held to underlie the human race; a unity which, though unrecognised in the past, must be made really operative in the future. To invite into a common inheritance of the earth and of all that civilization can give is perceived to be the vocation of the missionary; he indeed goes farther and proclaims a still more powerful idea in the unity of immortal destiny. Thus the unity of the race and a sense of community of interest between races hitherto sundered is being produced by the preaching of a single gospel for mankind.

(iii) AN UNSELFISH AIM after THEIR good, persistently and continuously pursued, has been exhibited to the Native races.

Among all the fierce competitions of the new-comers for the wealth the natives may have possessed or for the products of the lands where they lived, the natives might well stand aghast and alarmed at the 'Christian's thirst for gold.'

The Spaniards in America cannot have appeared to the cowering and plundered natives to have derived their power from a Good Being. The 'dregs of Spain' indeed were upon them, and suicide was over and over again their refuge. 'But,' writes Mr. Doyle (*America*, p. 30), 'there was at least one class of Spaniards who were not merely free from blame in this matter, but deserve the highest praise. For all that could be done to protect the natives, and to bring their grievances before the Government in Spain, and to improve their condition in every way, was done by the clergy. It is scarcely too much to say that no class of men ever suffered so much and toiled so unsparingly for the good of their fellow-creatures as the Spanish priests and missionaries in America.' This recognition of goodness is in its concluding sentence relatively excessive: but it is sufficient to show that amidst all the oppressions and villanies perpetrated upon the natives of America there was in Christian missionaries one set of men devoted to the natives' good. And it is the same in our own colonies in their early stages. The whalers who harassed New Zealand, the sandal-wood wretches of Polynesia, the convicts of Tasmania, the alcohol vendors who overrode native chieftains in South Africa and drenched to madness and death their tribesmen, stand at the extreme end, not only of European barbarity, but of all barbarity whatever, for there was in them the mercilessness of selfish greed, not the fanatical rejoicing in the blood of enemies. And amidst all these darkest doings Christian missionaries ever kept pressing in, and, as men of the Cross and men of the Bible, soothed and turned the spirit of despair and fear and hatred that seized upon the black men's minds in the early days of their contact with our fellow-countrymen. All these things are as much matters of fact as any which human history has to show. Let the early history of New Zealand be read: or let the autobiographical account of some men working in New Guinea and the New Hebrides Islands in the closing years of this century be read candidly, and the meaning of their lives as a demonstration of unselfish devotion to the good of the natives stands out clear. If they have taught them nothing else they have not left home and struggled there in vain.

Of course, to some extent, much missionary work has a character of officialism and of routine, which presents to the native mind the missionary as an ordinary professional man. But there are hundreds of lives which were not by routine, and which no sense of professional duties could have supported, even if it had given them their beginning. And lives of this kind have salted the whole history of Europeans. Even the Red Indians of North America have always had a succession of white men to reverence and trust. When men and women have learned the lesson of 'the washing of the disciples' feet,' and have gone out in that spirit, as in every colony some have done for every Church, the native has known it, and he has been partially redeemed from despair.

(iv) A HIGH TONE in DAILY LIFE. The *example* of some *merchants* and of some *Government officials* has been very effective as an educational influence, especially as they exhibit the standard at which men may be expected to aim. It is they who have shown how business could be conducted with honour, how servants could be employed with consideration, how want could be relieved with kindness; and when they have been able to take families with them they have shown them the Teutonic *unit of social life*, the '*home.*' These examples are of immeasurable importance, though their effect can hardly be regarded as penetrating so deeply as does the exhibition of self-devotion for others' good. The well-ordered lay household is in a colony a pearl of great price among the native peoples; but its place is intermediary in the order of ideas between the native's heathenism and the unselfish faith of the missionary. These in combination have often worked wonders; and in India especially the share of Christian laymen in drawing the Native mind towards union with what is best in the English mind constitutes a noble record. Is there to-day a fairer purpose open to a layman than that of living a just, upright, moral, and benevolent life as a merchant or a magistrate among these sensitive and impressible races? To demonstrate to them what integrity and industry can do is in every layman's power. The drawback to the organization of missions lies just in this, that they institute a delegation of functions, some of which ought not to be delegated. The missionary is taken as the semi-official representative of elementary virtues which the whole white community should show. An occasional subscription sets up the mission-station, and then frequently indifference and inactivity on the part of laymen are held to be justified thereby, or at least condoned.

Still, we may set down as one great influence of religion the setting before the natives examples of religious and moral men in mercantile and official positions living amongst them, and especially by such as have households, godly and orderly. Respect for law in the house and in the colony; temperance and chastity: these are virtues which the native can appreciate: he despises and loathes the white man who has them not, and is, by every testimony of travellers, docile and grateful to those who live by them.

There are some two hundred Protestant missionary societies in Britain, Germany, Switzerland, France, Denmark, Holland, and America, besides those of the Roman Church. Every movement of our colonization is now accompanied sooner or later by a religious embassy: often indeed, as in Fiji, Bechuanaland, Burmah, and New Guinea—to speak of extensions since 1870 only—the religious movement was made first.

Two isolated points may be noted :—

(1) The religious enterprise has *exceeded the bounds of Empire*. The civilization of Europe has not been confined

to the places where it has set up political sway: religion is taken to be part of civilization. While some societies are most anxious to recognise the imperial bond, and to make real our common citizenship, others, leaving this to those already in that field, take interest in China and Japan and the lands of Islam. Like commerce, Christianity ignores colour and government and clime.

(2) The amount of knowledge of our empire and of native races of the world possessed by ordinary English people is not really extensive: but it is considerable, and what there is has come to them more through the missionary societies in which they take part, than from any other source. Geography gives a start, but the races of mankind are mostly known to English people of the classes who do not travel, from the addresses and lectures of the missionaries who are at home for rest or in retirement. Thus we may say that the knowledge necessary for the proper exercise of citizenship is supplied to a great mass of the people of Great Britain chiefly by their religious organizations.

III. THE STATE AND RELIGION.

We distinguish three attitudes.

> STATE DIRECTION: For example, Spain and Portugal as lay arms of the Roman Church, with an Inquisition against heretics applied in Mexico more uncompromisingly than in Spain itself; England, while possessed of an undivided Church, sending out chaplains as a matter of course; New South Wales starting with its Government grants for chaplains; the West Indies with their endowed bishoprics.
>
> OPPOSITION: Government damping effort, and standing still when movement was desired by individuals: as from Berkeley's time throughout the eighteenth century, and especially in India until 1813.
>
> NEUTRALITY: Government standing aloof, but placing missionaries on the footing of ordinary subjects, and their churches and schools on that of ordinary property,

entitled to the ordinary protection of persons following lawful pursuits. This is rapidly becoming the universal method. Religious work is done after the analogy of our colonizing work in Africa, the 'Chartered Companies' finding their parallels in the 'Missionary Societies' of the home country. It should be observed that some colonies have begun to take an independent part; Canada, Nova Scotia, Australia, New Zealand, all have voluntary societies at work among native races within their borders, and even farther afield.

CHAPTER XII.

SOME GENERAL REFLECTIONS.

British Foreign Policy.

IN relation to the general history of the United Kingdom of Great Britain and Ireland we have seen how largely her foreign relations have been affected by the contest for commerce and empire beyond Europe. No one who rises from even a rapid perusal of Professor Seeley's *Expansion of England* can ever again look upon our history as determined by insular and internal influences only. It is said that we must be on our guard against the book carrying us too far; we are told that its formula is not complex enough, and that it only fits selected facts. This objection is not to be summarily disposed of. But the view is not peculiar to Professor Seeley; it is the view of the historians of the country most concerned in the contest. Michelet and Duruy say the same thing. They tell us that France and England entered upon the path of colonial enterprise together, and, *because they found they were rivals*, struck at each other's heart. France supported Cromwell against Charles I, Charles II against Cromwell, and James II against William of Orange. England could find no similar means of injuring France, for France suppressed her own internal feuds by the expulsion of Protestants: but we refused to allow Spain to open her colonies to France; we endeavoured to secure an unfair predominance on the seas; we compelled France to renounce her ally, Prussia, whom we assisted with our gold; and when she drew into alliance with Austria it was in reversal of her own policy of two hundred years' standing. France had once been the defender of liberty against Spain and the Emperor, and it was to her a fatal change of policy. It was her own recently-developed political absolutism that lured her along this ruinous path, but it did not prevent her from helping our republican colonies, and when her Revolution came, and she resumed the lead of Europe, we were still her foe, implacable, until Trafalgar and Waterloo ended the contest, and then there came a peace between us which has never been actively disturbed. From Germany Dr. Geffcken expresses the same view; every war since Cromwell between Great Britain and France or Holland has had as its guiding motive *colonial policy* (*British Empire*, p. 63).

In our general foreign policy in Europe the Peace of 1815 practically closed our period of activity. We guaranteed Belgium, and fought for Greece and for Turkey; but the cases of Belgium and Greece were peculiar, and we uphold Turkey for reasons connected with Asia rather than with Europe. The grounds for any other intervention among European nations would have been so platonic that it is no wonder that a policy of non-intervention replaced that of activity in the favour of the commercial classes, who before had been the mainstay of war. And looking at Europe only this policy has justified itself completely. When we look farther afield, however, we see that our non-intervention must be limited to non-intervention in French and Italian and German disputes; if we look outside Europe, over the world, such a policy has no meaning, except on the assumption that we are prepared to see our empire dismembered if any nation should choose to move. Thus the views of both non-interventionists and of those who have insisted on England being active in the councils of the world, are explained when we look to the quarter towards which each party is directing its gaze. As it stands now, it is difficult to imagine any purely European difficulty arising that would call us to arms. An attack upon Belgium hardly would do so, nor upon Denmark, nor even Holland; if they cannot stand alone it is difficult to persuade us now that Britain ought to prop them up, even if it were possible. The centre of gravity of our interest is certainly in our own kingdom, but as no Power desires to subjugate us in our home, our anxieties are only for the empire beyond, and our foreign policy is bound up with that.

Economic History.

Here the study of our colonial development is essential. The new sources of supply and raw material, the new demand for manufactures, the new fields for capital and labour, have affected interest and profits and wages, all the material of life at home, and have added new industrial communities to the realm. Our policy has been affected by the political union of these colonies with ourselves. An economic bond was attached to it, and theories of monopoly were secure in popular favour.

In the development of our industrial organization to its present leading position in the world our colonies, plantations, and factories have had great share. Other causes were operative in England, of course, such as that organization of capital in which, as Professor Marshall points out, we showed the way, and that organization of labour by means of money payments instead of dues, which rendered labour mobile, and therefore ready for the new era of inventions and improved processes. It is of England, taken together with her colonies, including America, that it is said that 'she has set the tone of modern business as well as of modern politics' (Prof. Marshall, *Economics*, p. 37).

Our colonies, again including America, have contributed, and are contributing, to the development of industrial processes. Not only has America already contributed more than her share of mechanical inventions, but in the invention of methods of combination for production and for trade she seems to be destined to take the lead amongst English communities. The powers of capital have never been so vigorously and effectively wielded in commerce and industry as they have been in America. The forms of activity long displayed in England by Jewish capitalists have been taken up and developed in America by English and German combinations. Our present colonies are as yet too young to take a leading position, but the signs point to their following in the vivacity and dexterity of American speculation and organization.

Political Science.

Political science has a rich field of material in the history of the political institutions which have been developed from the English model, and exist in great variety where other peoples than those of English blood have to be taken into account. And fields for fresh research are offered in the changes in social institutions due to changes of climate, to mixture of German, Dutch, and other European blood with English, to a rise in the level of comfort, to a freedom from ancient custom and from the slowly yielding habitudes of the Old World.

Knowledge and Art.

In the realm of knowledge and of art, as has been already said, no great achievements on the part of our colonies are to be recorded, nor is it easy to maintain that the historian of European philosophy or science or art would need to write a separate chapter for the colonial contribution up to the end of our present century. Materials for new science and new art have been presented in abundant variety, especially in new aspects of physical nature, in the opportunities of a period of great activity for the display of the vigour and energy of men, and in the knowledge gained of man himself in the new regions opened out. But that much of this material for knowledge or art is dependent upon empire, and that it might not have been attained by us without our having empire, is not certain; indeed, the contrary is shown by the fact that it is taken advantage of quite as much by the Germans as by ourselves. In knowledge of the languages, religions, and characters of the peoples of India, where we ought to have an advantage by reason of the great number of educated Englishmen who reside there and of Hindus who come here, our superiority over the Germans is by no means beyond dispute. But the time may come when the English will be first in interest, sympathy, and knowledge of these new peoples, their thoughts and ways, their needs and capacities, by reason of the responsibility which has been placed upon Englishmen, and upon them alone.

Religion.

At the opening of his work on Political Economy (*Economics*, p. 1) Professor Marshall writes: 'The two great forming agencies of the world's history have been the religious and the economic. Here and there the ardour of the military or the artistic spirit has been for a while predominant; but religious and economic influences have nowhere been displaced from the front rank even for a time; and they have nearly always been more important than all others put together.'

This weighty utterance finds signal verification in the history of English colonization; every word of it could be proved to be rigorously accurate as applied to this great chapter of European history. In the infancy of our colonization both of these agencies were operative, and they are both at work today. There are many who follow with interest the development of our colonies as fields for the employment of capital and labour; there are others who have not been moved to any personal interest in them until colonization is presented as a part of the provision for the religious education of the world. The spirit of military and naval conquest had its day, and has now passed by; the spirit of Art has not yet appeared as an agency, but the spirit of Science is very effective. But to-day, as in the days of Elizabeth, it is chiefly the economic and the religious impulses which draw Englishmen to participate in this movement.

The Six Great Empires.

Since 1815 the world has tended to aggregation of nationalities into great States, or of hitherto separated portions of nationalities. Of these six stand in the front rank of influence, and much must depend upon their mutual relationship and upon their several developments. The West of Europe contributes three—the British Empire, France, Germany; America, the United States; Asia, the Chinese Empire; and besides these, there is the semi-European, semi-Asiatic power, Russia.

Of these the UNITED STATES has hitherto endeavoured to live in a ring fence, with occasional demonstrations of hostility when other nations have threatened American territory. But this isolation cannot be entirely and consistently maintained. Seventy years ago President Monro enunciated the principle, which his successor formulated definitely, that the United States could not suffer European Governments to hinder the free development of important parts of the New World. The protest was mainly against the attempts of Spain to coerce her rebellious or already revolted colonies. Later the Americans entered a protest against a French occupation of Mexico, and no doubt they would, in some irregular manner, have prevented it, even if the Mexicans had failed to do so; they would not allow Spain to sell Cuba to any of the great empires if she wished; they could hardly suffer Denmark to part with Curaçao either; nor would they allow Hayti to settle its own fate if it desired a European protectorate; they have intervened in the Sandwich Islands sufficiently to prevent any protectorate being set up there; and have actually entered themselves into conjoint protectorship, with Britain and Germany, of Samoa. It is of very great importance to notice that the character of the United States population is becoming very cosmopolitan; the tables of immigration 1882-9 show an annual average of immigrants as follows:—

Great Britain and Ireland	145,000	Hungary	13,000
		Denmark	8,000
Germany	135,000	Switzerland	7,000
Sweden	37,000	Poland	4,000
Italy	30,000	France	4,000
Russia	21,000	Netherlands	4,000
Austria	21,000	Belgium	2,000
Norway	16,000		

i. e. British were only about one-third[1].

[1] A table of nationalities for 1880 gives American born 29 millions, German 5, Irish 4¾, English, Scotch, and Welsh 2, British Canadians, French Canadians, Scandinavians, each about ⅓. Other Europeans 1¼ millions, men of colour 6½, Indians ¼, Chinese ¼.

RUSSIA is restless: she has not found her limits in Asia yet, and cannot rest excluded from the south of Europe, and so she moves forward by intrigue or by war.

GERMANY is now strong at home. She colonizes by furnishing colonists on an extensive scale. She is moving also for herself, although she comes into the field very late and without much opening. But in Africa at three points, in remote New Guinea and neighbouring islands, and through a share in the protection of Samoa, she is on the alert. If she should aim at a protectorate in the Malay peninsula, she has already a strong outpost of a commercial kind in her trading-houses in Bangkok: possibly we may see Siam become her India.

FRANCE is restless, too, not from growth of population, but from self-respect and pride [1]. She feels the loss of pride of place. She is conscious of having high capacity for government of the administrative order, and foreign commerce is an essential of her life. Frenchmen contemplate fondly the long roll of the French possessions, meagre though the value of each item may be. They desire to colonize: their eminent economists and leading public men ponder over it; but they have always in their hearts the fear that their colonization cannot be on a worthy scale, because they see the population of the home-country at a standstill. They declare, however, that there is to be a new France at home, and ask the world not to judge her only by the past. They do not wish the present position to be acquiesced in by Frenchmen, or accepted as final by England or the other nations.

The CHINESE Empire presents the great problem of all, for it is by no means clear how long the State will be able to control the people. The *awakening of China* is what their leading men speak of, and with no bated breath. The opening of her ports to European trade has already proved to be quite as much an opportunity for their own people to go forth as for Europeans to enter in. The mobility of labour becomes indeed a stupendous problem if any substantial

---

[1] The total emigration from France during the years 1879–88 was not 5000 a year; that from Italy was 56,000.

fraction of four hundred million people begin to move. This mobility is certainly setting in; the Chinaman already is prepared to go anywhere. Soon we may find that he goes everywhere. In America and Australia men are practically acknowledging that the Chinaman was right in closing the ports of his country against men of different civilization, for they are now reverting to his policy. American ports are already closed, and the immigration has fallen from 30,000 a year to the few hundreds who can and will pay the heavy dues; but there seems to be an instability about this method if the four hundred million people do really 'awake,' unless, indeed, another military and naval era sets in, to which the wars of the eighteenth century will appear but domestic quarrels as a prelude to more serious antagonism, not of nations but of races.

In relation to the other great empires the BRITISH EMPIRE occupies a unique position by its close intimacy with them all. By the Freedom of our Trade we keep open house for them, and they all come in and go out. This unique position is a consequence of our pre-eminence in industrial and commercial pursuits. Hegel (*Philosophy of History*, p. 475) thus defines our character, and therefore our function in the world:—

'The material existence of England is based on commerce and industry, and the English have undertaken the weighty responsibility of being the missionaries of civilization to the world; for their commercial spirit urges them to traverse every sea and land, to form connexions with barbarous peoples, to create wants and stimulate industry, and, first and foremost, to establish among them the constitutions necessary to commerce, viz. the relinquishment of a type of lawless violence, respect for property, and civility to strangers.'

This is exactly in accordance with the testimony of M. Ernest Michel, who went through our colonies in order to investigate the reasons for our success. Our practical sense, our readiness to try experiments, and to abandon them if not successful, only to resume with new determination to succeed, and the respect for moral law shown in our colonies, deeply impressed him. This temper for order and regularity and soberness in fact underlies our industry and gives it substance and stability. It is the very quality noted among her roving adventurers by Queen Elizabeth, their 'so good order of government, so good agreement, every man ready in his calling,' which was discovered at the outset of our investigation, and is still found to characterize English colonists at its close.

The progressive character of our home development in political liberty and order has been reflected in our imperial history. The following brief summary shows how the place of the State in our colonial enterprise has varied with the stage of growth of our political constitution at home:—

(i) The Adventure period: typified by Raleigh—the State favours and assists colonization.
(ii) Beginning of Imperial assertion: Cromwell—the State directs colonization.
(iii) The Empire a basis for Trade: Chatham—the State an instrument for extending Trade colonies.
(iv) Exploration: Cook — the State an instrument for discovery of new lands.
(v) Trade pure and simple: Cobden and Bright—the State dispensed with and colonies disregarded.
(vi) Discharge of Duty: Mill—the State again found necessary.
(vii) Imperialism recognised: Beaconsfield[1] — the State widened and England's imperial position re-asserted.

Rocks Ahead.

It is alleged, however, that the British Empire is itself unstable and insecure. We are told that our armaments are not on a scale which would enable us to defend ourselves, and that we are practically retaining our present position at the mercy of other nations kept asunder by jealousy. Should any two combine to attack us our empire is ruined[2]. This is of course

[1] Lord Beaconsfield's voice it was that turned the attention of England outwards again.—Baron v. Hübner, p. 498.
[2] The comparative estimate of *Expenditure* is as follows:—
United Kingdom, *Army and Navy*, $38\frac{1}{2}$ millions a year (including

a current opinion in many branches of the fighting services: and not only there; so unbiassed an observer as Dr. Geffcken is as uncompromising a prophet of woe for us as any Admiral or General of our own. If France and Russia, he says—the nations most likely to ally themselves and to have ground of attack on us—were to join, and Germany and the United States were to stand aloof, our empire could not be preserved. This requires serious consideration from Englishmen. In presence of such a danger not a word should be written that would interfere with any citizen taking the right course with regard to supporting or opposing proposals for increased war expenditure. If we do not organize, and organize well, we shall certainly lose a great deal; if either (1) we are tired of our empire, or (2) we yearn so entirely for the tranquil enjoyments of peaceful trade that we will not organize a competent army or maintain a competent navy, with apparatus of coaling-stations and all such auxiliaries, our place in the world is lost. We have seen that it was defective organization, as a consequence of lack of public spirit, that lost France the first battle (La Hogue) in the great series of wars with England. French historians are unanimous in confessing that the loss of fine prospects in Canada and in India was due to unskilfulness of generals and admirals, to insubordination and lack of discipline among soldiers and sailors, and to a general enfeeblement of the military and naval departments of State. Disaster came upon France as a consequence of national carelessness and indolence under the rule of the unworthy successors of Colbert and Louvois.

On our part our successes gave us a force and a dash which proved irresistible. Heavy sacrifices of money were made, but we had determined not to stop until we were secure in the field. If the force and dash and the sacrifices should be on the side of our opponents now, and we should have the lethargy

some new debts); India, 17; the Colonies, 2; total British Empire, 57. France, 36 millions; Germany, 32; Russian, 29; United States (1886), 12. The expensiveness of our system and the dispersed character of our territory make these figures no correct measure of our comparative weakness. It looks as if it were not a question of raising more money, but of spending it differently.

and dulness and self-indulgence which lost France the fight from the very start, then England and her democracy would only be walking on the path which France and her court and effete aristocracy walked along two centuries ago, and the result for us now would be what it then was for them. Instances might easily be multiplied: Wellington driving the French out of the Peninsula; the Southern States laid at the mercy of the North; France at the feet of Germany in 1871; Dupleix driven out of India by Clive, are all examples of organization being the secret of success.

There are some considerations, going not far from the root of the matter, which may be taken into account by any who feel a shock at having to suppose that an empire and an influence constructed by gradual and apparently natural processes during three centuries are liable to overthrow by the chances of a single war. It may appear that Nature can produce nothing secure; that after all, wise men may stimulate and heroes may carry out great enterprises for generations together, and yet that the weakness or folly of a single generation may lose the whole. Certainly it is difficult to limit powers of destruction. York Minster was nearly ruined in a single night, and by one madman's act. But, on the whole, the weight of probability is against the possibility of such a catastrophe for our empire. We can see how it was built up; the piles and beams of the structure are evident, and the force that oversets such an edifice must be itself no mere national rivalry or sentimental jealousy on the part of other empires, but an overpowering necessity on their part to develop in directions where we stand in their way.

(1) The *military era tends to pass away, and to give place to the industrial*, and it is on the lines of industry that contests between nations are now likely to be waged. If France gave way before Germany, it was partly because Germany's industrial progress had fed her people and nerved them with an almost unconscious strength. And no military weakness on our part, of a temporary nature, could suddenly ruin our industrial position. It could do so only if the weakness became permanent. If it came from disregard of facts,

from indifference, from neglect, from national cowardice, a series of military defeats would without fail leave the empire a shattered wreck. But a single 'military' catastrophe could not do it; the folly of being unprepared would be our reproach, and it would have to be atoned for severely. But if the national heart was strong and sound, not one, nor two, nor three disasters would finally depose us from our place. The disaster which ruins comes upon nations from within rather than from without; prosperity has often acted as a cankerworm—Tyre, Carthage, Venice, what are they now? It is upon our national character as well as upon the strength of external forces that our permanent stability depends.

(2) Too much stress must not be laid on the political bond. Our 'empire' might be broken up, *our 'colonization' would still continue.* Nothing can now alter the position in that respect. We have colonized North America and Australia, we have secured a great start in Africa, we rule India, and our influence on the sea is as natural as the influence of the largest shareholder over the policy of a great company. The essential thing is already secured; a commercial 'empire' is laid down; English influence in the world is beyond cavil or attack, whether it be still exercised under the Crown of England or not. Even if the British empire is unstable, British commerce and British civilization are more likely to grow than to decline.

The alarms of Dr. Geffcken and of others are somewhat superficial. The immediate prospect may be threatening, and therefore immediate activity urgent; but if we are to be long-sighted, and to talk of days being numbered, we must remind ourselves that behind our political union there is a considerable economic union, and behind that a moral union, as results of our colonization and empire.

There is another danger, however, of a physical kind. What are we doing in view of the fact that in the British Isles we are living on capital in the shape of our coal and mineral resources? A chilly feeling comes over Englishmen as they reflect that all the cheaper sources are being rapidly exhausted, and that even the more expensive will not last for ever. The survey of our colonial history indicates an answer —the English race will be settled far and wide before that day comes; other coal-fields in other parts of the empire will be brought into use, and connexions with the old country will not be wanting. The relative position of that part of the race which will remain at home will not then be so commanding, but the future of the British nationality is not to be limited by the physical capacities of these islands.

SOME PROBLEMS OF IMPERIAL POLITICS.

The thoughts of public men in England and the colonies will be concerned in the future with some problems which at this moment (1891) are unsolved. They differ in urgency; any change in the world's politics may precipitate one or other of them.

In the province of GOVERNMENT:—

Imperial Federation.

Colonial Confederations: Australia, South Africa, the West Indies.

Relations of our *colonies with foreign countries*: especially liberty to make commercial treaties.

The method of allotting functions in government to *Native princes and chiefs* in our dependencies: especially to be studied for the Native States of India, with possibility of its resumption in some of the Provinces.

The candid renunciation of the idea of *equality* in our politics. We cannot carry it out, and are not doing so; but possibly we are hampered by pretending to do it.

The value of the *political* bond.

FOREIGN RELATIONS:—

The French rights on the *Newfoundland* shore; their position by Treaty of Utrecht, and colonial demands.

The Canadian claims to share in *Behring Sea Fisheries*

as against the United States doctrine that it is a private sea.

The *French in New Caledonia*, and Australian suspicion and dislike of their occupation.

The *threefold Protectorate of Samoa*.

The occupation of *Egypt*.

The *Opium traffic*.

The status of foreigners in such nations as *China* and *Japan*.

The position of *Portugal in Africa*, if it proves to be an obstacle to the development of African civilization.

The organization of our *National Defences*.

The co-operation of the colonies in *Imperial Defence*.

TRADE :—

A *Commercial Union* of the empire.

Commercial Confederations; e. g. Australia.

The *West Indies, Mauritius, and Natal* in relation to our *Free Trade* policy, in so far as it does not suit them but is compulsory upon them.

COLONIZATION :—

The *systematizing of Emigration* for reasons arising *at home*.

Its systematization for better development *of the colonies* themselves.

What will be done if Immigration is resisted? if the present colonists insist on closing their territories against further immigration? And if America, especially, insists on regarding British workmen as below the high standard of their own citizens, and therefore not to be admitted?

UNION OF THE ENGLISH RACE.

Is the existence of a *Dark England* to be a bar to our union with the more prosperous new communities? Do colonies mean to leave us to ourselves, and to decline union because of our large pauper class?

Is there any prospect of *union with the colonies for responsibilities* in the control of the destinies of India, for example; or any possibility of some course of combined action that would give Europeans and Americans together a recognised place in the direction of the Chinese Empire for a time?

The development of the *composite character* of the colonial communities. 'English-speaking' we have to call them, for 'English' is rapidly becoming a misnomer. The tide of German emigration will certainly influence the national character of the 'American' in ways which cannot be estimated, and the other colonies in varying extents are composite too. It is misleading for us to think that it is entirely to England that Americans and Colonists look as their home.

CONCLUSION.

Men whose minds are much occupied with the domestic interests of the nation suspect those who talk much of the 'empire' as high-flying patriots of an unsubstantial, not to say vapoury, temper; to be closely watched and kept from doing harm if they are employed in public affairs. And again, friends of liberty have a suspicion against these same Imperialists as friends and abettors of despotism and despoiling. What impression the record of Colonization and Empire as it has been sketched in this book may make on this prejudice in a reader's mind may be uncertain. But the record may be fittingly closed by reference to two men who more, perhaps, than any others have moulded Englishmen's thoughts about public affairs; men, both of them, distinguished amongst political thinkers for the very two qualities which are supposed to be lacking in the ordinary admirer of our imperial and colonial history.

BURKE:—'The Parliament of Great Britain sits at the head of her extensive empire in two capacities, one as the local legislature of this island; the other, and I think *her nobler capacity*, is what I call *her imperial character*, in which, as from the throne of heaven, she guides and controls them all.'

This shows what Burke thought of the relative importance of our insular and our imperial public duties; but Mill takes a still wider view when expressing his deliberate opinion upon our influence in the world at large.

MILL had before him the results of half a century of farther development, when he withstood the impulse which many of his own political friends were giving to the Separative movement. In 1836 Cobden had declared that Colonies, like Army and Navy and Church, were mere appendages of aristocracy, and that 'John Bull' had before him in the next fifty years the task of 'cleansing his house from this stuff.' Mill writes:—

'The imperial connexion has the advantage, specially valuable at the present time, of adding to the moral influence and weight in the councils of the world, of the Power which, of all in existence, best understands liberty, and, whatever may have been its errors in the past, has attained to more of conscience and moral principle in its dealings with foreigners than any other nation seems either to conceive as possible, or recognise as desirable.'

By the sobriety and solidity of judgment of Burke and Mill, by their experience of affairs and variety of intercourse with men competent to express opinions, and by their constant advocacy of the cause of liberty, we are entitled to claim for their deliverances a significance that should at least disarm prejudice against 'imperial' sympathies and principles.

The Greeks placed history under a muse, Clio, and they did right. The history of this empire of ours is an EPIC. The adventures, the discoveries, the privateering, the wealth, the contests, the victories over nature on sea and plain, and over opposing nations; the knowledge of new men and new scenes, the formation of new nations, their disunions and harmonies, how they traded and how they became independent,—all of these constitute a movement of humanity which makes our dullest prose, stiff with lists and figures, tell a story of the old heroic kind. The names of great men, and men who were not great but only interesting; of plain, good men, and of men of romantic and even of heroic mould, star its pages; and the movement of the peoples whom they led has inaugurated a new era for the race. Historians and biographers have done well for us; but perhaps if Shakspeare had had Hakluyt before him as well as Hollinshed we should in our youth have been won into profounder sympathy with this element of our national story, and we should have better understood the mission of England in the world.

APPENDIX: BOOKS.

THE literature of Colonial History is far too extensive to allow of a Bibliography being given. Frequent references to books are made in the text, and readers will find it easy to pursue the study by referring in the catalogues of the libraries to which they have access to the names (1) of the various Colonies, and (2) of the persons who have played prominent parts. The following lists are drawn up by way of suggestion :—

I. GENERAL WORKS.

Adam Smith, *Wealth of Nations*, Book IV. Chap. v.
Merivale's *Lectures on Colonization* (1841 and 1861). Out of print.
Payne, *European Colonies*.
Seeley, *Expansion of England*.
Geffcken, *The British Empire*.
von Hübner, *Through the British Empire*.
Dilke, *Greater Britain* (1868); *Problems* (1890).
Leroy-Beaulieu, *De la Colonisation* (Guillaumin, 10 fr.).
Roscher, *Kolonien, kolonial Politik und Auswanderung*.
Freeman, *General Sketch of European History*.

II. ORIGINAL SOURCES.

Voyages and Discoveries: *Collections of Hakluyt* (selections, 4 vols. H. Gray, 48s.); *Purchas*; *Harris* (1705); *Callander* (1766). *Dalrymple* (1770), and *Burney* (1803), Pacific Ocean; *Pinkerton*, 17 vols. (1808), and *Kerr*, 18 vols. (1811–24), general.

276 *Appendix.*

Voyages of Dampier, Anson, Byron and *Cook* (by Hawkesworth); *Cook, Second and Third Voyages*; *Tasman, Vancouver, Phillip, Flinders,* and *Darwin.*

Original Histories: John Smith's *Virginia*; Hutchinson's *Massachusetts*; Ligon's *Barbados*; *Calendar of State Papers*, 1574-1629, 6 vols. (ed. Sainsbury).

Travel and Discovery: under the names of the Countries and of the Travellers and Discoverers.

III. SPECIFIC SUBJECTS.

Helps, *Spanish Conquest of America*; Bryan Edwards, *West Indies*; *The European Settlements in America* (Burke or Campbell); Palfrey, *New England*; Bancroft, *America*; O'Callaghan, *New Netherlands*; H. Cabot Lodge, *The English Colonies in America*; Parkman, series of works on *The French in America*; Westgarth, *Australia* (1861); Jung, *Australia* (1884); Gisborne, *New Zealand* (1888); Greswell, *Our South African Empire*, 1885; Rambosson, *Les Colonies Françaises*, 1868; De Luque, *Historia de los Establecimientos Ultramarinos*, 3 vols. 1784 (a Spanish account of European Colonization); Lopes de Lima, *Possessões Portuguesas*, 3 vols., 1884 (Portuguese).

Histories of India: James Mill, Elphinstone, Hunter, Lethbridge, Wheeler; '*Rulers of India*' series (ed. Hunter).

Burke, *Speeches on America*; Mill, *Representative Government* and *Political Economy*; Macaulay, *Essays* on Clive, Chatham, Warren Hastings, Frederick the Great. Lives of Columbus, Franklin, Washington, Wilberforce, Colbert.

Wakefield, *Art of Colonization* (1849); Whately, on *Secondary Punishments* (1839).

Pownall, Brougham, Lewis, Grey, Creasy, Adderley, Mills, Todd, Munro, on *Colonial Government*.

Histories of Commerce and Industry: Macpherson, Porter, Leone Levi, Cunningham (1st edition).

Anthropology (Tylor), and *Ethnography* (Reclus) in *Encyclopædia Britannica*, and references.

Anderson, *History of the Colonial Church*, 3 vols., 1856; *Biographies of Missionaries*.

Applied Geography, J. S. Keltie (1890).

IV. Description and Statistics.

Her Majesty's Colonies, 1886.
Colonial Year Book (Annual).
The Colonial Office List (Annual).
The India Office List (Annual).
Statistical Abstracts for the Colonies, and *for India* (Annual). Government publications.
Lucas, *Historical Geography of the Colonies*.
Philip, *Atlas of the British Empire*, with Notes, 1s.

V. Discussions of Current Topics.

Royal Colonial Institute, Proceedings, Annual from 1869, containing Papers on every part of the empire by specialists, *e.g. New Zealand*, Sir. J. Vogel; *Canada*, Sir A. Galt; *South Africa*, Sir B. Frere and Sir C. Warren; *Australasian Finance*, Westgarth; *Australasian Defence*, Gen. Sir B. Edwards; *Native Princes of India*, Sir. L. Griffin; *New Industrial Era in India*, Sir W. Hunter; *Practical Colonization*, Sir F. deWinton; *Emigration*, Sir F. Young.

Colonization and Emigration; *State Colonization,* Earl of Meath; *Reports* of various *Commissions* and *Parliamentary Committees*.

Speeches of Lord Dufferin and *Sir H. Parkes.*

De Vogüé, *On Africa*, *Revue des deux Mondes*, Dec. 1st, 1890; White, A. S., *Development of Africa*, 1890.

Imperial Federation: Books, papers, or speeches by Lord Lorne, Lord Norton, Lord Thring, W. E. Forster, Professor Freeman, Goldwin Smith, Sir G. Bowen, Sir R. Temple, Sir F. Young, and by Colonists, Sir A. Galt, Sir J. Vogel, Sir G. Stout, Sir G. Berry, F. Labillière, W. Westgarth, and the publications of the Imperial Federation League.

Colonial Conference of 1887, *Report of Proceedings.*

UNIVERSITY EXTENSION MANUALS
A NEW SERIES OF USEFUL AND IMPORTANT BOOKS

EDITED BY PROFESSOR WM. KNIGHT

CHARLES SCRIBNER'S SONS, Publishers

THIS Series, to be published by John Murray in England and Charles Scribner's Sons in America, is the outgrowth of the University Extension movement, and is designed to supply the need so widely felt of authorized books for study and reference both by students and by the general public.

The aim of these Manuals is to educate rather than to inform. In their preparation, details will be avoided except when they illustrate the working of general laws and the development of principles; while the historical evolution of both the literary and scientific subjects, as well as their philosophical significance, will be kept in view.

The remarkable success which has attended University Extension in England has been largely due to the union of scientific with popular treatment, and of simplicity with thoroughness.

This movement, however, can only reach those resident in the larger centres of population, while all over the country there are thoughtful persons who desire the same kind of teaching. It is for them also that this Series is designed. Its aim is to supply the general reader with the same kind of teaching as is given in lectures, and to reflect the spirit which has characterized the movement, viz., the combination of principles with facts and of methods with results.

The Manuals are also intended to be contributions to the literature of the subjects with which they respectively deal quite apart from University Extension; and some of them will be found to meet a general rather than a special want.

They will be issued simultaneously in England and America. Volumes dealing with separate sections of Literature, Science, Philosophy, History, and Art, have been assigned to representative literary men, to University Professors, or to Extension Lecturers connected with Oxford, Cambridge, London, and the Universities of Scotland and Ireland.

NOW READY

THE USE AND ABUSE OF MONEY

By Dr. W. CUNNINGHAM, Trinity College, Cambridge. 12mo, $1.00, *net.*

CONTENTS—POLITICAL ECONOMY WITH ASSUMPTIONS AND WITHOUT — INDUSTRY WITHOUT CAPITAL — CAPITALIST ERA — MATERIAL PROGRESS AND MORAL INDIFFERENCE—THE CONTROL OF CAPITAL—THE FORMATION OF CAPITAL—THE INVESTMENT OF CAPITAL — CAPITAL IN ACTION — THE REPLACEMENT OF CAPITAL—THE DIRECTION OF CAPITAL—PERSONAL RESPONSIBILITY—DUTY IN REGARD TO EMPLOYING CAPITAL—DUTY IN REGARD TO THE RETURNS ON CAPITAL—THE ENJOYMENT OF WEALTH.

Dr. Cunningham's book is intended for those who are already familiar with the outlines of the subject, and is meant to help them to think on topics about which everybody talks. It is essentially a popular treatise, and the headings of the three parts, Social Problems, Practical Questions, and Personal Duty, give a broad view of the large scope of the book. The subject is Capital in its relation to Social Progress, and the title emphasizes the element of personal responsibility that enters into the questions raised. The discussion is as thorough as it is practical, the author's main purpose being to enlighten the lay reader. The novelty of his point of view and the clearness of his style unite to make the book both interesting and valuable. The volume contains a syllabus of subjects and a list of books for reference for the use of those who may wish to pursue the study further.

THE FINE ARTS

By G. BALDWIN BROWN, Professor of Fine Arts in the University of Edinburgh. 12mo, with Illustrations, $1.00, *net.*

CONTENTS—Part I.—ART AS THE EXPRESSION OF POPULAR FEELINGS AND IDEALS:—THE BEGINNINGS OF ART—THE FESTIVAL IN ITS RELATION TO THE FORM AND SPIRIT OF CLASSICAL ART—MEDIÆVAL FLORENCE AND HER PAINTERS. Part II.—THE FORMAL CONDITIONS OF ARTISTIC EXPRESSION: — SOME ELEMENTS OF EFFECT IN THE ARTS OF FORM—THE WORK OF ART AS SIGNIFICANT — THE WORK OF ART AS BEAUTIFUL. Part III.—THE ARTS OF FORM:—ARCHITECTURAL BEAUTY IN RELATION TO CONSTRUCTION—THE CONVENTIONS OF SCULPTURE—PAINTING OLD AND NEW.

The whole field of the fine-arts of painting, sculpture and architecture, their philosophy, function and historic accomplishment, is covered in Professor Baldwin Brown's compact but exhaustive manual. The work is divided into three parts, the first considering art as the expression of popular feelings and ideas—a most original investigation of the origin and development of the aesthetic impulse; the second discussing the formal conditions of artistic expression; and the third treating the "arts of form" in their theory and practice and giving a luminous exposition of the significance of the great historic movements in architecture, sculpture and painting from the earliest times to the present.

THE PHILOSOPHY OF THE BEAUTIFUL

Being the Outlines of the History of Aesthetics. By WILLIAM KNIGHT, Professor of Philosophy in the University of St. Andrews. 12mo, $1.00, *net.*

CONTENTS — INTRODUCTORY — PREHISTORIC ORIGINS — ORIENTAL ART AND SPECULATION—THE PHILOSOPHY OF GREECE

—THE NEOPLATONISTS—THE GRAECO-ROMAN PERIOD—MEDIAE-VALISM—THE PHILOSOPHY OF GERMANY—OF FRANCE—OF ITALY—OF HOLLAND—OF BRITAIN—OF AMERICA.

Not content with presenting an historical sketch of past opinion and tendency on the subject of the Beautiful, Prof. Knight shows how these philosophical theories have been evolved, how they have been the outcome of social as well as of intellectual causes, and have often been the product of obscure phenomena in the life of a nation. Thus a deep human interest is given to his synopsis of speculative thought on the subject of Beauty and to his analysis of the art school corresponding to each period from the time of the Egyptians down to the present day. He traces the sequence of opinion in each country as expressed in its literature and its art works, and shows how doctrines of art are based upon theories of Beauty, and how these theories often have their roots in the customs of society itself.

ENGLISH COLONIZATION AND EMPIRE

By ALFRED CALDECOTT, St. John's College, Cambridge. 12mo, with Maps and Diagrams, $1.00, *net*.

CONTENTS—PIONEER PERIOD—INTERNATIONAL STRUGGLE—DEVELOPMENT AND SEPARATION OF AMERICA—THE ENGLISH IN INDIA—RECONSTRUCTION AND FRESH DEVELOPMENT—GOVERNMENT OF THE EMPIRE—TRADE AND TRADE POLICY—SUPPLY OF LABOR—NATIVE RACES—EDUCATION AND RELIGION—GENERAL REFLECTIONS—BOOKS OF REFERENCE.

The diffusion of European, and, more particularly, of English, civilization over the face of the inhabited and habitable world is the subject of this book. The treatment of this great theme covers the origin and the historical, political, economical and ethnological development of the English colonies, the moral, intellectual, industrial and social aspects of the question being also considered. There is thus spread before the reader a bird's-eye view of the British colonies, great and small, from their origin until the present time, with a summary of the wars and other great events which have occurred in the progress of this colonizing work, and with a careful examination of some of the most important questions, economical, commercial and political, which now affect the relation of the colonies and the parent nation. The maps and diagrams are an instructive and valuable addition to the book.

IN PREPARATION

FRENCH LITERATURE. By H. G. KEENE.

THE REALM OF NATURE. With Maps and Illustrations. By HUGH R. MILL, University of Edinburgh.

THE STUDY OF ANIMAL LIFE. By T. ARTHUR THOMSON, University of Edinburgh.

THE DAILY LIFE OF THE GREEKS AND THE ROMANS. By W. ANDERSON, Oriel College, Oxford.

THE ELEMENTS OF ETHICS. By JOHN H. MUIRHEAD, Balliol College, Oxford.

OUTLINES OF ENGLISH LITERATURE. By WILLIAM RENTON, University of St. Andrews.

SHAKESPEARE AND HIS PREDECESSORS IN THE ENGLISH DRAMA. By F. S. BOAS, Balliol College, Oxford.

THE FRENCH REVOLUTION. By C. E. MALLEY, Balliol College, Oxford.

LOGIC, INDUCTIVE AND DEDUCTIVE. By WILLIAM MINTO, University of Aberdeen.

THE HISTORY OF ASTRONOMY. By ARTHUR BERRY, King's College, Cambridge.

THE ENGLISH POETS, FROM BLAKE TO TENNYSON. By the Rev. STOPFORD A. BROOKE, Trinity College, Dublin.

ENERGY IN NATURE. An Introduction to Physical Science. By JOHN COX, Trinity College, Cambridge.

OUTLINES OF MODERN BOTANY. By Prof. PATRICK GEDDES, University College, Dundee.

THE JACOBEAN POETS. By EDMUND GOSSE, Trinity College, Cambridge.

TEXT BOOK OF THE HISTORY OF EDUCATION. By Prof. SIMON S. LAURIE, University of Edinburgh.

BRITISH DOMINION IN INDIA. By Sir ALFRED LYALL, K. C. B., K. C. S. I.

THE PHYSIOLOGY OF THE SENSES. By Prof. MCKENDRICK, University of Glasgow, and Dr. SNODGRASS, Physiological Laboratory, Glasgow.

COMPARATIVE RELIGION. By Prof. MENZIES, University of St. Andrews.

THE ENGLISH NOVEL FROM ITS ORIGIN TO SIR WALTER SCOTT. By Prof. RALEIGH, University College, Liverpool.

STUDIES IN MODERN GEOLOGY. By Dr. R. D. ROBERTS, Clare College, Cambridge.

PROBLEMS OF POLITICAL ECONOMY. By M. E. SADLER, Senior Student of Christ Church, Oxford.

PSYCHOLOGY: A HISTORICAL SKETCH. By Prof. SETH, University of St. Andrews.

MECHANICS. By Prof. JAMES STUART, M. P., Trinity College, Cambridge.

THE GREAT EDUCATORS.

Edited by NICHOLAS MURRAY BUTLER, Ph.D. Sold separately. Each vol., 12mo, net, $1.00.

A series of volumes giving concise, comprehensive accounts of the leading movements in educational thought, grouped about the personalities that have influenced them. The treatment of each theme is to be individual and biographic as well as institutional. The writers are well-known students of education, and it is expected that the series, when completed, will furnish a genetic account of ancient education, the rise of the Christian schools, the foundation and growth of universities, and that the great modern movements suggested by the names of the Jesuit Order, Rousseau, Pestalozzi, Froebel, Herbart, Dr. Arnold and Horace Mann, will be adequately described and criticised.

ARISTOTLE, and the Ancient Educational Ideals. By THOMAS DAVIDSON, M.A , LL.D. *Nearly Ready.*

ALCUIN, and the Rise of the Christian Schools. By ANDREW F. WEST, Ph.D., Professor of Latin and Pedagogics in Princeton University. *Nearly Ready.*

ABELARD, and the Origin and Early History of Universities. By JULES GABRIEL COMPAYRÉ, Rector of the Academy of Poitiers, France. *Nearly Ready.*

LOYOLA, and the Educational System of the Jesuits. By Rev. THOMAS HUGHES, S. J., of Detroit College. *Ready.*

PESTALOZZI; or, the Friend and Student of Children. By J. G. FITCH, LL.D., Her Majesty's Inspector of Schools. *In Preparation.*

FROEBEL. By H. COURTHOPE BOWEN, M.A., Lecturer on Education in the University of Cambridge. *In Preparation.*

HORACE MANN; or, Public Education in the United States. By the Editor. *In Preparation.*

Other volumes on "Rousseau ; or, Education According to Nature," "Herbart ; or, Modern German Education," and on "Thomas Arnold ; or, the English Education of To-day," are in preparation.

CHARLES SCRIBNER'S SONS, Publishers,
743 & 745 Broadway, New York.

www.ingramcontent.com/pod-product-compliance
Lightning Source LLC
Chambersburg PA
CBHW032049230426
43672CB00009B/1532